THE WELSH MARCHES

COLLINS ARCHAEOLOGY

THE ARCHAEOLOGY OF
THE WELSH MARCHES

S. C. STANFORD

COLLINS
St James's Place, London
1980

William Collins Sons & Co Ltd
London · Glasgow · Sydney · Auckland
Toronto · Johannesburg

First published 1980
© S. C. Stanford 1980

ISBN 0 00 216251 2

Set in 11pt VIP Bembo
Made and Printed in Great Britain by
William Collins Sons & Co Ltd Glasgow

EDITORS' FOREWORD

Additions to the large and growing number of books on archaeological subjects may seem at first sight hard to justify; there would appear to be a book to meet every need and answer every question. Yet this overprovision is more apparent than real. Although certain subjects, for instance Roman Britain, are quite well provided for, others have scarcely been touched. But more than that, archaeology is moving so fast on all fronts that the rapid changes within it make it very difficult for the ordinary reader to keep up. In the last twenty years or so there has been a considerable increase in the number of professional archaeologists who are generating a great deal of new knowledge and many new ideas which often cannot be quickly shared with a wider public. Threats to sites by advancing development in town centres, building on new land and road works, as well as from agriculture and forestry, have grown to terrifying proportions, and are being at any rate partially met by extensive rescue operations. The volume of ancient material of all kinds and periods has multiplied enormously, and its interpretation in the light of new knowledge and techniques has altered, in most cases radically, the accepted picture of the past.

There is thus a real danger of the general reader being left out of the new developments while the professionals are absorbed in gathering and processing clues. This series is intended for the reader who wishes to know what is happening in a given field. He may not be a trained archaeologist, although he may be attending courses in some aspect of the subject; he may want to know more about his locality, or about some particular aspect, problem or technique; or he may be merely generally interested in the roots of our civilization, and how knowledge about them is obtained. It is indeed vital to maintain links with our past, not only for inner enrichment, but for the fuller understanding of the present, which will inform and guide the shaping of our future.

The series presents books of moderate length, well illustrated, on various aspects of archaeology, special topics, regions, techniques and problems. They are written in straightforward language by experts in their fields who, from a deep study of their subjects, have something fresh and stimulating to say about them. They are essentially up-to-date and down-to-earth. They point to sites and museums to visit, and to books which will enable the reader to follow up points which intrigue him. Finally, they do not avoid controversy, because the editors are convinced that the public enjoys being taken to the very frontiers of knowledge.

CHERRY LAVELL
ERIC WOOD

Some Forthcoming Titles

HOUSES   R. W. Brunskill
IRON AND STEEL   D. W. Crossley
CHURCH ARCHAEOLOGY   Ann Hamlin
THE FLOATING FRONTIER   Mark Hassall
MATHEMATICS IN ARCHAEOLOGY   Clive R. Orton
THE ARCHAEOLOGY OF SOUTH WEST BRITAIN   Susan Pearce
PREHISTORIC AND ROMAN AGRICULTURE   Peter Reynolds
SETTLEMENT IN BRITAIN   Christopher Taylor
GLASS   Ruth Hurst Vose

Already Published

VIKING AGE SCULPTURE   Richard N. Bailey

For Colin, Claire and Ann, who spent
their holidays on the spoil heaps

ACKNOWLEDGEMENTS

Most of the information summarized here has been obtained by others over many years, though I have sometimes given it a personal interpretation. Where this differs markedly from other views it should be clear in the discussion. I owe a great debt to the series editors, Cherry Lavell and Eric Wood, who have removed many errors and other shortcomings from the text, to the general editor, Hilary Davies, and to my wife, Yvonne, who has made many improvements while typing the script. The following colleagues, friends and organizations who have allowed me to adapt their drawings or use their photographs have helped me greatly: Aerofilms Ltd, W. A. Baker, the Birmingham Archaeological Society, G. C. Boon, the British Museum, the Cambrian Archaeological Association, M. O. Carver, G. Daniel, the Department of the Environment, P. S. Gelling, W. F. Grimes, the Grosvenor Museum, G. C. Guilbert, Hereford City Museums, Her Majesty's Stationery Office, D. Hibbert, M. J. T. Lewis, the National Museum of Wales, Helen O'Neil, D. F. Petch, L. A. Probert, Shrewsbury Museums, the Royal Commission on Historical Monuments (England), A. Saville, F. H. Thompson and G. S. G. Toms. To them all, and to the many friends on excavations and in extramural classes who have furthered my understanding of this region, I say a sincere thank-you which I extend to the publishers for putting this essay into print.

CONTENTS

PLATES

(Unless otherwise stated, all photographs were taken by the author.)

xi

FIGURES

PREFACE

In view of the abundance of imposing archaeological monuments in the Welsh Marches it is surprising that this is the first archaeological study of the region to be published. As an extramural tutor I have been specially aware of the need for something like this but would never have written it had not Cherry Lavell and Eric Wood focused their enthusiasm for the idea upon me. I have tried to make it readable for newcomers and useful to the older hands, both as an introduction to the detailed evidence in excavation reports and journals and as a forum for the discussion of some significant issues. It is not planned as either guide-book or elementary text-book (though some may so employ it); for I hope it will be used as an extended essay on how communities have striven to survive over the centuries within the geographical and political limitations of the Welsh Marches.

Over the past twenty years the pace of archaeological discovery in the Marches has quickened and some of the resulting changes in thought form major themes in this book. There are hints of a greater stability among Bronze Age communities than previously expected and exciting discoveries relating to the beginning of hillforts in the later part of that period. Our new appreciation of hillfort communities in the Iron Age is sufficiently detailed to permit some confident, though not dogmatic, conclusions to be drawn; and the multiplication of Roman military sites allows greater certainty in interpreting the conflict between Roman and native.

For other times evidence is accruing slowly and spasmodically. The Dark Ages, between Romans and Normans, may still be archaeologically gloomy; but the pursuit of sub-Roman problems continues annually at Wroxeter, and after this text had been first drafted the first Anglo-Saxon rural cemetery west of the Severn came to light at Bromfield. For the Middle Ages the recognition of scores of shrunken and deserted settlements demands new explanations for the process by which the present settlement pattern came into being.

The border is studded with castles and fortified manors, relatively rich in architectural and archival documentation but inviting a fuller archaeological understanding of many of their basic characteristics. These, along with boroughs and churches, villages and field systems, provide the material for investigating the physical evolution of our medieval communities. Nearer the present I have tried to indicate some of the archaeological interest arising from the countryside industries of the eighteenth century, and the monuments of transportation – the canals and railways.

With so much happening over such a wide front it is certain that some, and probably many, of the conclusions presented here will be overturned in the near future. I hope that sufficient evidence has been offered to show that I have not adopted any interpretations lightly; and that there is adequate indication of contrary arguments so that the reader will not feel cheated if other interpretations come to be preferred.

Boundaries

Most borderlands have somewhat uncertain margins, and with the Welsh Marches there is room for individual preference in placing the border here further west, or there further east. For the present study its eastern boundary is taken to lie along the plains of the lower Severn and Weaver and the western boundary to be the edge of the Welsh Massif, i.e. it comprises the whole of the former county of Hereford (now part of Hereford and Worcester), most of Shropshire and Gwent, west Cheshire and parts of Clwyd and Gloucestershire.

Although the coverage has generally been taken to county limits, sufficient latitude has been allowed to include sites beyond these that are essential elements of the Marches' pattern in particular periods. Thus, for the eighth century AD our boundary sweeps through Powys to take in the whole of Offa's Dyke and related works. Some will be disappointed to find that adherence to the topographical and county boundary of southern Powys has left the chamber tombs around Talgarth beyond our close scrutiny; and others that our medieval retreat from Offa's Dyke has left the castles of Hen Domen and Montgomery with only passing references. The same need to avoid being drawn too deeply into Wales has left Ffridd Faldwyn and the Clwydian hillforts outside the present survey.

Dating

Secure dates are scarce, particularly in the prehistoric periods where we rely mainly upon dates derived from the assay of radio-active carbon-14 in organic material from archaeological contexts. Such determinations involve statistical uncertainty so that for a date of 2000 ± 100 bc there is only a 2:1 chance of the correct date falling with the bracket 2100–1900 and a 19:1 chance of it lying between 2200 and 1800. There is always the possibility of incorrect archaeological recognition of the sample's context and often lack of information on how old the timber was when it was utilized in the building or hearth that it is now used to date.

Carbon-14 dates are conventionally quoted in terms of Libby's original estimation of the half-life of carbon-14 as 5568 ± 30 years, although a better half-life of 5730 ± 40 years has long been available. It has emerged in recent years that carbon-14 dates do not agree with the dendrochronological dates, established back to about 5000 BC, which derive from tree-ring counts using long-lived species like the bristlecone pine. Various correction-curves have been proposed to reconcile the two dating systems and so allow corrected carbon-14 dates to be quoted in calendar years. This introduces other uncertainties, but the overall effect seems advantageous and corrected dates are normally used in this study without further explanation and without indicating the standard deviations involved. For a convenient index to the original data the reader is directed to the C.B.A. *Archaeological Site Index to Radiocarbon Dates for Great Britain and Ireland*. Where uncorrected 'Libby' dates are quoted, 'bc' and 'ad' are used in lower case; corrected dates, like other calendar dates, are accompanied by capital 'BC' or 'AD'.

Fig 1 The Welsh Marches—counties,
relief and viewpoints. Land over
122m stippled

CHAPTER ONE

Viewpoints

The Welsh Marches is mainly a lowland area, but the hills are ever present, whether close on either hand in the lower Wye valley or rising sentry-like on the horizon of the Shrewsbury Plain. It is never difficult to imagine the scout of a pioneering party climbing the nearest hill to survey the land ahead; nor to picture the folded terrain as the refuge of rebels during some oppressive occupation. It is easy to understand the attraction of the fat farmlands of Herefordshire to raiders from the bald uplands of Radnor Forest; and equally to see how the wealth of the Marches could support land-grabbing expeditions into neighbouring territories.

In a land of hills it seems appropriate to use six hillforts, shown in fig 1, from which to assess the topography: from south to north, Sudbrook and Twyn y Gaer in Gwent, Midsummer Hill and Croft Ambrey in Herefordshire, the Wrekin in Shropshire, and Moel y Gaer in Clwyd. (They are all normally accessible to the public, though not all are in public ownership.) From these viewpoints the Marches appears to be divided into five distinct regions.

The Dean-Trelleck uplands (fig 2)

The southernmost region is bounded in the south by the narrow finger of the tidal Severn thrusting towards the Midlands and bringing in Atlantic influences, both climatic and cultural. As a result the growing season is long – eleven months with mean temperatures above 6°C at Usk, compared with only nine in Herefordshire at Ross-on-Wye and as few as eight in the central Marches at Church Stretton. Our viewpoint for this green land is the coastal hillfort of Sudbrook Camp, where the estuary has narrowed suddenly from thirteen to five kilometres. Here, at low tide, the Severn is confined to a narrow passage known as the Shoots, between broad platforms of rock; above and below are wide expanses of silt (pl 1). The rock outcrop was

19

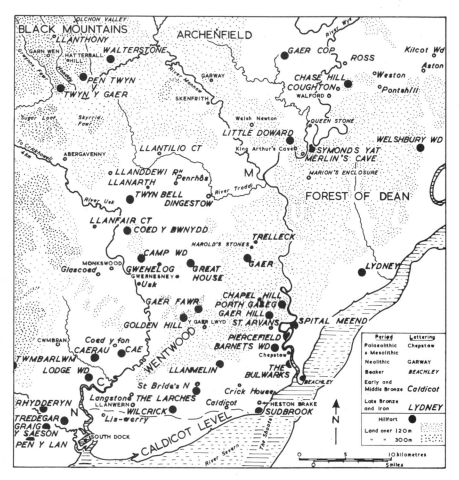

Fig 2 Selected prehistoric locations in the southern Marches. M-Monmouth, N-Newport, C-Caerleon

utilized for the railway tunnel between Bristol and Newport; and the next rocky constriction upstream by the mouth of the Wye has been seized upon for the Severn bridge. These are useful pointers to the former importance of the links between the opposing shores of the estuary.

In prehistoric times the Severn at Sudbrook was even narrower and this would have been the normal head of coastal navigation. Roman finds below three metres of estuarine clay on both sides of the channel attest to an extensive flooding, probably in post-Roman times which forced apart the communities of Somerset and Gwent, and

20

Plate 1 The Severn estuary at low tide from the rampart of Sudbrook camp (*David Hibbert*)

buried earlier settlements under coastal and valley silt; our distribution maps of Roman and prehistoric sites are consequently inadequate. With the drowning of the lower valleys of the Usk and Wye, the Severn now insinuates its saltiness deeply inland along their winding courses and leaves muddy banks bare as each tide ebbs. Between these rivers lies a wedge of coastal plain, the Caldicot Level, interrupted only at Sudbrook where a dry ridge runs down from the hills to the shore. On either side of this, the plain has all the characteristics of reclaimed marshland, protected by extensive sea-walls towards the mouth of the Usk, against the onslaught of extraordinarily high tides driven in by south-westerly gales. Most of the larger modern villages find a dry foothold on the cultivable strip of Keuper Marl along the plain's northern edge. According to the period in question this plain may be regarded as an eastward extension of the lowlands of Glamorgan, or as the attenuated extremity of the Severn lowlands; so it is not surprising that it holds a glorious miscellany of English and Welsh place-names: Nash, Bishton, Llanwern and Llanvihangel-near-Roggiett among them.

Much more decidedly Welsh in character and atmosphere are the uplands of Wentwood and Trelleck and the tributary valleys of the river Usk, an irregularly dissected area where the Usk and Wye cut indifferently across geologically contrasting provinces. Since these hills only rise to about 200–250 metres there are some extensive cultivated areas, noticeably on the plateau top around Trelleck itself; but the frequency of steep slopes in Old Red Sandstone and Carboniferous Limestone has led to large areas being put under forest. Patches of forest elsewhere show that the area generally is one of less intensive agricultural exploitation.

West of the Usk is the front of the South Wales moorlands which shield the coal valleys from our view. The foothills are followed by the Monmouthshire and Brecon Canal, in the wake of which have come the railways and new roads, the housing estates and glass-fronted factories of a very different Gwent from that described so far. Its modern history is tied to the coalfield and the ports.

The Carboniferous Limestone of Trelleck is separated from its continuation in Dean by the deep gorge of the Wye. On the English side too the plateau top is cultivated, though bordered by forested slopes on three sides and changing abruptly to forest on the east where rocks of the Coal Measures outcrop. The poor soils associated with the sandstone of the latter formation, the relics of centuries of iron working and coalmining, the acres of sessile oak woods and the distinctive rural scene of smallholdings with outbuildings of iron-

Plate 2 The Black Mountains and the Vale of Ewyas from Twyn y Gaer
(*David Hibbert*)

stained sandstone, combine to make the Forest of Dean distinct and isolated. Offa's Dyke and the later English boundary used the Wye valley to separate east from west; the broken terrain and sparse settlement have always tended to make the Forest, like Trelleck, a frontier zone between north and south.

With two major rivers crossing this southern region the emphasis given here on its negative role, as an obstacle rather than a gateway to the Marches, may seem strange; but above Caerleon the Usk is too small to have encouraged development, while the narrow twisting gorge of the Wye is often too narrow to take a road as well as the river. Most of this Dean-Trelleck area is therefore to be seen as a land of shorter perspectives and narrowly circumscribed opportunities, favouring the growth of small groups.

The Herefordshire basin (fig 2, fig 3)

Across the no-man's-land between southern Gwent and central Herefordshire flows the Monnow, a tumbling stream of no navigational potential that rises in the Black Mountains (*pl 2*). Here, above

23

Fig 3 Selected prehistoric locations in the central Marches

the Afon Honddu and 426 metres above sea-level, is the hillfort of Twyn y Gaer, from which we can survey this mountain region. It is a land of deep valleys whose chequered fields, cultivated mostly for hay, reach only a little way up the valley sides before changing to the broken green of steep rough grazing which continues to the plateau tops, about 500 metres, dark with seared bracken or the shadow of heather. To south, west and north the flat summits in Old Red Sandstone deny easy communication between the several valleys or with the Brecon lowland to the west. As a result the Black Mountains have acted as a breakwater diverting the movement of people and ideas. They narrow and emphasize the Talgarth route into the Herefordshire plain and give the Usk route a clearly defined role independent of the Wye.

The north-eastern ridges of the Black Mountains are lower and very much like the Old Red Sandstone uplands to the south-east, where the pasture is frequently interrupted by woodland. In antiquity this south Herefordshire district of Archenfield was Welsh and place-names like Llangarron, Llangrove and Llanrothal survive; but it has long been separated from the rest of Gwent by a frontier along the Monnow.

Beyond Archenfield and the Wye rise the Woolhope hills, bringing up Silurian limestone near the centre of the Herefordshire basin. The sky-line is held by the Malverns, fifty kilometres away on the far side of the border. We see how open northern Gwent is to the English lowlands to the north-east, but we have only to turn round to see the glint of the Severn estuary, the source of south-western influences in more than one period of prehistory, while eight kilometres south of Twyn y Gaer the Usk valley route from south-west Wales outflanks the Black Mountains and reaches the Marches at Abergavenny.

It is time to move our viewpoint eastward to Midsummer Hill (fig 3), near the southern end of the dramatic Malvern fault-line along which are upthrust rocks more ancient than any we have hitherto stood upon. Rivalling in age any in the world's geological history they cause the Malverns to stand up steeply from the Midland plain like the knuckles of a clenched fist; and looking along them we are left in no doubt about the significance of this topographical and cultural divide (pl 3). The clay lowlands of the Midlands lie to the east. In the distance, trending south-westwards, are the Cotswolds, an almost level horizon of Jurassic Limestone, 300 metres above sea-level, describing a geological uniformity on a scale unknown in the broken terrain of the Welsh Marches. Between them and the Marches is the uppermost part of the tidal Severn and Gloucester. In the north

25

Plate 3　The Malvern Hills looking south towards the Herefordshire Beacon hillfort, crowned by its medieval ring-work, with Midsummer Hill camp beyond

foreground is the Herefordshire Beacon, or British Camp hillfort; while beyond the Malvernian outcrop structural disturbances along the west bank of the Severn bring up successively the Suckley Hills, Bromyard Downs, and the Abberley Hills. This eastern margin of the Marches is steeply accidented, with deeply rejuvenated valleys plunging to the Severn.

In the centre of the Herefordshire basin to the west the upper layers of Old Red Sandstone have been widely removed by erosion, and residual table-lands like Credenhill and Dinmore Hill have steep scarped edges now covered by trees. Between such hills, which give a local relief of 60–180 metres, there are broad lowlands strewn with glacial drift. Outwash sands and gravels create many areas of lighter soil, but there are regions in the west with boulder clay on top of marl where drainage is impeded, and there are pro-glacial ponds in the north between Staunton-on-Arrow and Shobdon. Nevertheless this is a land generally regarded as rich for farming – although the farmer has not always been left in peace. The hillfort warriors must have created

26

problems for their neighbours, and the Romans disturbed the farming pattern. In pre-Conquest days, and subsequently, English raids and Welsh counter-attacks took their toll of livestock and personnel.

The central Marches (fig 3)

From the ramparts of Croft Ambrey, nearly 300 metres above sea-level, the Herefordshire basin lies displayed to the south. In fair weather the Black Mountains, Brecon Beacons, Forest of Dean, Malverns and Cotswolds can all be seen and the unity of Herefordshire is obvious.

South-westwards from our vantage point the wooded Silurian limestone escarpment merges with the hills of Wales beyond Kington. North-eastwards it curves to approach Ludlow, only to turn west again as Bringewood Chase before turning north-eastwards as the wooded escarpment of Wenlock Edge. The geological regularity presented by this escarpment is succeeded north-west of Croft Ambrey by a jumble of hills which extend in limestone, sandstone and shale northwards to the Camlad and the upper Onny. Although there are many hills up to 275 metres, cultivation has gone over the tops of most of them; and they offer today a tidy aspect of improved grassland between neat hedges, interrupted by patches of woodland with broader forests on the more extensive escarpments (pl 4).

In Roman times scouts probed westwards through these hills against resistant British tribes; and through them later, in medieval times, swept the armies of Owen Glyndwr to ravage the English settlements close to the border. At Mortimer's Cross, where the Lugg breaks out of the central hills, the Mortimers fought unsuccessfully against Edward of York in the struggle for the English throne.

At about the same latitude eastwards are the Clee Hills, of Old Red Sandstone capped by Coal Measures and basalt, which give rise to a considerable area of uncultivated land above 275 metres. A dissected plateau extends eastwards to overlook the valley of the Severn between the Wyre Forest and Bridgnorth; and to the north, sandwiched between the Clees and Wenlock Edge, lies fertile Corve Dale.

North-west of Wenlock Edge are the ancient hills of Caer Caradoc, the Long Mynd, Corndon, the Stiperstones, Earl's Hill and the Breidden. For the first time since leaving the Black Mountains we have come into a region with large areas of limited agricultural value; but it possesses mineral resources that attracted prehistoric stone battle-axe makers to Corndon Hill, and Roman miners to the neighbouring Shelve district. There, the abandoned pit-head gear of the

Plate 4 The south Shropshire hills looking east form Caer Caradoc hillfort, Clun

nineteenth century lies awkwardly beside sacred prehistoric stone circles. We should ponder the grandeur, personality and even majesty of such hills for early people who lived close to the land, for Caer Caradoc's crags rise precipitously to 460 metres, and clouds often envelop the Long Mynd. The Church Stretton valley provides the only easy way through this difficult terrain and along it went in turn the Roman and later roads, and then the railway, on their way to Viroconium or Shrewsbury; southwards, Herefordshire may be reached via Leintwardine or Ludlow. The Romans preferred the western route, whereas the English preference for the eastern one was confirmed by the establishment of the Court of the Marches at Ludlow in 1502.

These hills extend the uplands from Wales across the border and, by way of Titterstone Clee, to the very banks of the Severn, effectively separating the basins of Hereford and Shrewsbury.

Plate 5   The Wrekin from the south-west

The Shrewsbury plain (fig 4)

At the south-east corner of the plain of Shrewsbury is the rhyolitic hump of the Wrekin (*pl 5*). From its arched spine, within the hillfort's ramparts, the view south-eastwards is across gently undulating terrain towards the sky-scrapers of the new Wolverhampton. The Severn pours that way, towards the Midlands, through the Ironbridge gorge. To the south and south-west stand the hills of south Shropshire: the clean sweep of Wenlock Edge, the volcanic protrusion of Caer Caradoc and the flat summit of the Long Mynd. Further west rise Moel y Golfa and the Breidden, and past the latter, emerging from mid-Wales by way of Newtown the Severn holds these southern hills within its curving arm and leaves the greater part of the Shrewsbury plain north of its meandering circuit.

Diverted from its Irish Sea outlet during the last glaciation, the middle Severn flows uncertainly over the uneven morainic surface left by the ice-sheets. The area is generally poorly drained, although

between the hummocks of boulder clay are more amenable spreads of gravel and sand, remnants of river terraces, themselves the by-products of the last ice-age. Here and there, small areas of resistant sandstone form low but sharply sculptured hills, particularly along the edge of the Keuper Sandstone outcrop at Oliver's Point, Grinshill Hill and Hopley Hill, and an igneous pre-Cambrian inlier forms rounded knolls near Haughmond. Rising no more than 75 metres above the surrounding land, such hills provide the few upstanding viewpoints on these northern plains.

From the top of the Wrekin there is no discernible watershed between the Severn drainage in the foreground and that of the Dee to the north. The elongated heap of debris left on the ice margin 20,000 years ago and known as the Ellesmere or Woore moraine, separates the two river systems along a zone of poor drainage where peat bogs like Whixall Moss and Whattall Moss developed later. The moraine forms a land of limited opportunity, attracting fewer people and therefore less effective for communication between the communities to north and south.

The valleys of the Dee and Weaver (fig 4)

In the vicinity of Mold, at the north-west limit of the Marches, a small limestone hummock is occupied by the hillfort of Moel y Gaer. A land of low relief, smothered by boulder clay and very green, extends eastwards from it to the low sandstone ridge that runs north-south through the centre of Cheshire, between the Dee and Weaver. To the north the estuary of the Dee points the way out of the Welsh border to the Irish Sea, in which direction too leads the narrow coastal plain route to north-west Wales. The foreground of the Clwydian foothills between Ruabon and Holywell is a broken countryside developed on Coal Measures and Millstone Grit. Behind, formed of Carboniferous Limestone and rising to 300 metres, is the Clwydian Range itself (pl 6). Few roads cross it but it is easily outflanked by the northern coastal route, and may be bypassed along the upper Dee valley which opens the way to both Cardigan Bay and the coastal plains of Gwynedd. The northern Marches are thus exposed to western intruders, but are equally well placed as a base for the invasion of Wales.

Most of the boundaries of these five physical regions of the Marches

Fig 4   Selected prehistoric locations in the northern Marches.
PYC—Penycloddiau; MYG   Moel y Gaer, Bodfari

are approximately indicated on the political map by the southern boundary of Herefordshire and the northern and southern boundaries of Shropshire (*fig 1, p xviii*). The only line not translated into political terms is the one along the northern edge of the south Shropshire hills.

The physical divisions coincide with, and locally are emphasized by, climatic differences. The warm air from the North Atlantic creates in Gwent and Hereford a remarkably mild climate which is also characterized by lower rainfall than one might expect on this side of the country. By comparison it seems that north of Ludlow, at Church Stretton, the winter rain often turns to sleet and the frost lies longer on the fields. In the cooler lands of the northern border greater exposure to the north-westerly airstreams increases the number of stormy days with cloud and makes this a moister area throughout the year.

To oversimplify, it might be said that the arable lands of the border lie mainly in the south and that pastures are pre-eminently in the north; but whether under grass or plough the lands north and south of those central hills are rich by comparison with the bare uplands of Wales nearby, and also with much of the less fertile terrain of the Midlands – where in early times at least there seems to have been less ambitious agricultural pioneering. The border was therefore attractive to those on either side and its control was vital for the ultimate defence of the larger regions that lie at a distance from its frontiers.

Plate 6　The Clwydian Hills looking north to Moel Fammau (*David Hibbert*)

CHAPTER TWO

Palaeolithic Hunters and Their Descendants

For the greater part of his existence man has survived on the proceeds of the chase and left but a shadowy record of his activities. In most parts of the world little other than flint implements has survived. Just as Europe was one of the frontier areas to be reached at later stages following anatomical and cultural developments in Africa and Asia, so was Britain, although joined to the continent until 6000 or 5000 BC, marginal in turn to the rest of Europe. At a time when population was scant anyway it is understandable that the less well equipped representatives of our species should have been reluctant to press northwards into those misty lands that from time to time were largely covered by the extension of glaciers from the Polar ice-cap, and where the west European outcrop of chalk containing the flint from which most implements were made was restricted to the south and east. The Welsh Marches, being distant from the chalk outcrop and nearer the ultimate edge of the continent, stood remote in most respects from the mainstream of man's Palaeolithic endeavours in Europe as represented in the gravels of the Somme or, much later, in the caves of the Dordogne. Indeed it is only in the latest, Upper Palaeolithic, phases 26,000–8000 bc,* that the Marches can at present claim to have anything like adequate evidence of man's use of the area before the beginning of farming.

There are in addition some simple geological reasons why the evidence of early occupation of the Welsh Marches is thin. Most of Britain north of the Thames-Severn line was subjected to repeated advances of ice. The flint implements of the Lower and Middle Palaeolithic cultures belong to the older drift deposits associated with the earlier ice-sheets. With the spread of ice in the several phases of the

---

* The use of 'bc' and 'BC' is explained on p xvii.

last British glaciation, the Devensian, between about 70,000 and 8300 bc – broadly correlated with the last Alpine glaciation, the Würm, – such deposits would have been overridden in most of the Welsh border and either scraped away or smothered by new layers of boulder clay and outwash gravels.

The odds must therefore be high against finding Lower or Middle Palaeolithic tools in the Welsh Marches except in those regions in the south and south-east which were not reached by the final glaciation, and were high enough to escape burying by the detritus issuing from the melting margins of the ice. There is little chance of such implements being found on open sites north and west of this ice front, which lay approximately along the line Abergavenny – Hereford – Wenlock Edge – Bridgnorth. Some of the higher mountains, like the Black Mountains, Caer Caradoc, the Long Mynd and Long Mountain, would have protruded above the surrounding glaciers; but this final glaciation was sufficient to bury the western plains of Herefordshire beneath more than 200 metres of ice so that hills as high as 300 metres, like Merbach Hill near Hay, were overridden; and boulder clay was deposited at over 400 metres on the flanks of the Wrekin. Wherever the ice had extended the old soils would have been stripped from the hillsides, and the valley bottoms littered with boulder clay.

South and east of the ice front outwash sands and gravels were deposited in the valleys of the lower Usk, middle Wye, the middle Teme and the Severn below Bridgnorth. Beyond these, or at higher levels in the valleys, are the terrace gravels associated with earlier glaciations, particularly prominent in the valley of the Severn. From gravel pits between Bewdley and Gloucester have come five Lower Palaeolithic handaxes and an equal number of flake implements, but to the west and north, Lower and Middle Palaeolithic implements, covering more than 200,000 years of man's occupation of Britain, are rare indeed. In the Marches we may note the report of an ovate chert handaxe found at Welsh Newton in south Herefordshire, about 210 metres above sea-level and so clear of deposits associated with the Devensian glaciation. Also south-east of the final ice-front are a handaxe from Neen Sollars, Shropshire, and from Chepstow a flake from a tortoise-shaped flint core that had been prepared to enable several flakes to be struck from it – a method distinctive of the Middle Palaeolithic and known as the prepared-core or Levalloisian technique.

Rather more unusually located, at Sarnesfield in west Herefordshire, is a handaxe reported to have come from the digging of a gate-post hole. This is in a lowland area well behind the ice-front, and its survival close to the modern surface is either a remarkable coincidence or an indication that it has been re-deposited in post-glacial times. In the same account reference was made to an Upper Palaeolithic blade from the same farm.

We are accustomed to distinguishing our early cultures on the basis of their flint industries, and it may be that changes in the form of tools coincided with a change of population, with new racial groups or even distinct anatomical species in the earliest years; but the objects which loom large in our own studies were not necessarily those upon which most ingenuity and enterprise was spent by the people who used them. A hundred interesting developments in houses, costume and diet, let alone the possible intricacies of religion and community organization, may have taken place under the umbrella of 'Lower Palaeolithic handaxe cultures'. Nevertheless with the appearance of Upper Palaeolithic cultures we may expect a major advance in man's understanding of and exploitation of the environment, and the enrichment of his social life. A new method of converting cores of flint into tools was now introduced. Instead of a few flake tools being struck from each flint the core was now prepared in such a way that many narrow blades could be struck from it. These served, when trimmed, as knives, arrowheads, scrapers and points (*fig 5, 1–8*).

Homo sapiens sapiens, emerging as a distinct species by 35,000 or 40,000 bc (i.e. based on radio-carbon analysis; see p xvii), seems to have been in occupation of north-west Europe during the final phase of the last ice-age. His new techniques for preparing flint tools made much more economical use of the raw material and must have made it easier for him to shake himself free of the trammels of the chalk and explore regions at a distance from this outcrop. For this reason, if for no other, it is not surprising to find somewhat more evidence of Upper Palaeolithic hunters in Wales and the Pennines. Large parts of Britain were still under ice for much of the time, however, and it is likely that many of the finds reflect summer visits to the tundra along the ice-front, the hunters retreating southwards with the animals when winter froze the land once more. England was joined to the Continent and the estuary of the Severn was but a broad valley with a major river running through the middle. Migration could have taken place freely over hundreds of miles, but there may have been long periods when a local retreat of the ice allowed the hunters to establish themselves permanently, for centuries possibly, on the edge of the forest or in the shelter of caves. From such comfortable quarters they might have organized at their comparative leisure the hunting of the reindeer and mammoth which probably formed a major part of their

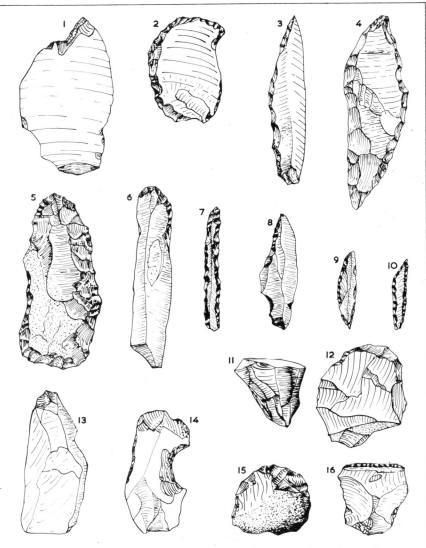

Fig 5 Upper Palaeolithic (1–8) and Mesolithic (9–10) flints from King
Arthur's Cave (after Taylor 1927) and Mesolithic-type flints from
east Shropshire (11–16, after Saville 1974)

1 Graver	7 & 8 Microlithic	13 Burin
2,6,15 & 16 Scrapers	points	14 Notched flake
3 & 4 Points	9 Crescentic microlith	All ¹/₁
5 Slug knife	10 Triangular microlith	
	11 & 12 Cores from	
	microlith production	

Plate 7 The Wye gorge from Seven Sisters' Rock near King Arthur's Cave
(*David Hibbert*)

diet. When such herds had migrated to other areas there were wild-fowl to be snared along numerous streams and ponds.

A major difficulty in assessing man's activities during this period is that we have little information about open-air sites. Instead, almost all our evidence comes from a few caves, the occurrence of which is circumscribed by the outcrop of cave-forming rock, principally the well-jointed Carboniferous Limestone which we have already met in the Forest of Dean. On the side of the Wye gorge between Dean and Trelleck a number of small caves occur in this limestone and from one of them – King Arthur's Cave, Whitchurch, – has come ample evidence of Upper Palaeolithic occupation. A return to our viewpoint at Sudbrook (*fig 2, p 20*) would remind us that the hills of Dean are but the re-emergent outcrop of the limestone of the Mendips, and that King Arthur's Cave is within the same Palaeolithic enclave as the caves of Cheddar Gorge in Somerset.

The Herefordshire cave is about 100 metres above the Wye (*pl 7*) and is included in a nature trail from the Biblins which also takes in a nearby rock-shelter that may have served as a Palaeolithic camp-site. The cave (*pl 8*) consists of two chambers, even the larger only extending about 12 metres, and its deposits were virtually cleared out by Symonds in 1870–1 and Taylor in 1925–7 (*fig 6*). In the passage to the second chamber Taylor found a hearth overlain by 300 millimetres of cave earth containing Upper Palaeolithic flints. At the mouth of the chamber Symonds had finished digging at three metres without reaching bed-rock. Under a recent stalactitic layer he found cave earth with late Pleistocene mammal bones, then a hearth layer which appeared to be a continuation of the one in the passage. Below this was a stratified red sand containing igneous pebbles which Symonds identified as

Plate 8   King Arthur's Cave, Whitchurch.

39

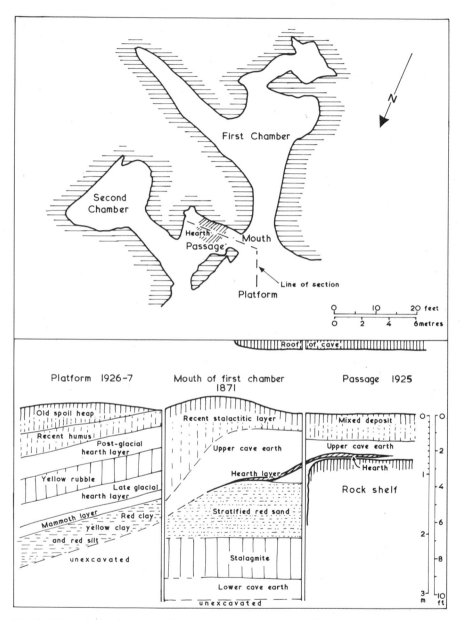

Fig 6 King Arthur's Cave: plan and schematic section of deposits, based on Taylor 1927

coming from the Builth and Rhayader areas in the upper Wye valley. He thought that the sand had been deposited by the river Wye flowing at this level, but it is more likely to have been carried to the cave from some superficial deposit by an underground stream. Below the red sand was stalagmite and then a lower cave earth containing an ice-age fauna that included cave lion, woolly rhinoceros, mammoth, hyena, horse, bison, the great Irish deer and reindeer.

On the platform outside, Taylor revealed a more detailed sequence of deposits, but his work too terminated before reaching bed-rock. Below Symonds' old spoil heap a layer of humus yielded a recent faunal assemblage and artefacts of Neolithic to Roman date. Below was a hearth with a recent fauna but lacking domestic animals; the flints indicate a modified Upper Palaeolithic industry which may represent the survival of a local Palaeolithic group in a post-glacial environment.

This occupation was separated from an earlier one by a layer of rubble, below which the cave earth contained a late glacial fauna including a giant deer, horse and bison, and Upper Palaeolithic flints comparable with those from other British caves and styled 'Creswellian' after the type site at Creswell Crags in the southern Pennines.

Below the second hearth was a thin layer with many mammoth bones indicative of deposition during a glacial phase, and in line with the expectation from analogous sites that the overlying Creswellian occupation dates from late in the last glaciation, perhaps around 8000 to 10,000 bc. Other bones from the mammoth layer and the underlying clay and silt included those of woolly rhinoceros, horse, bison, giant deer and hyena. We do not know whether the Creswellian occupation was permanent or intermittent, whether the periods of activity of these hunters of mammoth, horse and reindeer are to be counted in decades or centuries.

With the amelioration of climate the glaciers slowly melted from their outward margins, leaving a desolate landscape of unweathered gravel and boulder clay in the lowlands, while the hills in many places had been pared down to the native rock. Slowly, as sub-aerial weathering prepared the way for soil-rooted plants, the more accessible areas were colonized by dwarf shrubs and then by birch forest. While the conditions changed in this way there may have been some adaptation of Palaeolithic groups to the changing environment: amongst other things, they may have reduced the size of their flint tools, and changed their diet and hunting techniques as the large herds of big mammals dwindled and disappeared from southern Britain. Adaptation may

41

have taken place over a thousand years or more, for the improvement of climate was not a continuous process and from time to time there was probably a reversion to tundra conditions.

A rapid change is, however, apparent during the Pre–Boreal phase, 8300–7500 bc. The last of the ice thawed and Britain's climate became warm and dry with persistent south–eastern winds from the Continent giving mean July temperatures of the same order as those we enjoy today. Under such anticyclonic conditions vegetation would have been quick to invade the former tundra wastes with pioneer species like willow, aspen and birch preparing the way for deeper-rooted species and higher forest types. Red deer, wild oxen and wild pig now provided the basic needs of thinly spread hunter communities from places like King Arthur's Cave. Further afield there may have been a wide scatter of overnight camps, some of them visited regularly over many years.

It is possible that after about 7500 bc, with the onset of the Boreal phase and the spread of hazel, pine and oak forest, there may have been occasional intrusive Mesolithic groups competing for game and perhaps even herding deer and oxen; but it is more likely that they did not arrive in the Welsh Marches until the beginning of the Atlantic phase, 5500 bc, when a moister, maritime climate was accompanied by the spread of higher forest in which oak and elm were dominant. Their microlithic traditions may have continued with local groups for centuries after Neolithic colonists entered the area some time after 4200 BC.

It should be emphasized that although several new Mesolithic sites have been recorded recently in coastal and upland Wales and also in the valley of the Warwickshire Avon, Mesolithic finds in the Welsh Marches remain rare. While this may reflect a lack of field-work over much of the area, it has to be noted that only twelve microliths are recorded along the Clun-Clee Ridgeway zone, where field-workers have been particularly active. Chitty's comment that these do not entitle one to infer a Mesolithic occupation of the ridgeway regions is pertinent to any consideration of the few flints of this form from the Marches. These come from hilltop sites at 200 metres like Oreton, Salop and Chase Hill, Ross-on-Wye, and from valley locations like Arrow Court and Lower Harpton in west Herefordshire.

Hunting or herding parties, migrating with their chosen animals, may be expected to choose well-drained camp sites close to springs or streams. The majority of the microlith locations so far noted conform to these requirements; but apart from King Arthur's Cave there is insufficient material to locate any Mesolithic camp sites comparable with those of south-east and north-east England. The chance finds of microliths have come mostly from places producing a much larger quantity of material of later date. Chase Hill yielded only one microlith, a battered-back blade, among a quantity of Neolithic scrapers and other tools; Lower Harpton showed two possible mesolithic flints out of a total of 110 flakes; and from Arrow Court, in addition to the two flints that are regarded as Upper Palaeolithic survivals, there is one chert blade that is probably Mesolithic. At Gamage Farm, Much Marcle, a handful of Mesolithic flints accompanied a large number of Neolithic implements. Other Mesolithic-type flints have recently been found east of Bridgnorth (fig 5, 11–16).

Enough has been said to indicate our present ignorance of Mesolithic sites, but there may be much still to be discovered. In recent years more sites have been located on the valley gravels, whereas earlier field reconnaissance tended to concentrate on the hilltops and ridgeways. We may learn more when field-workers extend their activities more widely along the terrace gravels and look along the edges of the pro-glacial lakes around Wigmore and the middle valley of the Teme, among the Church Stretton hills and the valley of the middle Severn. Such places would have been favourite locations for hunting parties that could take wildfowl from the marshes to supplement a diet of venison and wild pig from the forest.

It may be thought with some justification that the Palaeolithic-Mesolithic period was not of great importance in the Marches. Nevertheless, those hunters whose remains are elusive had doubtless found their way beside streams and lakes, and along ridges, and had learned in detail the physical geography of the region. Their descendants may have been the guides, porters and perhaps stockmen for subsequent Neolithic colonists. To that extent the sparse Mesolithic occupation may have paved the way for the penetration of Neolithic ideas and trade. A more important effect of these millennia was the weathering of the raw detritus of the ice-sheets to form soils capable of sustaining a population of farmers.

CHAPTER THREE

Neolithic Settlers
and Traders

The assessment of the Neolithic period has in recent years been dominated and complicated by dating problems. On the basis of carbon-14 assays (see p xvii) the Neolithic in Britain is thought to have begun around 3500 bc (using the Libby half-life for carbon-14). This probably corresponds with 4200 BC on the dendrochronological calendar.

This long formative period, which saw the introduction of agriculture, continued until the appearance of new forms of pottery and the advent of metallurgy about 2500 BC. We have therefore something like 1700 years in which to dispose of Neolithic tombs and implements.

In the absence of enough dates the division between Neolithic and Beaker periods in the border can only be tentative. Ideas developed in Beaker communities elsewhere may have been introduced into late Neolithic communities without the widespread adoption of copper tools. Equally, however, there are indications that the border shared so much in the Beaker developments of religious, social and economic organization that the notion of a distinct Beaker period is justified. Accordingly most of the probable Beaker period finds are grouped in the next chapter; although in regions where they are especially rare occasional Beaker artefacts like barbed and tanged arrow-heads and battle-axes are mentioned to avoid repetition.

We know much about Neolithic tombs but little of their settlements, and in the Welsh Marches we know of no permanent examples of the latter. We do not know whether those who were buried in the chamber tombs came from the immediate vicinity, or whether the clusters of tombs that dominate the Neolithic map of western Britain simply emphasize the sacred nature of certain favoured areas to which the dead from miles around were taken. We cannot tell yet how many of their scattered implements were lost by settled communities working their fields or how many fell from the sacks of traders passing through deserted forests.

It is a characteristic of Neolithic communities in Europe that their economy is based upon agriculture; but recent research in some places has indicated that in the early years there may have been a balance between food taken from the farm and meat taken from the forest. In Britain we know that some Neolithic communities were certainly farming, even ploughing, at an early stage; but here too there may have been some whose main supply of food came from hunting. Surviving Mesolithic groups may have enjoyed the role of aboriginal hunters and taken on from time to time that of guides and porters; but until we have firmer evidence of such communities, distinguished by their own flint equipment or other acceptable fossils, there is no particular warrant for assuming that this was the case in the Welsh border.

Let us go back to the vicinity of Sudbrook Camp, to what would still have been the coast (fig 2, p 20). The greater width of the Caldicot Level downstream at this time is indicated by the finds of a Neolithic skull and animal bones at Newport, at the Alexandra South Dock and the Orb Works, about six metres below sea-level; the Neolithic coast line would probably have approximated to the present five-fathom contour. Numerous chamber tombs, the Severn-Cotswold Group, are distributed to the south-east over Mendip and the Cotswolds, and to the west in South Wales and beside the Black Mountains. Some have transepted stone chambers reached by a narrow passage from the broad end of a covering long mound; others have lateral chambers entered from the side of the mound. The transepted form has close parallels in north-west France, whence too the idea of lateral chambers may have come. It is therefore easy to imagine the types being introduced by settlers and missionaries arriving by sea along the Bristol Channel, and landing at the head of the estuary near Sudbrook. The existing pattern of tombs could have developed from nuclei established by small parties arriving here and dispersing to left and right. With so many centuries available most of the tombs could have resulted from subsequent local development; indeed the view has been put forward that the entire British tomb development was indigenous. Dating material is notoriously sparse in Wales and the border, but by comparing pottery from the Powys tombs with that from radio-carbon-dated contexts in southern England Lynch has argued that the main period of development there was between about 3200 and

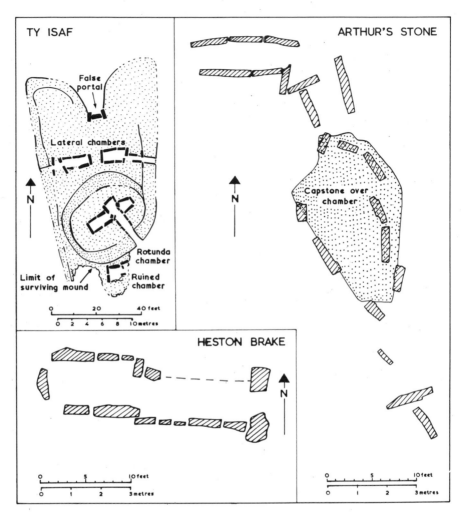

Fig 7 Chamber tomb plans—the remaining orthostats of the chambers of
Arthur's Stone (after Royal Commission on Historical Monuments
(England) 1932) and Heston Brake (after Daniel 1950), with the excavated
plan of Ty Isaf, Powys, for comparison (after Grimes 1939).

2800 BC. The earliest tombs may be considerably older.

When we consider the distribution of these tombs we are struck
first of all by the predominance of the form on the south-eastern side
of the estuary in Somerset and Gloucestershire. They are rare on the
north-western side and absent above the mouth of the Wye. A particular feature is the cluster of at least sixteen tombs far from the estuary at

Plate 9 Arthur's Stone chamber tomb, Dorstone, from the north-west.
Compare with fig 7

the foot of the Black Mountains, mostly in Powys. Savory has argued
that this area may, on occasion, have been approached by way of the
upper Usk valley from Dyfed, and it is possible that the Black Mountain group was established from this direction. On the other hand, the
occurrence of both terminally and laterally chambered tombs on both
sides of the Severn provides an argument for at least occasional parallel
development, if not unity, of the two parts of the Severn-Cotswold
region.

Despite the rarity of such tombs elsewhere in the Welsh Marches
there is, curiously enough, one sited as though to commemorate a
historic landing. Just a kilometre inland from Sudbrook Camp, on a
hillock only thirty metres above sea-level, the remnants of a gallery
grave are to be found in the scrubby woodland of Heston Brake,
Portskewett (*fig 7*). The surviving upright stones, or orthostats, indicate a terminal chamber measuring three metres by 1.5 metres at the
end of a 4.5-metre passage. Around it are the reduced remains of the
mound that would formerly have covered the tomb, now only about
twenty-one metres long and orientated east-west. An excavation in
1888 uncovered skeletons and some post-Neolithic artefacts.

North-west of Heston Brake, a ridge of rising ground leads to hills that cross southern Gwent from Chepstow Park Wood to Wentwood. Here, beside the modern road that mostly follows the ridge itself, we find the remains of another ruined megalithic chamber tomb, Y Gaer Llwyd in the parish of Newchurch West. Five orthostats and a partly collapsed capstone, along with some recumbent stones, mark this second monument to the piety of our Neolithic pioneers, 213 metres above sea-level in a col at the heads of valleys on either side of the north-westward heading ridge. It is well placed as a first stage on the path from Heston Brake to the tombs of the Black Mountains, but it stands alone and there is no other between here and the two tombs in the Usk valley by Crickhowell, forty-two kilometres from Heston Brake and little more than that from Swansea Bay.

Other evidence for the Neolithic occupation of the area between the Usk, Wye and Monnow is offered by casual finds of artefacts from eight sites, of which six are in or close to the valleys of the Usk and Wye. They include a flint axe from Gwernesney, Usk, and a polished stone axe from Chepstow. Another five sites have produced stone types appropriate to the late Neolithic or to the Beaker period, although beakers themselves are as yet unknown in the region; these implements show valley and hill distribution and include a flint sickle from Usk.

The chamber tombs of the Black Mountains, which include Ty Isaf (fig 7), are mostly located in Powys along the north-west and south-east sides of the mountains; but the north-east members just come into our present area of study. These are the ruined tomb of Arthur's Stone and the apparently intact long barrow presumed to cover such a tomb at Cross Lodge Farm, both in Dorstone parish. As though to emphasize the variety of site chosen for Neolithic activity the former is at 268 metres on the ridge between the Wye and the Dore, whereas the Cross Lodge barrow, twenty metres long, is on the lower slope, little more than two kilometres away, at 167 metres.

Arthur's Stone (fig 7; pl 9) has an irregular polygonal main chamber about 5.5 metres long covered by an enormous capstone of a local limestone concretion, cornstone, and parts of at least two passages or chambers at the north end. A wide orthostat with cup-marks, standing across the major axis south-east of the main chamber, looks like a false portal as would be appropriate in a laterally chambered member of the Severn-Cotswold group. From the varied alignments of the exposed stones it seems likely that more than one phase of construction is involved and any restoration of the plan would be highly speculative. Little remains of the mound that once covered the grave; Professor Grimes informs me that it formerly showed in the field to the south and it must have extended north of the modern road. We have no details of the skeletons or grave-goods that may have been taken when it was pillaged years ago.

In the same area on the Herefordshire side of the Black Mountains early literary accounts suggest there may have been a chamber tomb at one time in Park Wood, St Margarets/Others may await recognition, but in the Marches north of the Black Mountains the only accepted record of a chamber tomb, now destroyed, is of Llech y Wydhon on Llanymynech Hill/Powys. Three alleged chamber tombs in Shropshire in the parishes of Norton-in-Hales and Highley, and on Stapeley Hill, the Giant's Grave or Cave, have been discussed and rejected by Daniel.

With the Herefordshire tombs we therefore stand at the frontier of a Neolithic region and may consider how the remaining evidence for the period differs as between the foreground in the vicinity of the tombs and the middle distance among the Herefordshire plains and hills. In the Black Mountains, on the slopes of Cefn Hill at over 450 metres, Gavin-Robinson recovered material from a Neolithic occupation site. From beneath the superficial peat and humus came leaf-shaped arrow-heads, spindle-whorls and many flakes of flint. There was also a small sandstone mortar and a pebble hammerstone thought to have been used for cracking hazelnuts. Many other flint sites have been mapped on the ridge of this area and more recently many leaf-shaped arrow-heads and pieces of polished stone axe have been recorded at Vowchurch and on the Merbach ridge at Stockley Hill, Woodbury Hill and around Arthur's Stone, showing intensive use of this area persisting from the earlier Neolithic into the Beaker period.

Away from the Black Mountains, the few sites producing numerous flakes and arrow-heads include Fownhope, Wellington Heath, Keephill, and Hanley William, all on hills of medium altitude, from about 120 to 180 metres above sea-level. The presence of barbed and tanged flint arrow-heads of the Beaker period, along with leaf-shaped ones and fragments of polished flint axes (*fig 8*) on sites like Keephill, suggests they were used on more than one occasion and may have been the permanent dwelling sites of pastoralists, agriculturists, or communities combining hunting with either of these pursuits. A wealth of material may await discovery somewhere in their vicinity unless it has already been dispersed downhill by the plough.

Our attention has so far been directed to sites on hilltops and ridgeways, but many Neolithic finds and flints of uncertain date come from the middle slopes of hills and even from the valleys, most noticeably those of the Arrow above Kington and around Titley and Staunton, and the Teme around Bucknell and Buckton. They confirm that Neolithic activity, as shown already by the distribution of chamber tombs, is represented at various altitudes.

The ubiquity of Neolithic finds is further illustrated by polished stone and flint axes. From Herefordshire there are at least fifteen complete stone axes and four complete flint axes of this period in a total of thirty-three polished axe finds. They are scattered widely across the Hereford basin, coming from river valleys, the western clay plains and the sandstone and limestone uplands. Unassociated, as most are, with other artefacts, they cannot be used to indicate probable settlement sites; but there are too many to avoid the conclusion that they were destined for local use, and were not simply lost in transit on their way elsewhere.

Herefordshire received axes from most of the main British polished stone axe factories for which the rocks have been grouped and defined. The Group I greenstone axe found at St Margarets must have come from the neighbourhood of Penzance, Cornwall; a beautiful unused Group VI axe found at Upcott Farm, Almeley will have been made at Great Langdale in Cumbria; and three Group VII axes of a granite, augite granophyre, found near Weobley, at Mocktree and on Midsummer Hill are products of the Graig Lwyd factories in Gwynedd. Axes of Group VIII, a siliceous ash from south-west Wales, have turned up by the Garway Brook and at Tupsley. An acid welded tuff, of Group VIIIA from Dyfed, is the material of an axe found at Llanarfon Farm, Dorstone; while an altered shale utilized at the Group XXI axe factory, Mynydd Rhiw, Gwynedd, is identified in an axe from Craswall. Axe fragments of Group XXIII from Dyfed, have been found on Dinedor Hill. Flint axes, which must have come from the south or east of England, have been found at Weston Beggard, Woodbury Hill near Moccas, Weobley, Dorstone Hill and Hunderton.

Fig 8 Neolithic and Beaker stone tools from Herefordshire. All ½ except No. 10 (¼). All flint except Nos. 8, 10 and 11

1 & 2 Leaf-shaped arrow-heads	8 Polished stone axe showing
3 Petit-tranchet derivative	flaking scars
arrowhead	9 Polished flint axe
4 Barbed and tanged arrow-head	10 Perforated axe hammer and 11
5 Plano-convex knife	battle axe, (side and top views)
6 & 7 Scrapers	both of Corndon picrite

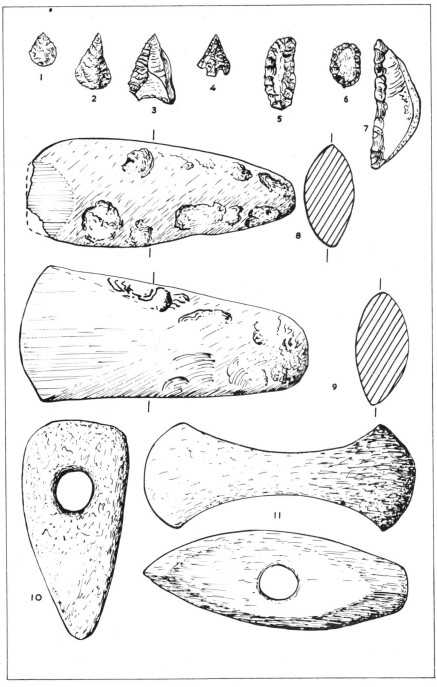

Briggs has recently reminded us of the likelihood that erratic boulders of glacial origin were used as quarries for axes, especially in the pioneering stages of Neolithic colonization. The development of the major axe factories may yet prove to be a secondary growth, and some of them may have been concerned with a fairly restricted local distribution. Such propositions are especially pertinent in the Welsh border where large surface erratics from the Lake District and various Welsh sources must have been very common; but in the writer's opinion the traditional view that most axes were fashioned at sites on or close to the rock outcrop and were then traded across country appears to be better founded.

The use of polished axes began early in the Neolithic and may have lasted for two thousand years. Against such a time-scale it would be idle to reconstruct from our few finds any particular routes that were followed by the traders or users of these implements. They were, after all, general purpose tools which may have been used more frequently in the carpenter's workshop than in the forest, and some of the finer specimens might have been reserved for display. All that we are entitled to suggest from their distribution is that Neolithic people travelled, however infrequently, into and through most parts of this varied region. It was not an unknown desert and for all we know by the end of the Neolithic there may have been considerable areas cleared for grazing and even agriculture. Whether the diet was won mostly by farming or by hunting there could have been some sizeable villages dispersed across the width of the central Marches; but with the exception of some trial excavations on the Dorstone ridge there has been no attempt to explore such sites by excavation.

Climbing north-westwards out of the Herefordshire plain to regain our viewpoint at Croft Ambrey (*fig 3,p 24*) we stand on the most extensive escarpment in the Welsh Marches. From where it begins against the Radnor Hills, west of Kington, to its end against the Severn near Much Wenlock, this limestone outcrop provides an obvious natural route that could have been used in any prehistoric period. It is at first surprising that few pre-Iron Age finds or structures are located along it, and we are bound to wonder whether this reflects a lack of detailed field-work. With this thought in mind we may turn to Chitty's map of the Clun-Clee Ridgeway, discussed in the next chapter, which shows clearly that the intensive utilization of the Clun and upper Teme valleys began in the Neolithic period. From Kerry Hill in Powys to Clungunford numerous finds have been made including leaf-shaped and barbed and tanged arrow-heads, and many other flint implements. There are several areas where prolific flints suggest possible settlements or camp sites. As Chitty has observed the finds are not restricted to the Ridgeway but occur broadly to north and south with the area of moderate density extending as much as six or seven kilometres from the ridge. It is impressive how in such a region of broken relief the prolific flint concentrations occur as close as a kilometre from one another and occur at all levels, from the flood plains of the rivers to the highest parts of the interfluves – from 150 to 400 metres. In an area of twenty square kilometres around Clunbury are some seventy sites where implements have been found, in other words one find-spot for every 3.5 square kilometres – a density unparalleled elsewhere in the Welsh Marches. Such a distribution would not result simply from the passage of traders; the area must have been closely settled by either hunting or agricultural communities. No Neolithic polished axes have been found along the ridgeway route itself, which is not therefore thought to have been in use until after the time of these axes. Recent finds of axes at Oakly Park and Kinlet are no closer than a kilometre from the route.

Small sherds of Neolithic pottery have been obtained from sites later used for hillforts in the central Marches at the Roveries near Bishop's Castle and Ffridd Faldwyn above modern Montgomery; and in 1978 Neolithic pottery was found in two small pits at Bromfield. Such finds may point to sites that were permanently occupied in this period, but we still lack information about the kind of houses or size of settlements concerned.

It is time to move northwards once again to the Wrekin where, in 1973, a barbed and tanged arrow-head was found. In the Shropshire lowlands before us (fig 4, p 30) Neolithic finds include a handful of polished axes: two from sites near Oswestry were possibly quarried at Mynydd Rhiw and there are flint axes from Shakeford, Hinstock, Hadnall and Uppington. Another polished stone axe from Hinstock is possibly from the Penzance factory, and an axe of Group XX from Harley near Much Wenlock (fig 3, p 24) is probably derived from Charnwood Forest, Leicestershire. Group XV rock, probably from the Lake District, was used for the polished cylindrical axe found in Attingham Park. Sherds of Neolithic bowls have been found on a lowland site by Sharpstone Hill at Weeping Cross near Shrewsbury and on the high Breidden. Chitty has often underlined the importance of the gravels of the Severn valley as routeways for prehistoric settlement and trade, and it will have been noticed that the examples mentioned lie, for the most part, close to the river. The riverside pattern of axes extends southwards to Leighton and into the central

Marches with a Great Langdale axe at Alveley (*fig 3, p 24*). The river route did not however have a monopoly of trade. The numerous axes scattered through the hills of the central Marches suggest there would have been dozens of trackways criss-crossing this territory.

In Cheshire fifteen polished stone axes were recorded by 1958 west of the river Weaver. Once more the distribution is widespread, including coastal sites in the Wirral, and both valley and hill locations inland. About the same number of finds had then been made in east Cheshire. Beyond the plain of the Dee and west of Moel y Gaer the ascent of the Clwydian Range takes us out of our region of study and into territory with more evidence of occupation: at the northern end of these hills, overlooking Prestatyn, sites like the North-West Cave at Gop, and King Charles Bowling Green, Gwaenysgor, have yielded quantities of Neolithic material.

We have been concerned to note and discuss the scattered finds in the Welsh border lowlands, but in the north, just as in the central Marches and the Black Mountains, the evidence for permanent settlement is mainly on the hills. We can only guess at the chain of camps in the lowland forests that may have served to link the upland communities of Wales and the border with distant centres of religious activity and axe manufacture.

CHAPTER FOUR

The Border in Beaker Times

Around 2500 BC the working of copper and gold was introduced into Ireland by adventurous artisans who came probably from the Beaker groups of Atlantic Europe. While they were persuading their Neolithic hosts that a cast copper axe was more efficient than the old polished stone implements the influence of Beaker cultures in the south and east of Britain led to the development of a large market for the new tools. The raw material was restricted to the west – exploited first in Ireland, but later in Cornwall, Wales and the Lake District. There was thus set up an interesting trading position with major markets in the south and east and the main source of supply in the far west. The trade in stone axes had already shown the way to bring western products into south-eastern markets, and the trade in metal was a natural succession to that earlier traffic. In the earliest days the distribution of Irish-type copper flat axes, often elaborately decorated, indicated that the craftsmen themselves took their inspiration from the area where the ores were extracted. Later, with the increasing exploitation of metal and the change to bronze, the artisans established themselves permanently in their trading areas.

We have seen that the Welsh Marches was only lightly populated in Neolithic times and many areas may have been virtually deserted for most of that period. The rarity of beakers and copper tools makes it unlikely that there was a sudden change in population now. Beaker sherds have been found as secondary deposits in the south Powys chamber tombs, and many open sites in the Black Mountains and elsewhere that have yielded leaf-shaped arrow-heads have also produced the barbed and tanged form which was introduced at the same time as beakers. Changes in burial custom that are associated with beakers elsewhere are illustrated locally by two stone-lined cists discovered on the side of the Olchon valley, each containing a skeleton and a beaker (*pl 10*). In a cairn over 600 metres above sea-level near the summit of Pen Gloch y Pibwr, north of Crickhowell, a handled

Plate 10   A beaker from the Olchon valley cist
burials, 190 mm high (*Hereford City
Museums*)

beaker was found. In east Herefordshire a beaker is recorded at
Mathon and beaker sherds have been found on Midsummer Hill
Camp. Beaker sherds recently found at Bromfield suggest a lowland
settlement there, as at Sharpstone Hill, Shrewsbury where, too,
beaker sherds have been found, as well as an enlarged food vessel
containing a later cremation. The cremation found in the Bicton burial
circle near Clun may belong to the Beaker period.

Certain areas which had an attraction in the Neolithic period
probably continued as foci of activity and served both as markets for
the new tools and as stopping places on the routes between the western
ores and the south-eastern consumers. It is therefore appropriate that
we now look at the Clun-Clee Ridgeway route, which Chitty saw as
becoming important with the trade in perforated battle-axes and
axe-hammers, – probably, then, during the Beaker period.

Lying for the most part on the ridge between the rivers Clun and

Teme, and coming down from the south-east slopes of Kerry Hill, it passed by the destroyed stone circle of the Grey Stones and Bettws-Y-Crwyn church and over Spoad Hill to the Llwyn, then to Rock Hill and Cwm on Black Hill, whence it descended to cross the Clun at Clungunford. It is then argued to go over May Hill and Brand Hill, where one prolific flint site and a handful of other find-spots lie reasonably close, and then descend to cross the Onny at Onibury. The suggested course lies along the terrace of the Teme and Onny, through the Bromfield barrow area and across the Corve near Ludlow, whence it follows the present road on to the western slopes of Titterstone Clee and over this hill towards Farlow and Prescott. Beyond here it is seen to veer to the right and descend south-eastwards towards Bewdley and the Severn valley. Along the whole of the track east of May Hill, the only areas of concentrated finds are at Bromfield and around Farlow, Oreton and Prescott on the north-east flanks of the Clees.

Five perforated battle-axes and axe-hammers have been found within a kilometre of this route: at Hopton Castle, Bromfield, Bitterley, east of Titterstone Clee and Farlow. The few datable associations of these implements in eastern and southern England are of the Copper or Early Bronze Age and they have a general association with beakers. A number of different igneous rocks were employed for their manufacture and the finished articles were disseminated widely in southern Britain. In our own areas, sixteen kilometres north of the Ridgeway, and on the southern slopes of Corndon Hill in Powys near Cwm Mawr Farm, two factory sites have been suggested for a large group of implements made from the local outcrop of picrite. Their distribution to the Midlands might have involved the use of the Ridgeway to reach the Severn and help explain the importance of this route. However, they are widely scattered in the Welsh Marches and the discovery of nearly seventy per cent of those identified in the original account of this axe type within thirty-two kilometres of the picrite outcrop implies that they were being used in the central Marches and not simply lost there. Like the Neolithic implements they point to increased local activity as well as to trade between the quarries and more distant communities. Moreover, there are several axe-hammers and battle-axes of foreign rock confirming that this area was also importing material; Group XXIIIb quartz-dolerite from Dyfed (see p 50) was used for the Kington axe-hammer.

Four picrite axes have been found along the Severn between Montford Bridge and Shrewsbury, perhaps emphasizing the focus of routes from Corndon on fordable stretches of the river. Two implements of rock other than picrite were found beside the river at Wroxeter; and at Brompton Ford nearby, a large broken axe-hammer was of Group XV rock. In Shropshire north of the Severn there are at least nine such tools of various rocks; and many occur along the central Cheshire ridge as well as in the Wirral and other parts of that county.

Stone circles, like axe-hammers, may span the Copper and Early Bronze Age like other constructions and artefacts of the Beaker culture. They are regarded as later than the chamber tombs because of their geographical separateness and greater altitude, normally 300 metres or more, as though taking the opportunity offered by a drier climate to exploit the uplands.

Two circles are found a few kilometres north of the Cwm Mawr axe-factory, on the broad ridge north of Corndon Hill. They are Mitchell's Fold (*fig 9*) and the Hoarstones, and they presumably had

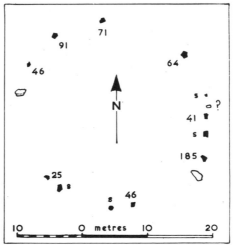

Fig 9 Mitchell's Fold stone circle, after Grimes 1963. Height of standing stones in cms; stone stumps marked 's'; recumbent stones unshaded.

some ritual or astronomical significance in the ceremonies of the period. The former is the better exposed, about 366 metres above sea-level with a wide and exciting view westwards over the uplands of Wales. Here on the roof of their world the local prehistoric inhabitants erected a circle 26–27.4 metres in diameter of which fourteen or fifteen stones survive in place, most of them less than a metre high and the highest nearly two metres. Two and a half kilometres north-east of Mitchell's Fold, in a broad and partly swampy hollow just to the east of the ridge, is the Hoarstones circle, 23–24 metres in diameter, established as having originally had thirty-eight stones, most of which are buried in the surrounding peat.

Surviving stone circles are not all that common and Grimes's map of those in Wales and the border shows that the few there are tend to occur in small groups as though either the worshipping population was restricted to few areas, or, more likely, that a few important centres served a much more widespread population. Mitchell's Fold and the Hoarstones mark the Corndon-Shelve area as one of these; perhaps the concentration of the axe-factory products within about thirty-two kilometres of the hill indicates the area that it served.

A related type of monument, the embanked earth circle, combining a setting of stones with an earth ring-work, was also possibly present in south Shropshire along the Clun-Clee Ridgeway. The Grey Stones, near the boundary with Wales, has been destroyed but originally had a ring-wall about thirty metres in diameter overall, with kerbs of large blocks. A second circle on the same route, at Pen-y-Wern, Clun may be the remains of a denuded cairn of twenty-seven metres diameter; and near the summit of Titterstone Clee O'Neil excavated an 'Earth Circle' which had a wall of local dolerite blocks in clay, one metre high and eighteen metres across the top. No grave was found in the centre of either the Grey Stones or the Tittersone Clee circles. Like the Corndon circles these are all high: Pen-y-Wern 381 metres, The Grey Stones 441 metres, and Titterstone Clee 533 metres.

Other possible examples of circles in the Welsh Border include Garn-Wen in the Black Mountains at 472 metres, a doubtful record of three stones said once to have been known as the Whetstones in Church Stoke south of Mitchell's Fold, and another on the north-western fringe of the Marches, at the watershed of the Clwyd and Dee drainage in Penbedw Park, Cilcain. At the latter, five stones of an original eleven survive of what may doubtfully have been a genuine prehistoric circle of about 27.4 metres diameter at 167 metres above sea-level. Of course, over much of the Welsh Border it is not easy to come by massive stones suitable for such circles and it could be that there were other religious centres marked by circles of posts, like totem poles; unless they were surrounded by a ditch, they are unlikely ever to be discovered.

Standing stones may also be part of the Beaker contribution to the landscape. In east Gwent by Trelleck, three large ones, Harold's Stones, are set up in line, and cup-marks carved on them include two

Plate 11   Harold's Stones, Trelleck from the south

on the centre stone about 180 millimetres in diameter (*pl 11*). Here on the limestone plateau 213 metres above sea-level, the modern village is a centre for the surrounding area; perhaps this spot was a focus in prehistoric times too. At the north-west extremity of the Forest of Dean, two single standing stones at Staunton and Huntsham may also date to this period or later in the Bronze Age. In Marion's Enclosure, Staunton, the stone is on the north side of the road at about 206 metres; but by contrast the Queen Stone at Huntsham stands beside the river Wye. It is of local sandstone 4.5 metres long with 2.4 metres below the modern ground level, and unusual in having sharply cut grooves, about fifty millimetres wide and up to 170 millimetres deep, running vertically down the four faces to ground level, but not below. There are five on the south-east face, three on the opposite face and two and one on the others. The grooves may have originated from natural weathering since the stone was erected, but their depth and sharp form suggest artificial improvement, though not necessarily in ancient times.

CHAPTER FIVE

Bronze Age Developments

Following its introduction during the Beaker period, bronze came to replace copper generally for cutting tools by about 2000 BC. In the succeeding Bronze Age the metalwork of the border has parallels, in most phases, in distant parts of Britain. Many of these items, examples of which are shown in fig 10, may have been brought thither by traders, although some, and possibly most, were made locally. The early metal axes were flat, but in the Middle Bronze Age the palstave was developed, with provision for the seating of the haft. Chitty long ago saw that the metallurgical similarity of the flat axe and unlooped palstave from Asterton Prolley Moor pointed to the use of local ores; and the discovery of the multiple flat axe mould at Longden Common close to copper-bearing pre-Cambrian rocks near Pontesbury adds to the case for a Shropshire industry in the Early Bronze Age.

Whereas Rowlands has been able to demonstrate the development of regional bronze-working traditions in many parts of southern England during the Middle Bronze Age, it is not yet clear whether the Marches had traditions distinct from neighbouring parts of England and Wales. The uncertainty continues into the Late Bronze Age, i.e. after 1000 BC, when the similarity of border weapons with others far away led Burgess to propound one attenuated cultural and political region stretching from Cardigan Bay to the Wash, dominated and distinguished by warriors armed with spears of the type best known from Broadward, Shropshire. It has, however, become increasingly clear that it will be misleading to use bronze-work, or any other single artefactual criterion, in this way to distinguish Bronze Age cultures and thereby imply political regions.

There have been attempts to interpret the distribution of Bronze Age finds, and particularly barrows, as areas of agricultural exploitation reflecting the suitability of local soils and climate. Consequently there have been suggestions that the mountain-top barrows in areas since covered by peat reflect an uphill movement during a drier period

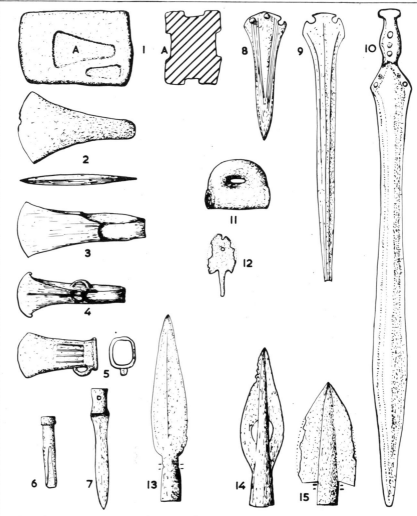

Fig 10 Bronze Age implements from the Welsh Marches. All x¹/₅ except
Nos 1 (⁴/₂₅) and 11 (²/₅). All bronze except 1.

1 Multiple flat-axe mould of stone
  from Longden Common: one face
  and cross-section
2 Flat axe, Newcastle-on-Clun
3 Flanged axe, Bucknell
4 Looped palstave, Ross
5 Socketed axe, St. Arvans
6 Socketed gouge, Brogyntyn
7 Socketed knife, Minera

8 Ogival dagger, Ebnal
9 Rapier, Aston Ingham
10 Leaf-shaped sword, Cwm-du
11 D-shaped tube, purpose uncertain,
   Broadward
12 Tanged razor, Merlin's Cave
13 Socketed spearhead, Guilsfield
14 Socketed spearhead, Willowmoor
15 Barbed spearhead, Broadward

in the Early Bronze Age with a subsequent retreat from the plateau tops during the Late Bronze Age. Among the weaknesses of this interpretation are the inadequacy of dating for most barrows and the general lack of recognized settlements to go with them. Until we have a clearer picture of settlement it is better to acknowledge that barrows and other cemeteries might be located for special religious or topographical reasons, related only distantly to the former homes and farms of those buried there. It is relevant to notice that in the lowlands of the Welsh Marches there are sufficient dated burials to show that the hilltops never had a monopoly in this respect.

A convenient summary of Bronze Age distributions in the border was provided by Chitty and Fox, as map C in *Personality of Britain*. This included Beaker period implements so that the distribution of actual Bronze Age objects is even sparser than shown; subsequent finds have hardly affected the relative densities of different regions, though new studies and distribution maps of individual metal types have been made recently by Burgess and Cowen, Rowlands and also by Burgess, Coombs and Davies.

Chitty's map shows a scatter of finds along the uplands of the southern border with a concentration on the Black Mountains, and there is a cluster of finds from and beside the Severn between Bridgnorth and Worcester. By contrast, the Herefordshire plains and the uplands to the west are almost empty. Finds recur in some number again across the hills of the central Marches between the middle Teme and the Severn, providing a zone of continuity with finds across central Wales to Cardigan Bay. To the north again, the western sides of the Shropshire and Cheshire plains show an overflow from the dense patches recorded over the hills and many of the valleys of North Wales. Apart from these foothill finds the main occurrence of Bronze Age material in the northern Marches is along the sandstone ridge from the Mersey near Helsby to the hills between Wem and Hodnet. As Chitty's detailed maps for Cheshire show, the majority of the finds along this ridge are the perforated Beaker implements already discussed. For the Bronze Age itself the evidence is more scattered and will be detailed below. Although it is possible that this ridge provided a trade link between the Mersey and middle Severn, many of the finds can be derived from sources to east or west, and could have been supplied to settlers on the ridge itself.

The Dean–Trelleck uplands (fig 2, p 20; fig 10)

In the Early and Middle Bronze Age the coastal zone appears to have been more important than the interior uplands. Savory has seen the few coastal barrows as evidence for settlement from Somerset and southern England in the Early Bronze Age, although an alternative interpretation by Grimes drew especially upon the evidence from the Crick House, Caerwent, bell barrow where a leaf-shaped arrow-head and two plano-convex knives were found. Like the cup-marked stones found in the ring around the barrow these tools are regarded as the product of local Neolithic people who had simply adopted the new fashion in burial mounds. Other barrows known in this area are the one at St Bride's Netherwent, the excavation of which in 1860 produced fragments of a bronze dagger blade, and the mound at Langstone, thirty metres in diameter and just over a metre high. Two collared urns of the Early Bronze Age come from the site of the Roman fortress in Usk and a flat bronze axe is recorded from near Usk. Middle Bronze Age palstaves without loops have been found at Liswerry, Caldicot, and Penrhôs, Llantilio Crossenny.

Most of the finds from the uplands between the Usk and Wye belong to the Late Bronze Age. By the park gate of Llantilio Court a fragmentary leaf-shaped spearhead was found, and socketed axes have been found near Trelleck, at Castle Hill Usk, Gwehelog near Usk, Llanarth and Llanfair Court. Founders' hoards containing out-of-date implements and scrap for reworking are particularly common in the Late Bronze Age; the one from Church Farm, Llanddewi Rhydderch included two socketed axes with loops. Two more of these axes, of Breton type, were found on Chapel Hill, Tintern; and a hoard of seven looped socketed axes were found near Liveoaks Farm, St Arvans. Even allowing for the greater abundance of bronze work generally in the Late Bronze Age the increased number of find sites for these axes compared with the earlier forms seems to betoken an increasing amount of colonizing, and it is tempting to associate this with the first appearance of hillforts. Savory has pointed to the possibility of a Late Bronze Age date for some of the promontory sites of the Wye valley, drawing our attention in particular to the finds from Merlin's Cave near Symonds Yat, which included a disc-headed and a rolled-strip headed pin of the type associated with continental Late Bronze Age Urnfield cultures. A slotted spool from the same cave is similar to the form found at Dinorben hillfort, Clwyd, and there was also a maple-leaf bronze razor. In the north-west of this region, ten kilometres west of Garn Wen at 427 metres on the Black Mountains at Pen-tir, Cwm-du, a leaf-shaped sword attests a continuing interest in high places in the Late Bronze Age.

The Herefordshire basin (fig 2, p 20; fig 3, p 24)

The agricultural potential of the Herefordshire basin was not to be realized during the Bronze Age. Although there are artefacts and round barrows occurring equally on upland and lowland sites most of them are around the sides of the basin where hill and valley intermingle; the centre seems to have been neglected. In the absence of settlements we can only consider the stray finds of bronze tools and the distribution of round barrows, and neither of these categories of evidence is without its problems. For example there is considerable doubt about the numerous bronze artefacts, including palstaves and spearheads, reported from Netherwood and Kyre Park. They are possibly from a hoard uncovered in a quarry near St Michael's College, Tenbury Wells – a hoard that some have thought was deposited there after being stolen from the collection of one of the masters at the College.

The difficulties with the presumed round barrows arise from the lack of dating evidence; for round barrows, though most common in the Bronze Age, may cover burials of any period from Neolithic to Saxon. That there may be a few of the latter in this area is suggested by the place-name Wolferlow in north-east Herefordshire, meaning 'Wulfhere's burial mound'. Apart from these questions, which can hardly be resolved without excavation, burial mounds are occasionally confused with small castle mounds, or mottes. The two can sometimes be distinguished by the presence of an attached enclosure indicating the bailey of a castle site, and where the mound lies next to the medieval church it is likely to be a motte; the mound of St Weonards, ten kilometres west of Ross, is a case in point. Subject to the individual re-assessment of particular barrows there would seem to be something like twenty-six mounds in the county of Herefordshire that warrant consideration as possible Bronze Age barrows, and another four are indicated by ring-ditches recorded on aerial photographs. In addition to the barrows there is evidence of two cemeteries, one in the sand quarry by Southend Farm, Mathon and the other at Pontshill, south-east of Ross.

The Mathon cemetery came to light as a result of quarrying operations from 1910 onwards and the records of the finds are casual indeed. Fragments of two looped spearheads were found in black deposits suggestive of cremation burials and many urns with cremated bones were found, some arranged in lines. The few urns that survive include a fine collared one in Hereford Museum and parts of other vessels that recall the material discussed below from the Bromfield cemetery; other pottery included a beaker and some Iron Age and Roman sherds. The ring-ditch of a probable barrow was photographed nearby by Baker. The Mathon finds are sufficient to indicate the possibility of other intensively utilized locations appearing elsewhere. They form part of a small group of material around the Malverns which includes a bronze palstave from Midsummer Hill and two barrows on the ridge at Colwall. From within Midsummer Hill Camp also come some sherds that are probably Bronze Age.

From Midsummer Hill the Bronze Age view to the north and west would have been mostly across unutilized forest, all the way to the Radnor and Wigmore hills, featureless save for a couple of ring-ditches photographed by the author near Wellington. In contrast to the deserted nature of most of north Herefordshire the land between Midsummer Hill and the Black Mountains has considerable evidence for this period. On Oldbury Camp in the Woolhope hills a looped palstave was found; a barrow, Bagpiper's Tump, is at the north end of the hills near Mordiford. To the south is an interesting group of finds in the Ross area which includes a flanged axe, rapier and spearhead from Aston Ingham, a palstave from Weston-under-Penyard, a Late Bronze Age spearhead from Coughton Marsh near Walford, and a further palstave from somewhere unspecified near Ross, shown on fig 10, 4, p 62. These suggest settlement around Ross; and confirmation of this may be seen in the discovery at Pontshill of a finger-decorated urn 450 millimetres below the surface lying on 200 millimetres of charcoal. This sounds like a cremation grave and the decoration of the vessel is paralleled at Bromfield. It seems likely that there was a cemetery at Pontshill too.

Near Tram Inn, in the valley between the Archenfield uplands and the north-eastern foothills of the Black Mountains, was found an unlooped palstave with ribbed shield ornament; still in Herefordshire to the west two palstaves and a socketed axe are recorded from Vowchurch and another socketed axe from Llanthony Abbey. There are two barrows on the Herefordshire plain at Madley, two more at Michaelchurch and others at Tyberton, Turnastone, Abbey Dore, Craswall and Dorstone.

These signs of Bronze Age activity across south Herefordshire may relate to the sandier soils in contrast to the clays that cover most of north Herefordshire. Reference has already been made to the paucity of evidence in the lowlands and it should be stressed that the only bronze artefacts found in Herefordshire away from the hills are a bronze ferrule from St Margaret's Park, Hereford, a leaf-shaped sword found with a spatulate dagger at Fayre Oaks, Hereford and a socketed knife from Lyonshall. Although the dagger is of Middle Bronze Age form, the rest are all late types and consistent with a Late Bronze Age initiative in the exploitation of the lowlands.

The central Marches (fig 3, p 24)

The excavation of Croft Ambrey produced only one sherd of pottery comparable in form and temper with that used in the Bronze Age cemetery at Bromfield. It was found over the top of late Iron Age deposits and no other Bronze Age artefacts were found, although a Bronze Age date was obtained for some carbonized grain found in an Iron Age deposit. South of the Ambrey near Croft Castle, at about 152 metres, a ring-ditch that possibly belongs to a barrow is known from an aerial photograph. But for a further view of the Bronze Age settlement of this area we need to look northwards and westwards – noting that although we are in a hilly district, most of the barrows presently known are on valley floors. There are three recorded in the valley of the Lugg around Kinsham and the barrow near Walford is probably the survivor of three formerly there.

Although hilltop locations were occasionally employed for barrows in this area, as on the Black Mountains and Malverns, the incidence of valleyward barrows is sufficiently high to show that the rivers held a special place in the minds of the Bronze Age inhabitants. It may be that they farmed the lighter soils of the sands and gravels beside the rivers and buried their dead no distance from their farms; but equally the deceased may have been brought down to the river from afar for their final resting place. In this connection it is particularly interesting to notice that the round barrow at Jacket's Well, Knighton, which produced two collared urns and cremated bones, was placed at the confluence of two streams. In the area of the Clun-Teme confluence by Leintwardine there are at least eight ring-ditches known from aerial photographs in addition to the Walford barrows. None of these has been systematically excavated, but there can be little doubt that this junction of river valleys was an important focus of activity.

The Bromfield necropolis

The limestone hills above Leintwardine decline eastwards to the valley of the Teme north-west of Ludlow, beyond which the ground rises again to the dominating brow of Titterstone Clee Hill. Between the Corve to the east and the Onny and Teme to the west there is, near

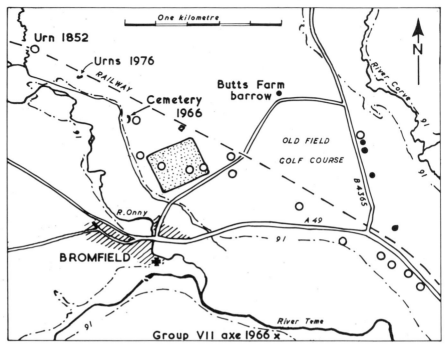

Fig 11 The Bromfield necropolis. The five upstanding barrows are marked by large dots and the fourteen ploughed-down barrows by circles. The Roman marching camp with a farm enclosure north of it are stippled

Bromfield, an extensive level gravel terrace, utilized as a golf course and race-track and crossed by the railway and the A49. Widely dispersed over this oval area about 1500 metres long and 750 metres wide are some twenty barrows and a flat cemetery *(fig 11)*. Of the barrows two particularly prominent examples stand at the edge of the golf course, topped by large trees, while an even larger one, much reduced by ploughing, stands in the angle between the railway and the B 4365.

When Fortey mapped and excavated the barrows here in 1884 there were six still standing; another to the north-west had been cut through by the railway in 1852. He found cremated bone and part of a bronze knife at the bottom of the large barrow by Butts Farm, while from the other tree-crowned mound at the eastern end of the golf course a large urn forming a secondary deposit near the top was broken by the excavators. This urn and the heavily decorated enlarged food vessel from the barrow in the railway cutting show that these large barrows belong to the Early Bronze Age; but the area was already in use in the Neolithic and Beaker periods. A Group VII Graig Lwyd axe and a perforated battle-axe have been found in the vicinity; and

Neolithic and beaker sherds have been excavated close to the small enclosure shown in fig 11.

Further evidence of such early activity is given by a carbon-14 date of 2560 BC for charcoal in a pit cut by a barrow ditch examined in 1967 following the enlargement of the Bromfield sand and gravel quarry. No artefacts survived in the shallow remains of the barrow's central grave, but around the barrow and up to about twenty metres from it were a number of grave deposits, including four urns, three of them upright and one on its side. There were also four small isolated deposits of washed cremated bone and two shallow pits containing charcoal.

About thirty metres north-west of the barrow a cemetery was uncovered during an earlier stage of quarry extension in 1966. Here some 130 shallow pits, up to about 400 millimetres deep and 600 millimetres in diameter, had survived the age-long ploughing. Their contents revealed a complexity of burial routine, the significance of which still escapes our understanding. Three carbon-14 dates show that the cemetery was in use for over 800 years, the earliest being calibrated to the period 1770–1870 BC and the latest to 910 BC. Proof of continuity of use is offered by the rarity of instances where earlier cremation pits are cut by later ones; it would seem in most cases that the small heap of earth that was surplus to filling requirements after the cremation deposit had been put in the pit remained adequately prominent, like a large mole-hill, to ensure that its position was respected, even over hundreds of years.

Only two graves had a deposit of cremated bones in an urn. In both cases, as in the burials around the barrow, the empty urn had been placed in a hole dug about 600 millimetres deep from the ancient surface; into it was then poured a token of cremated bone and the grave was backfilled. There were instances where only a compact deposit of clean cremated bone was encountered, as though it had been deposited in a leather or cloth bag; and there were twenty-two pits with nothing but charcoal below their backfilling. The other 100 pits contained various amounts of comminuted cremated bone in a charcoal deposit, and of these thirty-one also included some pottery. In many cases it was clear that most of the pot had been buried but that it had been broken before burial; there was no evidence of more than one vessel being represented in any pit.

The pottery is particularly interesting as it contains several of the ornamental features – such as imitation horseshoe handles, bosses and finger-tip decoration – found on urns of the Deverel-Rimbury tradition of southern Britain (fig 12). Although the models for these forms

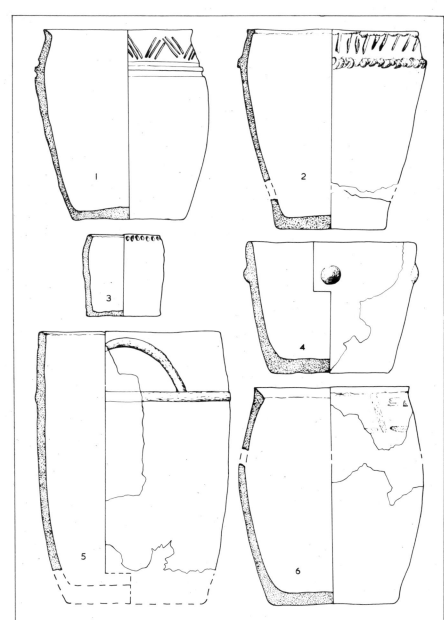

Fig 12   A selection of pottery from the Bromfield cemetery (x¼) Nos 1, 2
and 6 from pits 1770–1870 BC, 1030 BC and 910 BC
respectively. Note the finger-tipping on No. 3, the bosses on
No. 4 and the applied 'horse-shoe' decoration above the cordon
on No. 5.

may have been brought into the area from outside it is clear that the Bromfield pots themselves were made nearby; most of them are tempered with dolerite such as is found capping Titterstone and Brown Clee Hills ten and twelve kilometres to the east. It seems reasonable to conclude that the vessels used for these burials were brought from the vicinity of the Clees, but we may speculate whether they were provided for the use of the lowlanders by a Clee Hill firm of professional potters or funeral directors, or whether the cemetery was reserved for people from the Clees.

In view of the concentration of barrows and the focal position of this necropolis where Corve Dale joins the valleys of the Onny and the Teme, the use of the same burial area by neighbouring groups is not unlikely. We may look forward to testing this hypothesis if the quarry uncovers further cemeteries where different rock is used for tempering the pottery. Fortunately, the area to the south and west of Bromfield is limestone and that to the north and east mostly sandstone; the dolerite is narrowly restricted to the tops of the Clees.

There are few other Bronze Age burial sites in this sector of the Marches. A barrow containing three skeletons in separate stone cists was removed when Ludlow church was built. On Titterstone Clee is a cairn close to the crag known as the Giant's Chair, and there is a group of round barrows nearby on Hoar Edge and another barrow at Coreley. A seated skeleton was found in a mound when the new church was built at Farlow; and near Bewdley there is the old record of a probable cemetery at Dowles and more recent air photographs of ploughed-out barrow ditches on the terrace gravels there.

This transect of the central Marches, the area crossed by the Clun-Clee Ridgeway, has emphasized the interest of Bronze Age people both in the high tops of the finest hills and the valley floors of the main rivers. A similarly contrasting distribution of barrows is to be found in south-west Shropshire and east Powys. A barrow is mapped beside the river at Eaton in Lydbury North parish and another between the Unk and Clun south of Bicton where two barrows have shown as circular crop marks caused by improved growth over the deeper soil provided by their ditches. There are barrows in the hills to the sides of the Camlad valley east of Church Stoke and several more scattered over the hills of the Shropshire/Powys border; but the greatest concentration is on top of the Long Mynd where about twenty occur at around 427 metres, often placed near the edge where they would be seen from the neighbouring lowlands. In view of its height and steep slopes it is difficult to regard the Long Mynd as a favoured centre of exploitation for Bronze Age settlers whether they relied most upon cattle or crops for their diet. It would seem rather that this magnificent hill mass was held in awe by people who went to the special trouble of burying their dead, though perhaps only their most respected leaders, close to the clouds.

Although the barrows of the central hills are in general unlikely to have been constructed on the site of settlements, they must show that the area around was populated. As Chitty has demonstrated so vividly, the products of many workshops came into this area, and many of them were presumably destined for local inhabitants. So it is that we find early in the metal age decorated flat axes of Irish type lost on Titterstone Clee and in Clunbury village, and other flat axes by the Severn at Arley and nearer the western end of the Ridgeway at Newcastle-on-Clun and eight kilometres further west at Castle Bryn Amlwg. The more developed form of axe, the palstave, was essentially a tool of the Middle Bronze Age but survived into the Late Bronze Age. It is recorded around Bewdley where four have been found, and at Eardington near Bridgnorth; another group appears around Leintwardine with provenanced finds from Walford and Buckton; and at Bucknell a flanged axe was found. Palstaves have also been found to the west at Upper Woodhouse Farm, Knighton and at Bryn Shop near Castle Bryn Amlwg. A palstave is recorded from Titterstone Clee and a socketed axe from Upper House Farm, Silvington, on the east side of the Clee Hills.

Reference has already been made to the frequency of metalwork hoards in the later Bronze Age and two such hoards have been found during draining operations in the central Marches. The small one from the Bloody Romans' Field, Lydham Heath, near Bishop's Castle, included a lunate spearhead, other spearheads and fragments of three more as well as part of three swords, one of them being leaf-shaped. The other hoard was found at Broadward Hall, Clungunford, in 1867, nearly two metres down and accompanied by a great number of animal bones including many complete skulls. The surviving part of the hoard, now in the British Museum, includes parts of at least forty-six spearheads, twenty being barbed. There were also seven fragments of spearhead sockets, five ferrules, two bugle-shaped objects, a tanged chisel and eleven leaf-shaped sword fragments.

As with barrows, the location of these hoards on valley floors may reflect a special interest in water for ritual acts, the hoards resulting from the frequent deposition of weapons to propitiate the gods. Burgess has suggested that the Broadward tradition of metalwork, found across Britain from Dyfed to Lincolnshire, was established in a society in which a water cult was an important feature. An alternative explanation, – not necessarily to be preferred to the exclusion of the cult idea, – would be that the deforestation of the hillsides in the later years of the Bronze Age resulted in greatly increased run-off. The extra production from the new land and the attendant population increase, which may account for the first hillforts, coincided roughly with a climatic change around 800 BC, from the drier sub-Boreal continental-type climate to the wet and cloudy Atlantic phase. Together the several factors could have combined to produce flooding of valleys where bronze-smiths may have had their workshops beside convenient streams. With the drowning of the artisan and the covering of his workplace with silt his store of scrap metal, old implements and newly fashioned ones could have been forgotten. Such founders' hoards are, however, widespread and not confined to the valley floors. Two dug-out canoes found in Marton Pool, Chirbury may belong to the same period.

The Shrewsbury plain and the valleys of the Dee and Weaver (fig 4, p 30)

For the evidence of Bronze Age activity over the lowlands of Shropshire and Cheshire our Wrekin viewpoint is particularly convenient. For the earlier part of the metal ages, until about 1400 BC, there are few finds; but those that are recorded lie across the south-west part of the area from Hadley near the Wrekin to the Oswestry area and beyond in the valley of the Ceiriog. The finds are too few to indicate that they lie along a popular route, and they are not closely datable.

Of the same early period as the Longden Common mould (p 62) are the flat axes from Hadley and Battlefield. North-westwards, on the western edge of the lowlands where the Ellesmere moraine abuts the hills of Wales at Ebnal, was found a small group of interesting fifteenth-century bronzes. There were originally two ogival daggers of Camerton-Snowshill type, and a cast flanged axe of Arreton type, both forms that were most popular in the south-east. One of the other items, an end-looped spearhead, is rare to the south and east but common in Ireland.

It is convenient to take next all those finds that have been ascribed to the Middle and Late Bronze Age, from about 1400 until 600 BC. The transition from Middle to Late Bronze Age around 1000 BC involved some notable technological developments, including the use of lead bronzes; but the implement forms are mostly regarded as developments from Middle Bronze Age antecedents.

Although many areas in the northern Marches remain empty, the

73

incidence of finds of the latter half of the Bronze Age is much more intense than for the earlier years. Moreover, a certain degree of grouping is apparent. This may be examined at the Wrekin. It is easy to see here the significance of the Severn gorge at Buildwas as the way into or out of the plain of Shrewsbury; and it seems likely that this important geographical focus – where the river route is narrowly confined and breaches a transverse hill route from south Shropshire to the Pennines – was appreciated and, in the later years at least, commanded by the Bronze Age inhabitants. The several individual finds in this area include five palstaves from Preston-on-the-Weald Moors, a looped palstave from the Ercall Quarry, a spearhead from Dayhouse Moor, Cherrington, a socketed axe from Hadley and a leaf-shaped sword from the Severn at Buildwas around which place three palstaves have also been found. We meet here too our first bronze hoard in the northern Marches, at Willowmoor at the foot of the Wrekin. The area from which the finds came has a number of mounds which may be barrows, so that it may have had some long-standing religious significance – the hoard possibly representing votive offerings deposited in the marsh. The large number of spear fragments perhaps argues against this, and a more exciting suggestion has been that the finds came from a Bronze Age battlefield. They included two spearheads, one of them lunate, a socketed axe, some swords and about 150 fragments of spearheads. The lunate spearhead places the hoard in the same general horizon as the Broadward and Guilsfield hoards, in the eighth century or later.

From the Wrekin it is possible to trace with some confidence two trails of later Bronze Age finds, one north, the other north-west. The first of these takes us via the Tern valley to the Ellesmere moraine and then beyond Whitchurch along Cheshire's Central Ridge. In the south, in the upper Tern basin, are two hoards containing socketed axes, an isolated socketed axe and a sword. At the north end of the ridge at Ince on the side of the Mersey a socketed axe was found. Between these two extremes there are several finds of the Middle or Late Bronze Age. Most are in and around Delamere Forest, where they include burials at Houndslow, containing three urns and a pigmy vessel, a highly ornamented small cup that often accompanied urns. Other burials were found at Castlehill and Seven Lows, where a collared urn was discovered. Undated barrows in this area are found at Galowsclough, Monarchy Hall, Tiverton and Tilstone Fearnall. South-west of this group there are barrows at Coddington and Carden Hall, while to the south-east, at Egerton Hall, were found two gold twisted bar torcs of the later phases of the Middle Bronze Age. It is

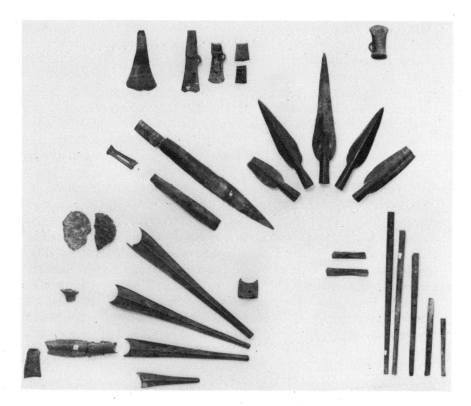

Plate 12   The Guilsfield Bronze Age hoard (*National Museum of Wales*)

likely that the ridge served both as an area of colonization and as a route from the Mersey to the middle Severn.

The second trail lies along the Severn north-westwards from the Wrekin with a palstave and a looped spearhead from Wroxeter, two palstaves and a trunnion chisel from Meole Brace, a socketed axe and a palstave near Shrewsbury and then a scatter of finds along the valley of the Perry including four socketed axes, a shield, rapier and knife from Hordley, and a spearhead from Petton/At Knockin Castle a palstave was found. By way of these finds we reach a small hoard at Brogyntyn, Selattyn, just north-west of Oswestry in the vicinity of which have been found a flanged axe, a flanged chisel and four palstaves/The route so described will have brought us by way of the Severn and Perry close to a major breach in the front of the Welsh massif, the valley of the Dee at Llangollen. Here the focus of routes from the south-east and those from north and south along the edge of the

75

highland are marked by clusters of finds including two hoards/Chitty has mapped no fewer than eight socketed axe finds along the Dee valley from Llangollen to Ddôl; it will always have been an important route for penetrating North Wales/

To the south of this famous corridor a similar situation can be discerned in north-east Powys where the Severn enters the Shropshire plain. From the Breidden hillfort overlooking the bend of the Severn comes a socketed axe; and a spearhead is recorded from the Severn valley nearer Welshpool. The major find here however is the hoard from Guilsfield (*pl 12*) on the hillside just above the Severn and only 100 metres from Crowther's Camp. The hoard contained originally more than 120 objects dated very widely through the Bronze Age; they included a flat axe, palstaves, a looped socketed axe, a lunate spearhead, a hollow spearhead, a leaf-shaped spearhead, ferrules and fragments of leaf-shaped swords, ogival sword chapes and socketed gouges as well as partially worked and unworked bronze. A collection of this kind looks like the stock-in-trade of a bronze-smith and it is possible that the finds came from his actual work site.

/ North of the Vale of Llangollen a number of finds cluster around Wrexham and Mold, on the rising ground between the Cheshire plain and the Clwydian Range. They include the hoard of six unlooped palstaves and a chisel from Acton Park, an unlooped palstave from

Plate 13　The Mold cape of gold (*Reproduced by courtesy of the Trustees of the British Museum*)

Buckley and a socketed knife from Minera. Evidence for Early Bronze Age settlement on the plains of this area is provided by fragments of a food vessel, two cinerary urns and a pigmy cup from Holt. Burials on the hills of north Clwyd include a barrow at Ffrith y Garreg-Wen, Whitford, which yielded a dagger and food vessel sherds; six secon-

Plate 14   The Caergwrle bowl, of oak with gold leaf decoration. Height 79 mm
(*National Museum of Wales*)

dary cremations were inserted into the mound. At Rhydwen in the same parish a food vessel and a pigmy cup were found in a barrow, and at Brynford an Early Bronze Age cremation contained in an encrusted urn was accompanied by segmented blue faience beads that may have been imported from Egypt or some other eastern Mediterranean source around 1450 BC, though an alternative view is that such beads were also made in Britain. At Lower Stables Farm, Ysceifiog, Fox excavated a cairn surrounded by a ditch. There was a primary crema- tion and three secondary deposits of cremated bone, one contained in a cinerary urn.

It is interesting that in addition to the lost torcs from Egerton Hall we have in this north-western part of the border three other gold objects of the Bronze Age. There is first a twisted bar torc from Holywell similar to the Egerton Hall ones. Then from Mold comes a gold cape (*pl 13*) found in 1833 with human bones in a cist under a cairn known as Bryn-yr-Ellyllon. Many amber beads were also found in the cist, presumably from the fringe of the cape. There can be little doubt that this was the grave of an important person, indicating the increasing prosperity of the northern Marches during the period around 1200–1000 BC.

Dated a little later, perhaps around 800 BC, is a remarkable oval oak bowl with gold inlaid patterns (*pl 14*) recovered from a boggy field south-west of the Rhydyn, west of Caergwrle Castle. There is general agreement that the concentrically circular devices around its rim represent shields hung from the side of a boat, while a zigzag inlay near the base is taken to represent the choppy surface of the sea, towards which dip golden oars. This schematic representation seems to show knowledge of galleys such as were used in the eastern Mediterranean about this time and the bowl may be seen to be yet another of the items, like the buckets and cauldrons of Ireland and Wales, that were influenced by, if not imported from, Mediterranean workshops.

Nowhere in our survey of the Bronze Age artefacts and burials in the Welsh Marches have we come across a house or settlement. The apparent paradox of the Bronze Age, replete with burials but lacking settlements, has been partially reconciled in recent years by the recognition that hilltop settlements, defended by palisades and often succeeded by hillforts, probably formed a common settlement type during the Middle and Late Bronze Age. It is easier therefore now to see the finds of the centuries after 1200 as a reflection of increasing settlement that was to lead to the establishment of palisaded sites. That is to say, the hillfort story, which has been reserved for the following chapter, begins, however uncertainly, in the Middle Bronze Age and is going strong through the Late Bronze Age, from around 800 BC. Against this background it seems significant that the clustering of Bronze Age finds is more noticeable north of Broadward, whereas it is only sporadic in the south. For this reason alone it would be appropriate to begin an enquiry into the relationship between Bronze Age settlement and hillforts in the north of the border country, but it also happens that the earliest dates we have for border hillforts have come from the northern Marches.

CHAPTER SIX

The Hillforts

The hillforts are in many respects the most striking and important archaeological monuments in the Welsh border. In certain areas between the Severn and the Dee these ancient camps occur with a density, proportionate to size, as great as anywhere in the world and display fortifications whose extent and complexity are rarely surpassed in Europe. Between them they encompass a period of occupation of more than a thousand years. For many decades they have been the targets of archaeological research, and we probably now know more about Welsh border hillforts than about any comparable group in the whole Celtic hillfort province from Caithness to Asia Minor. This appreciation has been greatly aided by the compilation of the Ordnance Survey *Map of Southern Britain in the Iron Age* (1962) and it is likely that the general density and distribution of hillforts shown on that map is substantially complete. Nevertheless, there are some additions necessary in the Welsh Marches including Oakmere Camp in Cheshire, the Berth north-west of Shrewsbury, Colstey Bank near Bishop's Castle, Dinmore Hill, Westington and Uphampton Camps near Leominster, and Eaton Camp near Kenchester.

Whereas these camps were once viewed as a late reaction to the Roman invasion, the chronological bracket has expanded dramatically in recent years to show that the earliest, palisaded, sites go back to the Middle Bronze Age, perhaps as early as 1200 BC, and that substantial ramparts were being built around 800 BC; so hillfort constructions overlap the technological change from bronze to iron. Accordingly, it seems appropriate to think of the period covering the Late Bronze and Iron Ages as the Hillfort period. Some sites remained in use during the Roman occupation, and some may have been occupied during the Dark Ages.

There are considerable differences in the density and size of hillforts from one part of the border to another, and differences too in history. Foremost, after matters of date, are questions of function.

Were they permanent settlements, or temporary refuges, or simply meeting places for occasional tribal gatherings? How independent were they of one another, and how extensive were the tribal territories? To answer any of these questions we have to seek evidence for continuity of activity or of abandonment and neglect, evidence that is both difficult to discover and uncertain to interpret.

Our study so far has indicated that prehistoric communities on the border often acquired objects and ideas from afar and communications seem to have been comparatively efficient. We may therefore assume that comparable tools and structures should bear comparable initial dates in neighbouring areas, permitting the construction of a relative chronology based on defensive features that can be supported by the increasing number of carbon-14 dates. It is unfashionable these days to explain new phenomena by invoking invasions, but we should not spurn them when other explanations seem inadequate. The pre-Roman Celtic period in Europe was one in which numerous folk migrations are historically documented, and even in Caesar's time groups from Gaul were migrating to Britain; so there is no reason why earlier migrations should not be accepted for Britain as they have to be for continental Europe.

The valleys of the Dee and Weaver (fig 4, p 30)

From Moel y Gaer one is conscious that much of the terrain to the east is unsuitable for hillfort construction. Nevertheless, if we leave the close-set Clwydian forts between Foel Fenlli and Moel Hiraddug near Prestatyn as part of the Welsh upland pattern, placed to exploit the Vale of Clwyd, there still remain in the northern border some upland areas that are less intensively utilized for hillforts than is the case south of the Severn/North of the Ellesmere moraine the Cambrian foothills have only some seven hillforts along a front that is over fifty kilometres long, and four of these are close together in the valley of the Alun. The Central Ridge has a cluster of six hillforts including Eddisbury Camp and Helsby; but south of Kellsboro' Castle there is only the tiny Maiden Castle, Bickerton, standing alone to control south Cheshire. North and east of the Weaver hillforts are unmapped until the scattered sites of the high Pennines are reached fifty kilometres or more away. The Eddisbury group therefore marks the north-eastern limit of border hillforts/

Moel y Gaer forms the best starting point for a discussion of the excavated evidence from these hillforts, for Guilbert has shown that there was a settlement on this hillock before the standing rampart was built. A ring of posts beneath the rampart indicated a round hut of normal Bronze Age form that is assumed to be contemporary with a continuous palisade slot several metres outside the standing rampart. This is a well-documented example of a palisaded hilltop enclosure with round huts inside. Charcoal from the occupation surface of the hut indicates that it was in use until about 820 BC or later, and this date is likely to fall within the life of the surrounding palisade. A palisade at Dinorben, Clwyd, is dated 1170 BC, and that at the Breidden, Powys, 975 BC. Eddisbury too has a pre-rampart palisade. The lack of harmony in the palisade dates may indicate that they were constructed as a local response to changing conditions and are not to be regarded as

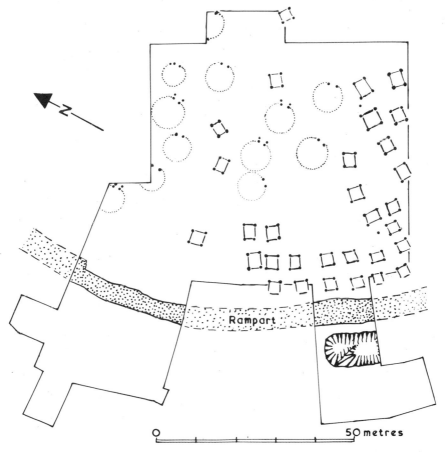

Fig 13 Sketch plan of buildings in part of Moel y Gaer, Rhosesmor, in phase 2, showing four-posters and stake-walled round houses, four of them with porch posts (After Guilbert 1975)

simultaneous introduction from outside. A fence is, after all, a simple and common means of delimiting a settlement, keeping stock and children in, and keeping cattle raiders and wild animals at bay (there would certainly have been bears and wolves in the forests at this time).

Other post-ring round huts at Moel y Gaer show continued use of this form of building down to about 450 BC. The whole settlement was remodelled about 370 BC, when a large rampart was constructed within the line of the former palisade (fig 13). Its course lay across the ruins of the earlier round hut, which may have been demolished to allow the defence to be so set. The impressive construction of the new rampart involved front posts with narrow infillings of masonry between them (pl 15) and apparently some horizontal timbering between these posts and a back row. The whole rampart was about six metres wide and had in front of it an irregular quarry-like ditch. The elaborate Moel y Gaer rampart is broadly within the same family of timber-laced ramparts found by Varley at Eddisbury and Maiden Castle, Bickerton. Together they may indicate a major phase of hillfort building in the northern border, using a technique that was used on sites as far apart as Finavon, Angus and Crickley Hill, Gloucestershire. Its long popularity in North Wales was demonstrated by Savory at Dinorben, where the second timber-laced rampart was built not earlier than about 500 BC, although the underlying original timber-laced rampart produced material dated around 975 BC.

Guilbert's demonstration that the post-ring round huts of Moel y Gaer were replaced now by a grid of four-post square huts encourages the view that the refortification reflects radical changes in the settlement pattern, perhaps as the result of folk movement. Also thought to be present now are less substantial round buildings provided with door posts as the stoutest component in a ring-wall of stakes, presumably with wattle and daub covering. This settlement does not seem to have lasted long, for the four-posters were dismantled while their timber was still worth salvaging. If all the four-posters were contemporary they would have been taken down before about 250 BC. There would probably have been a long period of disuse before the somewhat shadowy later re-occupation that involved rectangular buildings with no surviving foundations or post-holes and a rampart reconstruction that is dated not earlier than about 200 BC. There is no evidence on which to postulate continued occupation beyond this time.

At some stage Eddisbury Camp was provided with paired rectangular guard-rooms at its south-east entrance. Although less regular in plan, they are clearly in the Welsh border tradition of what Savory has

Plate 15   The revetment of Moel y Gaer hillfort rampart showing the stone piles set between post-holes (*G. C. Guilbert*)

called 'Cornovian' guard-rooms, after the tribe that occupied Shropshire; and they may be expected to belong to the same general period established for such structures in Herefordshire, i.e. the fourth to third centuries BC (*fig 15*). It is interesting that there are surface indications of guard-room recesses at Moel y Gaer too; and it may be supposed that they were contemporary with the rampart of 370 BC.

Although Varley was convinced that these Cheshire hillforts were permanently occupied, there is insufficient evidence to indicate the intensity and duration of such settlement. It could be that some, or all, of these sites were occupied from time to time, involving widely separated periods of rebuilding and occupation. The hillfort experiment may have been tried and not found popular; or they may have served for seasonal gatherings of communities of scattered farmers, involving only light and sporadic occupation. It is worth noting that the sum of the enclosed areas of all seven Cheshire forts only amounts to 11.5 hectares, less than a tenth of the Shropshire or Herefordshire equivalents.

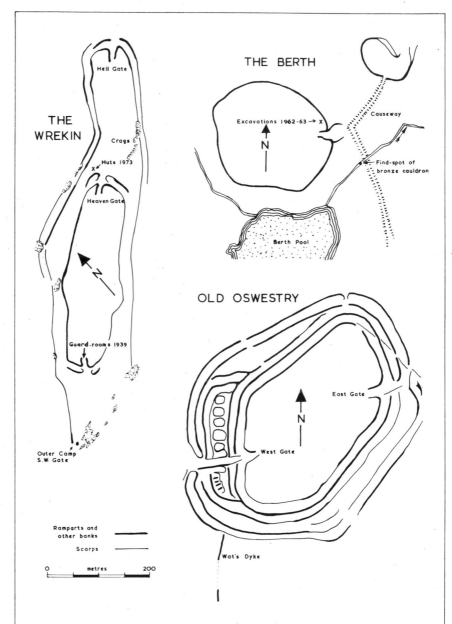

Fig 14   Three Shropshire hillforts: The Wrekin, the Berth and Old Oswestry
(Adapted from Ordanance Survey plans)

The Shrewsbury plain

South of the Ellesmere moraine we enter territory where the hillforts are in general large although very widely separated. Several hold defensive positions on hills that permit exploitation of the lowlands, like Oliver's Point, Bury Walls, Ebury, Haughmond Castle and the Burgs. Others demonstrate the contrast in hillfort location that is so common in the British scene; thus Old Oswestry is only 164 metres above sea-level, whereas the windswept Wrekin is at about 408 metres. What Old Oswestry lacks in altitude it makes up for in the magnificence and complexity of the ramparts. The outer defences of the Wrekin may be little more than a ledge, but the hillside beyond is nearly precipitous. The unusual site of the Berth, Baschurch, consists of two hillocks in a marsh, connected by a causeway to the firm ground nearby.

It is possible that there was also an extramural population in scattered farmsteads like those in the Sharpstone Hill area, but no convincing dating evidence for them is yet published. It seems unlikely in any case that such farms formed a major element in the population compared with the hillfort communities; but they are of more than a little interest since they include round houses and four-posters.

The early history of the Severn hillforts must begin with the Breidden in Powys, where Musson has obtained a date of around 1000 BC for a somewhat irregular double palisade, with posts one metre apart laterally and longitudinally, found beneath a stone rampart, and presumably related to some of the Bronze Age metalwork, including a socketed axe, found there. It recalls the double palisade of more regular construction with posts about 1.5 metres apart, under the timber-laced inner rampart of Ffridd Faldwyn Camp, twenty kilometres to the south. A single palisade, associated with post-ring round houses, was found below the rampart of Old Oswestry, where too there was Bronze Age material. There is thus good reason to believe that much of the Late Bronze Age metalwork found in this part of the Marches is in some way related to the establishment of hillforts. The buildings inside the Breidden include timber round-houses presumably associated with the palisade and rectangular four-post and six-post structures, related to the stone rampart and carrying late fourth-century dates, as did the four-posters at Moel y Gaer. Associated with the rectangular huts were also some stake-walled round huts, comparable with those at Moel y Gaer.

From excavations in 1939 and 1973 it would seem that the Wrekin was first defended by a simple dump rampart thrown forward on the

85

natural steep slope, enclosing something more than six hectares. Excavations at the north-west corner, the most exposed part of the site, showed that four-post houses, no more than about three metres square and with hearths inside, had been constructed and rebuilt two or three times on terraces cut into the hillside. Working back from the carbon-14 dates obtained from the posts involved in the burning of the final hut, it seems likely that the first buildings were put up some time early in the seventh century. There are embayments discernible on either side of the northern inturned entrance corridor of this camp, Hell Gate, which suggest that by the end of its occupation this first Wrekin hillfort had rectangular guard-chambers. These might be expected around 400 BC and so conform with the carbon-14 dates for the burning of the huts.

A smaller perimeter enclosing about four hectares was then constructed higher up the slope, the outer lower areas being abandoned. The southern entrance of the new defence had rectangular timber and stone 'Cornovian' guard-rooms, so it may be assumed there was no long gap in occupation between the burning of the larger hillfort and the construction of the new defences. It is not known what form of house was used for this later camp but the apparent continuity of guard-room tradition might lead us to expect similar buildings to those just described. Nor do we know how much longer permanent occupation of the Wrekin continued, although a carbon-14 date for some burnt grain lying on a terrace in the outer camp shows that there was another fire about AD 50, when the Romans would have been operating nearby. The absence of Romano-British sherds shows that the hillfort did not continue as a village during the Roman period.

From the discussion of hillforts so far it will have been apparent that the earthworks we see today are the remnants of centuries of use and alteration. They were extended and retracted; sometimes old defence lines were actually obliterated. At the Wrekin there was substantial contraction but the rebuilt defences still consisted of a single rampart, or merely a fighting platform, and ditch. On some multivallate sites there is insufficient evidence to decide between different interpretations of the function of the earthworks./At the Breidden the rampart already mentioned has another stone rampart outside, sixty to ninety metres away down the slope. The space between the two is wide enough to have served as a corral, but it is interesting to notice that it is approximately the same distance as across the defences of Old Oswestry, where banks and ditches succeed one another without intervening space, leaving no doubt that the final defence there was multivallate. Four banks with intervening ditches protect Old Oswestry for most of its perimeter, but at the west gate the number is increased to seven and part of the area beside the corridor is further complicated by several transverse banks which would serve to confuse anyone trying to escape from the entrance corridor into the shelter of the ditches. This is the most northerly example of developed multivallation of the form that occurs spasmodically between Shropshire and Dorset. There are relatively few hillforts that exhibit such extensive corrugation of terrain aimed, presumably, at holding the enemy about ninety metres away from the defenders on the innermost rampart, and perhaps related to the developed use of the sling as argued by Wheeler for Maiden Castle, Dorset. In its own spectacular way Old Oswestry thus draws our attention to the individual quality of border hillforts reflecting a society in which personal preference and initiative often overrode traditional forms of defence and organization. Such multivallation must belong to the later years of the Iron Age and allow Old Oswestry to join the Wrekin as a hillfort that probably remained in use until the Roman conquest./

The central Marches (fig 3, p 24)

This area contains the greatest variety of hillforts. There is the mountain-top eyrie of Caer Caradoc by Church Stretton, an ideal example, one might think, of a hillfort refuge. Yet this uncomfortable enclosure has within it numerous hut platforms, and its inturned entrance, with guard-room recesses, is approached from the moor below by a fine graded path cut obliquely into the hillside. There can be little doubt that, like the Wrekin, Caer Caradoc was a permanent settlement.

With this in mind one might turn to the largest hillfort in the area, Titterstone Clee, where a ruined stone rampart lies sprawled across the moor, encompassing originally more than twenty-eight hectares (pl 16). It was thus about three times as large as any other hillfort in the central Marches and on grounds of size alone must be assumed to have had some special importance. Its imposing aspect would have made it a well-known landmark at any time and it will be remembered that dolerite, probably from this hill, was utilized in the Bronze Age pottery found at Bromfield. We have however little evidence to help us distinguish the function of this hillfort from that of any other in the border. O'Neil's excavations were mainly concerned with the defences that were going to be quarried away and in the course of his work he showed that a timber wall had fronted the rampart at an early

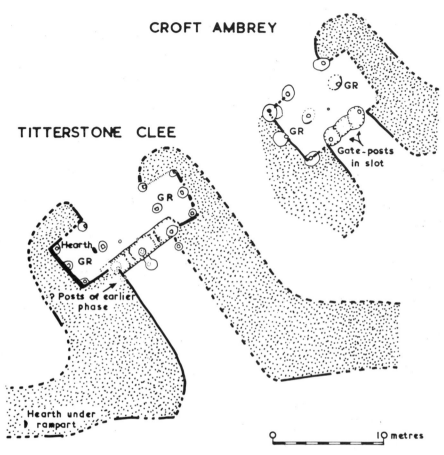

Fig 15 Guard-room phase gates at Croft Ambrey and Titterstone Clee Hill Camp. Croft Ambrey, South-West Gate period VA (based on Stanford 1974, fig 16); Titterstone Clee, main entrance, period III (based on O'Neil 1934, pl X with the addition of the gate slot from his periods I & II)

stage before the existing stone revetment was built. More than one period was involved at the South Gate, which was approached by a six-metre wide corridor with paired rectangular 'Cornovian' guard-rooms of composite wood and stone construction behind its twin portals. We can therefore assume that Titterstone Clee was partly contemporary at least with the Wrekin, and also the Roveries by Bishop's Castle where Thomas re-excavated twin guard-rooms of similar form. At both the Roveries and Titterstone Clee no Iron Age artefacts were found and there was no evidence to show whether they remained occupied until the Roman conquest.

Plate 16 Titterstone Clee hillfort rampart

Another site with important evidence for the early occupation of hillforts in the central Marches is Caynham Camp near Ludlow, which has produced unstratified sherds of two vessels tempered with dolerite (*fig 16*). Caynham Camp itself is on a narrow upfolded outcrop of Silurian limestone, surrounded by Old Red Sandstone; the nearest outcrop of dolerite is four kilometres away. In these circumstances it would seem that Caynham was being supplied by professional potters working on the Clee Hills, whence came the temper for the Bronze Age potters at Bromfield. It becomes increasingly significant therefore that one of the sherds from Caynham (*fig 16, 7*) has been regarded by Gelling as a close parallel to a Bromfield vessel found in a pit dated 910 BC. It would seem likely that the occupation of Caynham goes back to the early centuries of the first millennium BC, although in view of the undistinguished character of the pot in question it would be unwise to regard the parallel as offering more than a general chronological horizon for comparison; a vessel of this simple kind could have been in vogue for three or four centuries. Nevertheless, it may point to the possible occupation of Caynham at a time when palisade defences were in use elsewhere in the northern border. Such a defence, not clearly substantiated by excavation at Caynham, would have preceded the first rampart which was apparently strengthened with horizontal timbers. We may speculate that the firing of this rampart, comparable with the destruction of other timber-laced ramparts on the Cotswolds at Crickley Hill and Leckhampton Camp, was the work of hostile newcomers.

In front of the degraded remains of the burnt Caynham rampart a small bank was built, possibly with a crude stone revetment at its front and a stockade on top. This work preceded a massive rampart built over the remains of both earlier works. A lot of its spoil must have come from internal scooping, and it was associated with a deeply inturned entrance that must be expected to contain guard-rooms and to be broadly contemporary with the fifth-century Main Camp defences at Croft Ambrey. It is not possible to be more precise about the duration and nature of the later Caynham occupation, though the limited excavations in the corridor of the East Gate hinted at a complexity of features, and some of the unstratified sherds from the camp interior look typologically late in terms of the Croft Ambrey sequ-

Fig 16 Pottery from hillforts in the northern Marches, 1–10, and southern Marches, 11–17 (¼)
Nos 1–3, the Wrekin; 4–6 the Breidden; 7–10 Caynham Camp; 11–14 Llanmelin Wood Camp; 15–17 Lydney Park Camp

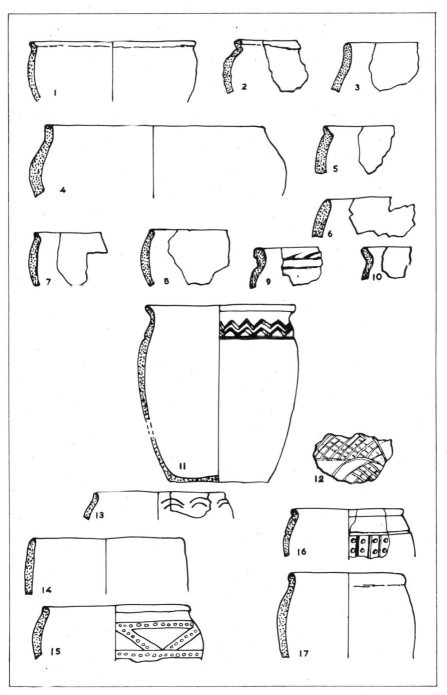

ence. We may guess that it remained occupied until about the time of the Roman conquest, though the absence of Romano-British sherds shows that it was not fully utilized as a village during the Roman period.

On the sloping interior at Caynham was a terrace with a slot for the wall of a semicircular building, eight metres in diameter, with several large posts across its front (fig 17). It presumably belongs to the hillfort occupation and its lack of parallels on other border hillforts may indicate an unusual function, perhaps as a temple. The same area had numerous other post-holes, difficult to interpret but probably including at least two four-post buildings. Even small trenches usually exposed post-holes, often re-cut many times so that it looks certain that Caynham was closely built upon. Especially interesting was the finding of quantities of carbonized wheat in many post-holes and the charred remains of post stumps as well. The two terminal posts of the semicircular building were burnt, but so too were the two western posts of a four-poster, 3.3 by 2.4 metres overall, that lay across the western side of this building. Clearly at least two fires were involved. If the burning of the four-poster was at the end of the occupation, perhaps at the time of the Roman conquest, the destruction of the semi-circular building may relate to the earlier burning of the timbered rampart.

The discovery of quantities of wheat at Caynham Camp is important evidence for the use, and presumably the growing, of wheat in the Welsh border; and although the occurrence at Caynham is not closely dated, its presence in numerous post-holes, which can hardly all belong to the same period, makes it likely that it was normally in use in the hillfort. Evidence pointing in the same direction was obtained at the Wrekin, where samples of carbonized grain from two terraces were dated around 675 BC and AD 50. The communities of the central Welsh Marches were growing corn from an early stage in the hillfort period and still cultivating it when the Romans arrived.

We have seen that it is only at Caynham Camp that some evidence has been found in the form of potsherds to permit speculation that the hillforts of this central area remained occupied after the widespread construction of large ramparts, inturned entrances and guard-rooms. There is however one site where surviving earthwork indicates activity near the end of the hillfort period./At Bury Ditches, south of Bishop's Castle, the Forestry Commission's conifers have been felled to reveal the proud defences of a multivallate camp which has a defence zone about as wide as that at Old Oswestry, another example of the most developed form of multivallation in Iron Age Britain.

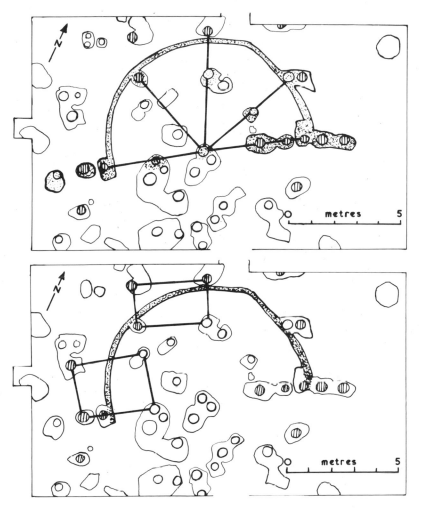

Fig 17   The semicircular building at Caynham Camp
   Above   As envisaged by Gelling (1962–3, 98) with an extended facade
   and possible main rafters shown; semicircular slot and postholes of this
   building stippled. Vertical shading shows post-sockets where clearly
   indicated.
   Below   the author's interpretation, involving at least two four-post
   buildings superimposed on the semicircular plan. Note the large number
   of unexplained post-holes under either interpretation

In this typical hillfort country of the central hills there are more
hillforts per square kilometre than in the border areas to the north. At
the same time there is more evidence for the long-continued use of

hillforts south of the Ellesmere moraine than to the north. It seems that the hillfort form of settlement was better suited to the social and economic needs of the hill tribes than it was to the people of the northern plains; but the reasons for this are not yet easy to discern/ There remains great scope for dating and relating individual sites, for the area includes not only several large hillforts but also a fair sprinkling of the smaller ones that are more appropriate to the Welsh valleys than to the border. It remains to be seen whether the tiny hillforts of south-west Shropshire – places like Wart Hill and the outpost by the Roveries – were continually occupied throughout the hillfort period or whether they represent a particular phase in which small settlements, enclosing only half a hectare or so, were preferred to larger units. Guilbert regards the earthworks on Stitt Hill and Ratlinghope Hill on the Long Mynd as non-hillfort enclosures related to nearby cross-dykes, thus pointing to a possible Bronze Age origin as argued for comparable plateau sites in southern England. The early camp at Ffridd Faldwyn only held about 1.2 hectare; and elsewhere, as there, a small unit may have given way to a larger nucleation when stronger political elements arrived or emerged to reorganize the people of the hills.

The Herefordshire basin

We have earlier seen how the historic county of Herefordshire consists of a region, the Hereford basin, that is itself a geographical unit. Cultural and political boundaries do not necessarily follow topographical divides but there is a strong case for believing that the tribal boundaries of the hillfort period followed the same course as the later county boundaries around the rim of Herefordshire.

This is an area where large camps, mostly over two hectares and about half over six hectares, predominate, and are furnished with large ramparts. Central to it is the largest member, Credenhill Camp, enclosing twenty hectares (fig 18) and twice as large as its nearest Herefordshire contender, Sutton Walls. The central position of Credenhill, in the middle of the basin and in the same area that was used for a Roman town at Kenchester and for the English county capital at Hereford, supports geographically its claim to be the capital hillfort of this tribe. It is difficult to know what kind of evidence would be compelling for the view of a capital function, and certainly the limited excavations undertaken as a rescue operation before afforestation at Credenhill Camp produced nothing exceptional. They merely established that the hillfort shared several characteristics with other excavated hillforts in the area. Before we turn to such detail we may extend our view from the central capital to the hillforts of the perimeter and notice that there are a number of large hillforts established, perhaps significantly, on or close to the county boundary (fig 19). Burfa Camp in Powys, Garmsley Camp in Worcestershire, Herefordshire Beacon and Midsummer Hill Camp in Herefordshire, Symonds Yat Camp in Gloucestershire and the Little Doward Camp in Herefordshire actually lie beside the boundary, while the hillforts of Pen Twyn and Twyn y Gaer are in a part of Gwent that was once a detached portion of Herefordshire.

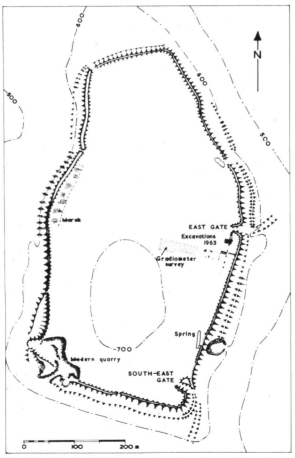

Fig 18   Credenhill Camp, plan showing earthworks and site of excavations 1963. Based upon the Royal Commission on Historical Monuments (England) plan. Same scale as fig 14

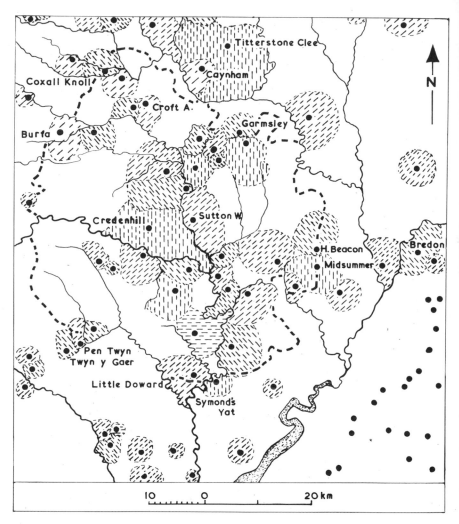

Fig 19 Hillforts of the Decangi and their neighbours with territories
proportionate to the enclosed areas of the hillforts, and the boundary of
Herefordshire shown as a pecked line. Cotswolds hillforts are shown by
dots alone. (Based on Stanford 1972 with modifications)

It is important to notice that excavation of sites within this area has
produced, with the exception of Twyn y Gaer and Capler Camp, a
remarkably consistent pattern of structural and artefactual evidence.
The comparisons are particularly strong for Croft Ambrey, Midsummer Hill and Credenhill, where there are similarities in defence,
houses and pottery to support their inclusion in the same cultural

group from at least the fifth century BC. Although less specific, the finds of pottery and the form of the defences at Sutton Walls, Poston Camp, Dinedor Camp and Aconbury Camp bring them in too. Twyn y Gaer exhibits in its earlier years at least fairly close similarities in gateway structures with the sequence found on the Herefordshire sites, and during this period it too was supplied with pottery from the Malverns. In later years, however, Twyn y Gaer appears to have come under more southerly influences, perhaps indicating a change of political allegiance to the Silures of South Wales.

Capler Camp has been set apart because it is the one hillfort in this area where excavation has failed to find evidence of permanent occupation; however there are special circumstances that may have influenced the blank record obtained by Jack in 1924. The hillfort is on Old Red Sandstone, with soil that is particularly injurious to pottery,

CROFT AMBREY — RESTORED PROFILES OF THE DEFENCES

PERIOD I — 7th century B.C.

PERIOD IV — 5th century B.C.

PERIOD VII — 1st century B.C.

Fig 20 Restored profiles of the defences of Croft Ambrey with ramparts based on the spoil available from contemporary ditches and quarry scoops (After Stanford 1974a, fig 11)

so that few sherds are likely to survive. The absence of sherds, and equally of animal bones which are dissolved in these acid soils, is therefore no criterion to show whether a site has been permanently occupied. Furthermore, we must remember that ideas on what was to be expected inside a hillfort were shadowy indeed in the 1920s. and it is questionable if many of the post-holes and dirt surfaces which now form the evidence for the long history of hillforts would have been recognized. Lastly, the excavation was restricted to long trenches only 0.6 metres wide, giving the excavators, who were professional labourers, little chance of recognizing post-holes even if they had been there. In these circumstances it seems better to regard the excavations at Capler Camp as inconclusive rather than negative, and not to pose it against the prima facie case for treating this area as a unit, with its hillforts sharing a common history.

The beginnings of their story seem to be in the seventh century, if we use calibrated carbon-14 dates rather than the uncalibrated forms preferred in 1974 when the Croft Ambrey excavations were published. The seventh century establishment on that site was a fresh settlement on virgin ground, to judge by the cleanliness of the turf below the first rampart. The defensive ditch that was dug 2.4 metres wide and 1.2 metres deep would have been too small to provide adequate spoil for the rampart which must have received additional spoil from small internal terraces prepared for houses (*fig 20*). The first houses were four-posters, including some at the tail of the rampart. They were set out in lines and occupied sites to which most of those excavated adhered throughout the long occupation. After their initial emplacement some of these buildings were rebuilt as many as six times with the posts going in within half a metre of the original locations (*fig 21*).

The total area excavated on the upper part of the hillfort was small, but it included a variety of terrain, with similar buildings being found on the steepest slope – about one in seven – on the highest part of the hill above 305 metres and on the largest area of flat ground beside the West Gate. Even small trenches dug within this area usually picked up part of a post-hole complex. The topographical variety coupled with the repeated re-digging of post-holes provides us with good reason to think that the circumstances here were different from those obtaining on sites like Moel y Gaer and that before the end of the Iron Age the greater part of the interior was closely covered by rows of buildings separated by narrow paths.

It is interesting that these four-post buildings, ranging in size from 1.8 to 3.6 metres square, are similar to those at the Breidden, Moel y

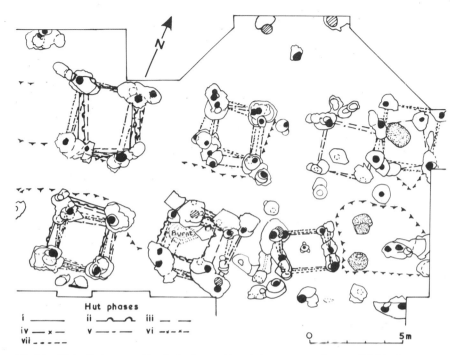

Hut phases

i _____ ii __∿_∿_ iii _ _

iv __ x __ v __ · __ vi _·_·_

vii _ · _ · _ _

0 _____ 5 m

Fig 21   Rebuilt huts at Croft Ambrey. Surviving post-sockets solid black. Pits
stippled (After Stanford 1974a figs 50 and 51)

Gaer and the Wrekin, where the four-posters have also been more or
less square. Mention has already been made of the discovery of hearths
within such small buildings on the Wrekin, but on these bare hillsides
the preservation of hearths is rare. There were however areas of burnt
bedrock indicative of hearths inside one or two huts at Croft Ambrey.
In the absence of other structures for dwellings and on the assumption
that hearths would normally be found in houses it is concluded that
some of these buildings, perhaps as many as half of them, were used as
dwellings. The others, and almost certainly the small examples, will
have served as granaries or as stores for other materials.

   These early inhabitants of Croft Ambrey do not seem to have used
much pottery and indeed the only sherd from the whole site that is
possibly to be dated before the enlargement of the camp about 470 BC
is an unstratified rim tempered with Clee Hill dolerite. It may be that
the manufacture of pottery in the Clee Hill area continued long after
the days of the Bromfield cemetery; although with the exception of
the sherds from Caynham Camp and a single sherd from Sutton Walls
tempered with the same rock there is little evidence of such a survival.

Nowhere in Herefordshire is there yet any evidence of prehistoric timber-laced or timber-framed ramparts, and the only indication of a possible palisade phase preceding earthwork defences is a post-hole in one of the sections at Sutton Walls. It seems likely therefore that this area was not in general entered upon until the seventh century. The other carbon-14 dates obtained support this. At Twyn y Gaer the calibrated date for the fenced annexe in a very early stage of the hillfort's history is 390 BC, which makes the earliest fence on the site, and the foundations of the hillfort, about 470 BC. This is the same as the calibrated date for small twigs from the floor of the quarry inside the rampart of Midsummer Hill Camp, a quarry dug when the camp was established. Both hillforts seem to belong to the same wave of hillfort building that brought in its train a number of changes.

The introduction of new ideas at this horizon is indicated in the first place by the construction of small sub-rectangular paired timber guard-rooms in the new inturned entrance at Midsummer Hill Camp. Although alone in the Welsh Marches, except possibly at Credenhill, the Midsummer gateway was probably paralleled in Dorset at Maiden Castle. Now began the history of guard-rooms and the construction of inturned entrances which are found from the Severn to the Dee.

Credenhill Camp is believed to have been established at this time, its rampart raised mainly from the spoil of an internal quarry. At the same time a new large rampart was put up outside the old circuit at Croft Ambrey, raised from an enormous quarry-ditch to provide a bank that still stands five metres high above its old ground surface and is some seventeen metres wide at the base. It demonstrates considerable concern for defence, along with an adequacy of labour. Although these signs are generally in accord with the evidence from Credenhill and Midsummer Hill Camp, at Croft Ambrey the native culture continued with the re-use of the old square buildings; and, for a while, there were no guard-rooms. Within the century however Midsummer Hill and Croft Ambrey had their gates provided with rectangular stone and timber guard-rooms in the same style as hillforts in Shropshire and Cheshire. The contemporary gate at Twyn y Gaer had no guard-rooms but utilized a slot across the corridor in the same way as the contemporary gates at Croft Ambrey and Midsummer Hill. Neither the transverse slot nor the guard-rooms were used as gateway devices in any subsequent period on any of these hillforts, so the structural parallels between these sites support the carbon-14 dating for their parallel development in the period 470–300 BC. There are, moreover, for the first time in this area, ceramic similarities in that all four sites just mentioned started, around 470 BC, to utilize pottery

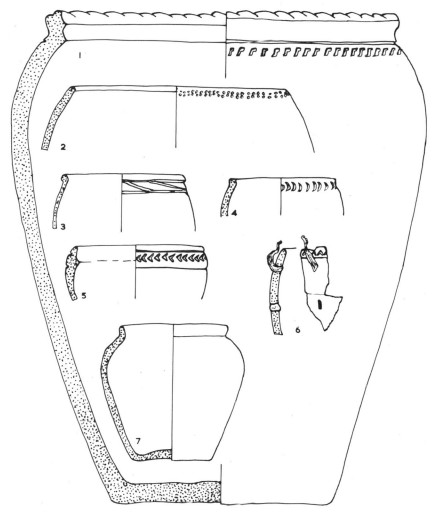

Fig 22 Examples of Iron Age pottery from the Malvern Hills workshops, found
at Sutton Walls (No 1) and Croft Ambrey, including an iron repair strap
on No 6. All approximately x¼

manufactured somewhere near the Malvern Hills.

The recognition by Peacock of the professional nature of pottery
manufacture in the West Midlands during the Iron Age marked a most
important advance in our understanding of these hillfort communities. As with the Bromfield pottery, it has proved possible to
identify the manufacturing area of different vessels from the rock
fragments included in them as tempering. For the hillfort pottery of

this region three geological outcrops are involved. First of all, used in pots mostly found westwards in the Herefordshire hillforts and Twyn y Gaer, is a limestone that must originate close to the Malvern Hills since it includes fragments of Malvernian rock. There is appropriately a narrow outcrop of Silurian limestones along the western side of the Malverns and the workshops of these, Peacock's Group B1 potters would probably have been located somewhere on them. The vessels made in this way were normally stamped with a single, or rarely a double, line of simple motifs, including arrow-heads or chevron designs, occasionally S-stamps, and rather rarely zigzags (*fig 22*). This decoration was normally placed between two tooled grooves close to the rim of barrel-shaped jars or bowls. A very high percentage of the vessels was decorated, and encrustations of soot, trapped in the hollow stamps, show that they were used for cooking, probably by the side of a low charcoal fire.

On the Malverns, at Midsummer Hill, the B1 pots were in competition with vessels tempered with Malvernian rock fragments, which must obviously have been made nearby. These Group A potters also made use of stamped designs, but more commonly relied on linear-tooled patterns, simple trellis designs or crescent marks, not unlike finger-nail decoration. Their pots in the early years were comparable in form and rim treatment with the limestone-tempered vessels, having the same internal grooves, but a tendency developed to produce simpler rim forms, and less careful decoration. Although these Group A potters were the poorer craftsmen, it was they who infiltrated the market to the west, perhaps from about 330 BC, but with increased effect during the first century BC. By the end of the Iron Age they had virtually ousted the limestone-tempered stamped wares from this area. There is a third, much less important group, C, whose designs appear to be related closely to those of Group A potters but who used crushed sandstone, probably from a Cambrian deposit, the Cowleigh Park beds just west of the Malverns. This firm seems to have come into the picture late in the Iron Age and produced simple saucepan-like pots with thickened rims and linear-tooled trellis decoration that remained in use in the early years of the Roman occupation.

Although numerous vessels from the Malvern Hills potters have been found on Bredon Hill and Conderton Camp, and elsewhere on the Cotswolds, their distribution in quantity west of the Severn is limited approximately to the area of Herefordshire. Croft Ambrey's folk were the most northerly of their regular customers and it is therefore easy to understand why they went to the trouble of repairing their broken pots with iron dogs to save waiting until the potter came

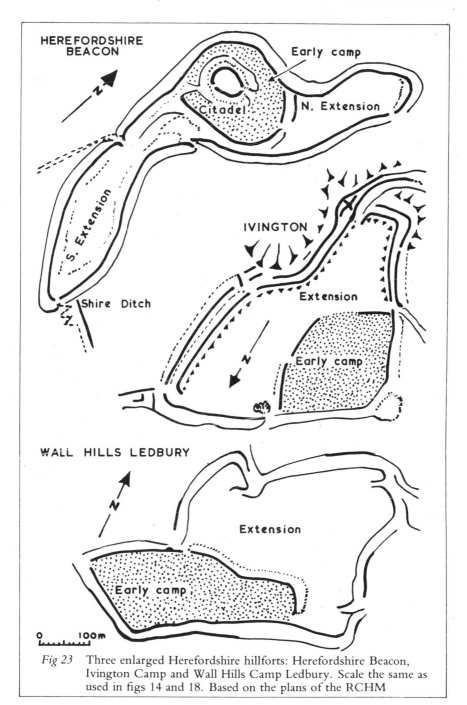

Fig 23　Three enlarged Herefordshire hillforts: Herefordshire Beacon, Ivington Camp and Wall Hills Camp Ledbury. Scale the same as used in figs 14 and 18. Based on the plans of the RCHM

round again. There was much stamped pottery at Poston Camp and it appeared in the early years at Twyn y Gaer. Other sites receiving it in the heartland of Decangian territory were Credenhill, Sutton Walls, Dinedor and Oldbury. The competence of the potting and the occurrence of stamped motifs in north-western France at the same time, in the fifth and fourth centuries, makes it likely that there was a connection between continental potters and these Malvern Hills craftsmen.

The introduction of this professional pottery industry will have been at about the time of a reorganization of hillforts which may have included some new establishments. A number of sites were enlarged at some stage from under four hectares to around eight hectares, and whereas the smaller, earlier enclosures have simple straight entrances the larger ones about them have markedly inturned entrances. Hillforts that were enlarged in this way – conjecturally when the inturned entrance idea was introduced early in the fifth century – are the Herefordshire Beacon, Ivington Camp, Wall Hills Ledbury, and the Little Doward Camp (fig 23). Other sites that are between 6.5 and 10.5 hectares and may have been established now are Aconbury, Eaton Camp, Gaer Cop, Oldbury, Chase Wood Camp, Wall Hills Thornbury, Sutton Walls and Dinmore Hill Camp. It is not, of course, suggested that all the early hillforts in the Herefordshire area were under four hectares and all the later ones over 6.5 hectares, but there is reason to think that in the fifth century larger units were preferred. Thus the fifth century defences at Credenhill enclosed twenty hectares and Midsummer Hill was set out to hold nearly eight hectares. At the same time such an interpretation would involve either the uniting of smaller nucleations in larger units or an infusion of new settlers. In view of the arguments already adduced for the late penetration of the Herefordshire basin, it seems likely that if there were invaders at this time in western Britain they would have looked towards this relatively empty area. It could be that the early fifth century saw one of the last major acts of colonization in lowland Britain before the arrival of the English settlers.

Another pointer to the arrival of new people at this time may be the form of buildings discovered at Credenhill Camp and Midsummer Hill Camp. On both sites the first buildings to be erected were oblong, with four posts making structures about 3.6 by 2.4 metres. This is in contrast to the persistently squarish forms of the four-post buildings found at Croft Ambrey and other locations in the northern part of the border; and four-post buildings in contexts earlier than 500 BC elsewhere in Britain all seem to be square.

Post-holes at Credenhill show that the buildings were rebuilt

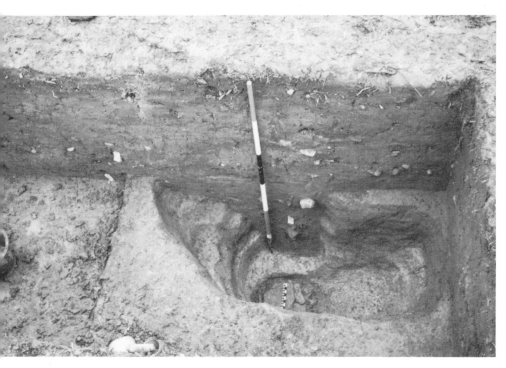

Plate 17   Credenhill Camp, a re-dug post-hole

several times (*pl 17*) but there were no traces of hearths; the huts probably had raised wooden floors. They were only three metres apart, set in rows besides streets that were five metres wide. The building density was thus comparable with that at Croft Ambrey, and at Midsummer Hill Camp, where most of the hillfort has gradients of one in three and one in four. Numerous hut terraces are visible on the latter slopes and have been surveyed twice, once in 1870 by Lines, whose magnificent manuscript plan is preserved in Birmingham City Museum, and again in 1965. The two surveys concur in showing about 230 such terraces on that part of the hill that is sufficiently free of undergrowth and tree cover to permit detailed observations (*fig 24*). If the population of the camp was restricted to these terraces it would have been considerable enough, but the excavation in 1969–70 of a flat area on the Hollybush Hill side of the camp, where no terraces were apparent, showed that four-post structures of the Credenhill type were closely set here and repeatedly rebuilt. The original structures were about 3.6 by 2.4 metres, although there was a tendency for later reconstructions to become square in plan. There was however very

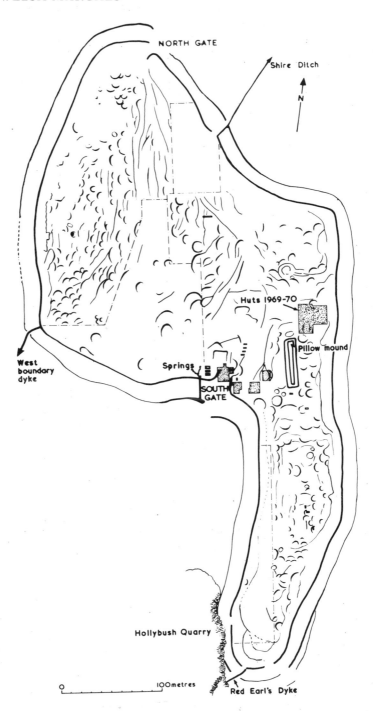

NORTH GATE

Shire Ditch

N

Huts 1969-70

Pillow mound

West
boundary
dyke

Springs

SOUTH
GATE

Hollybush Quarry

Red Earl's Dyke

0   100metres

little movement of huts from their original sites, so that the intervening spaces mostly remained open. In the original plan the buildings were just 4.5 metres apart in both directions, but late infilling reduced this in places. Of the nine buildings explored on this part of the site, the remains of sub-hearth burnt areas survived in five of them, offering some support for the view that approximately every other building on this kind of site was used as a dwelling hut. Taken together with the evidence of the terraces, the excavated huts indicate that Midsummer Hill Camp must have been virtually covered by buildings with little space for other activities save in the relatively narrow quarry scoops behind the rampart.

There is insufficient information available to know whether the same house forms and density prevailed on the other excavated Herefordshire hillforts, notably Sutton Walls and Poston Camp; equally there is no reason to postulate any different state of affairs on those sites. As a starting point for a general assessment of the hillfort occupation of this area it will be assumed that the building densities deduced above were the norm for the other hillforts of this area. Assuming further that every other hut at Croft Ambrey was a dwelling housing four people, the density of population within the main camp ramparts would have been between 180 and 240 persons per hectare, appreciably higher than some of the estimates made for hillforts elsewhere in Britain. Using the lower estimate of 180 persons per hectare enclosed for all the Herefordshire hillforts the total population would have been about 25,000, if we allow 2000 between them for the recently recognized but unsurveyed forts of Dinmore Hill and Uphampton Camp. The overall density for the county would then have been twelve per square kilometre compared with nine per square kilometre estimated for Domesday Herefordshire and twelve per square kilometre estimated from the 1337 Poll Tax returns. I had previously thought it likely that the same density of occupation that characterizes Herefordshire hillforts would obtain in Shropshire, where similar estimates would involve a hillfort population of about 18,000, and the evidence that has since accrued from the Wrekin and the Breidden does not contradict this conclusion.

Of course there are uncertainties involved in all such estimates, but at least they indicate the possibility that population in this area reached a peak in the late Iron Age and probably suffered a decline during the

Fig 24   Plan of Midsummer Hill Camp showing presumed hut terraces and other breaks of slope. 1965–70 excavation areas stippled. Limits of detailed survey shown by broken lines. (Simplified from an unpublished survey undertaken in 1965 by the writer)

Roman period from which it only recovered by the end of the Middle Ages. The implications of these findings, though they may require further refinement, are clear enough. The idea that the lowlands remained a sea of forest into Roman times sadly underestimates the power and organization of the hillfort communities, for by the end of the Iron Age large areas of Herefordshire must have been cleared of trees and the ground used for farming.

There is no way of knowing what the balance was between arable and pastoral farming, though geographical factors might be expected to have resulted in a lesser emphasis on arable in the north of the border and on the higher ground everywhere. The recognition of a 'storage-pit economy' in southern and eastern England has led some to presume that storage-pits are an inevitable concomitant of large-scale arable farming in Iron Age Britain. Yet while carbonized grain is common on Welsh Marches hillforts, pits are rare, only being found at Sutton Walls, Credenhill and Croft Ambrey. Even then they are very small and few and very late in the Iron Age. Grain was mostly stored above ground in four-post granaries measuring up to 2.4 by two metres, like those at Croft Ambrey and Midsummer Hill. This is hardly surprising in a region where a damper climate and less porous soils made general use of storage-pits impracticable.

The climate may also explain the monopoly of wheat in the carbonized grain at Caynham, Croft and Midsummer Hill, whereas elsewhere in southern Britain barley has also proved to be important in Iron Age samples. Corn was thus widespread and may have been general. It was ground on saddle querns, although rotary querns as well appear at Twyn y Gaer during the life of the hillfort; and wheaten buns were probably baked under flower-pot shaped stoves heated by a covering fire of sticks (though Hunt has found similar vessels, associated with the Droitwich salt industry, which may have been used as disposable containers). The coarse earthenware from which these crudely shaped objects were made has been dubbed VCP to distinguish it from ordinary domestic pottery (fig 25). It is found widely through the border from Twyn y Gaer and Midsummer Hill to Moel Hiraddug, but it is noticeably absent from the south Gwent forts and from Caynham and Moel y Gaer. Some of the other items of Iron Age equipment are illustrated in fig 25.

Animal bones are seldom preserved in the acid soils of the border, but Sutton Walls and Croft Ambrey give some indication of the relative importance of various domesticated animals. At Croft Ambrey cattle, sheep and swine were represented in almost equal numbers, whereas at Sutton Walls cattle accounted for half, sheep for a

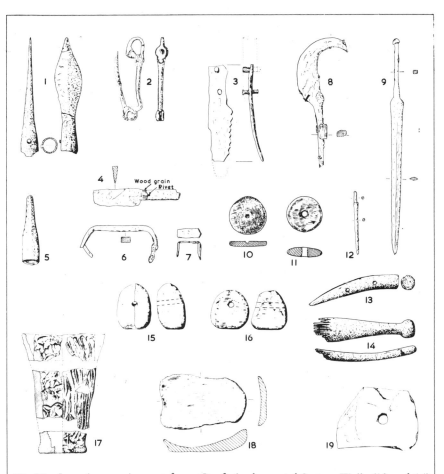

Fig 25 Iron Age equipment from Croft Ambrey and Sutton Walls (13 and 14)

Iron: 1 Spearhead   Antler: 13 Cheek-piece
2 Brooch   Bone: 14 'Weaving-comb'
3 Saw   Baked clay: 15 & 16 Loom-weights
4 Knife   17 Conjectural restoration of
5 Ox goad   a VCP 'oven' (or salt container)
6 & 7 Dogs   Stone: 10 Disc
8 Sickle   11 Spindle whorl
9 Dagger   18 Saddle quern
12 Awl   19 Thatch weight

Scales: 1–7 x$\frac{1}{3}$ 8–14 x$\frac{1}{6}$ 15 & 16 x$\frac{1}{12}$ 18 & 19 x$\frac{1}{24}$

third and swine for a sixth. The high proportion of swine at Croft Ambrey, compared with other English Iron Age sites, may reflect more forest for pannage, or a distinct dietary tradition, or the use of pigs for breaking up rough ground and reducing scrub, even as substitute ploughs. The Whitehouses' study of the Croft Ambrey bones showed that a majority of all species were over-wintered at least once; and the small number of immature sheep represented may show that they were largely bred for wool.

Forest clearance would have been a slow process caused mainly by grazing and the consequent non-regeneration of trees, with ring-barking and pigs playing a larger part than clear-felling. Gradually, modification in the economy and farm routine would have become possible. Flocks may have increased, or been concentrated in areas more conveniently placed for supervision. The arable area might have been extended, giving greater productivity per hectare and making even more pasture superfluous. Such a process may be seen, theoretically at least, to allow the area required by early hillforts to contract towards them and so permit either their own enlargement or the insertion of new settlements in the marginally exploited areas between old centres.

Against a background of thinning forest any sudden demand for structural timber would remove the surviving trees over a wide area. This would happen when a new hillfort was established, particularly if it was to have a timber-laced rampart, though it would normally be required, in any case, to meet the needs of rampart breastworks and houses; and the renewal of these would keep some pressure on the woodlands at all times.

Before we leave the Herefordshire area mention must be made of four hillforts whose defences are amongst the most magnificent of their kind (fig 26). First of these is Wapley Camp in the north-west of the county, occupying the top of an escarpment and protecting its enclosure with five banks on the east side where the slope is negligible, but reducing them to four on the steeper slope west of the South Gate. At their most extensive these defences extend over ninety metres like those of Old Oswestry and Bury Ditches, and the entrance itself is one of the finest in the border with a ninety-metre passage that turns left at the top of the rise towards a hidden gate position. Neither Wapley Camp nor its rival in earthwork, Risbury Camp near Leominster, has been excavated. Risbury Camp is remarkable for its low lying position on a boulder clay covered hillock beside a marsh, overlooked at a distance by higher ground. On the almost flat eastern side are four or five banks and ditches spread out over ninety metres. By contrast the

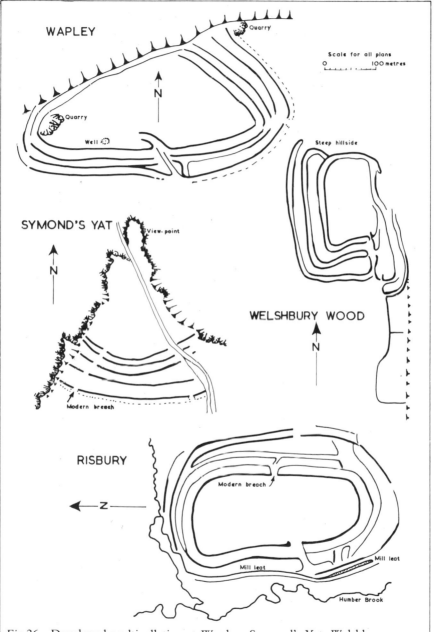

Fig 26 Developed multivallation at Wapley, Symond's Yat, Welshbury Wood and Risbury camps. Scale as on figures 14, 18 and 23. Based on OS and RCHM plans

defence zone is contracted to about seventy-three metres on the steep western side where the main, and possibly only original, entrance is located. These two hillforts demonstrate clearly how vast was the work put into the defence of relatively small communities. Wapley encloses a habitable area of about three hectares, but the defences that protect it extend over another six hectares. Risbury Camp covers 10.5 hectares, but encloses only 3.6 hectares of habitable area. The third site in the region that has defences over a comparable range, although somewhat mutilated, is the promontory fort at Symonds Yat which commands a magnificent view of the river Wye 106 metres below. The neighbouring fort in Welshbury Wood is similarly protected by extended defences along its west side although it encloses only 1.3 hectares.

The Dean-Trelleck uplands

The Roman canton of the Silures had its capital at Caerwent, Venta Silurum, but the territory of the tribe that for so long resisted the Roman army must have extended far to the west to include Glamorgan and southern Powys. The hillforts of the southern Marches may be seen to represent an eastward extension of the Silurian pattern from Glamorgan. The most common element throughout this territory is the small hillfort with less than 1.2 hectare enclosed – often with only a single rampart, though there are numerous multivallate forts as well. There are only a few hillforts between 1.2 and six hectares and only two with more than six hectares, both at the limits of Silurian territory: Y Gaer Fawr in the Tywi valley in Dyfed and Spital Meend overlooking the Wye in Gloucestershire.

It is interesting to notice that when, in its final phase, Twyn y Gaer's ceramic links were with the south rather than the east, the hillfort had been reduced to its smallest extent, an enclosure of no more than half a hectare. The change in pottery involved the abandonment of the Malvern stamped wares, and at the same time the gateway sequence diverged from that of the Herefordshire forts. These developments provide likely grounds for seeing a change in the cultural and possibly political allegiance of Twyn y Gaer, and thereby indicate a site that changed hands in the course of the Iron Age. It should thus lie close to the boundary of Silurian territory, and its characteristics provide further support for the traditional view that the hillforts of the Powys lowlands to the west, which include many small camps with small-scale defences also belonged to that tribe. In the east the division between tribes should lie somewhere on the Wye between

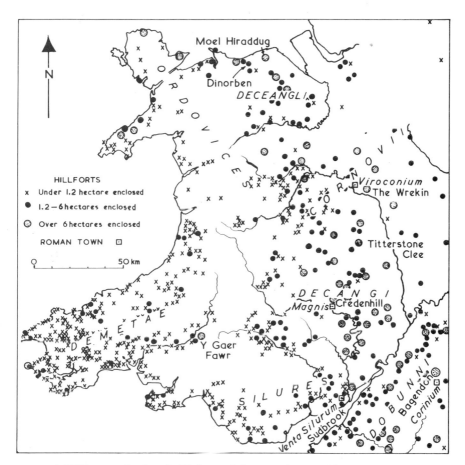

Fig 27 Hillforts and tribes in Wales and the Marches (Hillfort distribution as on OS *Map of S. Britain in the Iron Age* with additions in the Marches)

the Decangian forts of the Little Doward and Symonds Yat and the Silurian forts around Piercefield and Spital Meend. There is a marked break in the distribution of hillforts between the Herefordshire and Gwent groups and a rarity of sites on the Gloucestershire side of the Wye. Across north Gwent, between the Monnow and the Troddi and extending into the Forest of Dean, was a little-developed region that would have formed a no-man's land about ten kilometres wide.

While the distributional pattern thus permits the ready separation of this southern group of hillforts, the various elements that are recorded from them show that they, like Twyn y Gaer, both share certain border characteristics but also reflect other traditions and

113

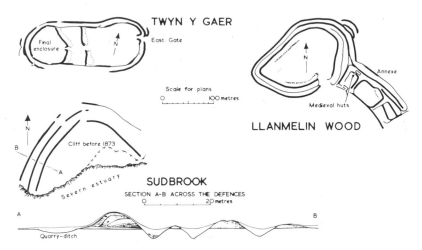

Fig 28   Hillfort varieties in the southern Marches: Simplified plans of
Twyn y Gaer (after Probert 1976), Llanmelin Wood and Sudbrook
Camps (after Nash-Williams 1933 and 1939). Scale as for figures 14, 18,
23 and 26.

influences. There is, for example, no evidence of timber-laced ramparts in the five excavated hillforts in this part of Gwent, or indeed of
any woodwork involved in rampart construction. In this respect too
the similarity with the state of affairs in Herefordshire, and the contrast with the northern border, is marked.

The early stages of hillfort construction in Gwent, although not
widely documented in detail, do seem to reflect traditions similar to
those employed in Herefordshire. At Twyn y Gaer (*fig 28*), following
the use of a fenced enclosure, an inturned entrance was constructed
with a gate that utilized a transverse slot after the manner of those
employed in the stone guard-room phases of the Herefordshire and
Shropshire hillforts. Inturned entrances are also recorded on the
Gloucestershire side of the Wye at Spital Meend and Lydney, and in
Gwent at Llanmelin Wood and Twyn Bell. Only Twyn y Gaer and
Llanmelin Wood have had excavations on their entrances, but at
neither have guard-rooms been found.

A feature that is common to many border hillforts is the use of an
internal quarry-ditch to build ramparts, which has been found on the
southern sites of Llanmelin Wood, Sudbrook (*fig 28*), Lydney and
Coed y Bwnydd. At the latter site dates of 450 and 480 BC were
obtained for timber from a round house built over the silt of a
quarry-ditch/Round houses have not been found in Herefordshire but
were used in the northern Marches in early phases at Moel y Gaer, Old

114

Oswestry and the Breidden/No four-post buildings are yet recorded from Silurian territory, and the only post-holes found within the hillfort of Twyn y Gaer are thought to belong to circular turf-walled houses.

In its pottery too this region is quite distinct from Herefordshire. Only in the early phases at Twyn y Gaer has any stamped pottery emanating from the Malvern workshops been found. Otherwise the contemporary pottery of the Gwent hillforts, what used to be called Iron Age B wares, has general affinities with Glastonbury wares of south-western England. Peacock has noted that at least one Glastonbury sherd from Llanmelin Wood is tempered with calcite and probably came from workshops in the Mendip area. Most of the pottery consists of plain jars with simple rounded or bead-rims, while the few decorated pots from Llanmelin, Sudbrook, Lydney and Twyn y Gaer exhibit simplified motifs from the Glastonbury repertoire, including incised eyebrow ornament and zigzags. The connections with south-western England are clear and are that much easier to appreciate if one bears in mind the likelihood that Sudbrook Camp would have been about the head of the estuary during the Iron Age when the Severn would have presented a narrow crossing for any trader coming over from the Somerset side.

The importance of Sudbrook Camp as a trading post and route centre is perhaps reflected in the attention given to its defence (*fig 28*). A massive rampart, eventually at least 5.2 metres high and 15 metres wide, of similar proportions to those at Croft Ambrey and Caynham Camp, utilized spoil from both its defensive ditch and from internal quarrying. The site must have been already occupied when the rampart was built, for it contained massive deposits of occupation soil. The defences eventually comprised three parallel ditches with low accompanying banks in addition to this main rampart, and the distance from rampart top to the outside of the fourth bank is fifty-eight metres. It is not clear what, if any, was the original defence on the site, but its later history is much complicated by activity during the early Roman period, when pits seem to have been dug into the quarry-ditch through hard trodden areas described as floors. As a result Roman coins and pottery were recovered low down in the quarry-ditch in excavation trenches that were too narrow to allow proper appreciation of the stratification.

Probably to be associated with the Roman pottery, although just possibly an aspect of late Iron Age trade, are numerous sherds of wheel-turned Iron Age material, in general comparable with that being made amongst the latest Iron Age communities on the Cots-

115

wolds and elsewhere in south-eastern England. Only further excavation could show which of these explanations is correct, in any case the contrast between the wealth of material at Sudbrook and the paucity at Llanmelin and Lydney point to the promontory fort having a special role and importance. The sea has encroached deeply upon the camp, the ramparts of which are truncated by modern or former cliff lines; now only some 1.6 hectare of the camp remains, although it must once have been appreciably larger.

The theory that the wheel-turned Iron Age pottery at Sudbrook Camp may have arrived there following the Roman occupation is supported by the rarity of British coins in Gwent. In general the area, along with south-west Gloucestershire and the rest of the Welsh Marches, lies outside the main distribution of the nearest coin-using community, the Dobunni of the Cotswolds. We have noted already that the few finds of Dobunnic coins in Herefordshire are probably the result of dispersion during the course of the Roman conquest, and the same is likely to be true of those in Gwent. The only certain finds are the gold staters of *Catti* from Chepstow and *Anted* from Dingestow and Chepstow. These carry on the obverse the branched emblem that is peculiar to Dobunnic gold staters, and on the reverse a schematized triple-tailed horse. A gold stater of *Corio* similarly designed came from Llanthony Abbey, though it is not known whether it was the Black Mountains Abbey or the one by Gloucester; and from somewhere in the Forest of Dean came two uninscribed Dobunnic coins.

This discussion has shown a mixture of different elements, many inadequately understood from earlier excavations, indicating some affinities with the Welsh border forts to the north but more commonly with lowland South Wales and the territory of the Silures. Many of the difficulties in understanding the history of the area underline the need for more detailed accounts from two or three major sites comparable to the one that has emerged from Probert's excavations at Twyn y Gaer. Only then can we hope to establish whether this area served as a springboard for ideas coming into the Welsh Marches, or whether, as at present seems more likely, it was isolated by forest from northern and eastern influences.

CHAPTER SEVEN

A Roman Frontier

Although there is plenty of evidence throughout prehistory for the movement of goods and the adoption of ideas in the Welsh Marches, most problems relating to its economy and politics are doubtless to be understood within the circumstances of the immediate neighbourhood: the necessary organization for most purposes is likely to have been limited to the range of visibility from our chosen vantage points (*see p xviii*). With the coming of the Romans, the individuality of these areas was subordinated to the requirements of the area as an Imperial frontier. Accordingly, we will abandon the regional subdivisions of the territory and look at the border as a whole through the eyes of the Roman invaders (*fig 29*).

Until now the story of the Welsh border has had to be told solely through archaeological sources using only the material remains of the past; but a somewhat different process of interpretation is required in the historic period. We can still do very little without archaeological discovery, for the surviving pieces of written history for this part of the world are few and generalized; but the archaeological and historical evidence has to be matched so that together they provide a reasonable interpretation of both records. The changes in interpretation over the years are more easily appreciated when it is remembered that Tacitus' account of the conquest of this part of Britain is not only incomplete but lacks accompanying maps; the only geographical locations to which he makes any reference are the river Severn and the tribal territories of the Silures, 'Decangi' and 'Ordovices'. Our task is to try to put archaeological sites in an appropriate context within this account.

The Roman invasion of Britain in AD 43 led quickly to the defeat of the British forces in the south-east. After his brother Togodumnus had been killed in the battle on the Thames, the surviving British leader Caratacus fled westwards. By AD 47 a frontier had been established roughly along the Jurassic escarpment, the subsequent line of

117

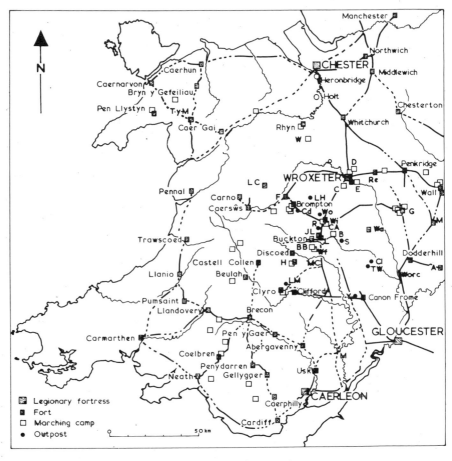

Fig 29 Roman military sites in Wales and the Marches

A Alcester	H Hindwell	TW Tedstone Wafer
B Bromfield	JL Jay Lane	TyM Tomen y Mur
BB Brampton Bryan	L Leintwardine	W Whittington
C Cound	LC Llanfair Caereinion	Wa Walltown
CA Craven Arms	LH Linley Hill	Wf Walford
Cd Caer-din	LM Little Mountain	Wi Wistanstow
Cl Clifton-on-Teme	M Monmouth	Wo Woolston
D Duncote	MC Mortimer's Cross	Worc Worcester
E Eaton Constantine	R Rowton	Y Yarkhill
F Forden Gaer	Re Redhill	
G Greensforge	S Sheet, Ludford	

the Fosse Way. Legio II Augusta was eventually to establish a fortress at Exeter, and Legio IX Hispana one at Lincoln. Somewhere between the two, the Midlands would have been under the control of Legio XIV Gemina, who were eventually to appear at Wroxeter/The years following the Thames battle saw the reduction of at least twenty hillforts in southern Britain by Legio II under Vespasian, hillforts that included places like Maiden Castle, Dorset, with its developed multivallate defences. This may be the context in which similar defensive techniques were introduced into a few Welsh Marches hillforts like Old Oswestry, Bury Ditches, Wapley Camp, Risbury Camp/Welshbury Wood Camp and Symonds Yat Camp. A counter argument is that refugees from hillforts that had just been overrun by the Romans would not have been ideal ambassadors to sell a new system of defence to those Britons who yet remained free. Again, the border sites too may go back some time before the conquest and represent the partial success of professional military architects. Similar professionals may have been responsible for the spread of the guard-room idea in the fifth and fourth centuries BC; and for the wave of broch building in Scotland.

In the winter of AD 47–48, when the governor Aulus Plautius was replaced by Ostorius Scapula, tribes from outside the occupied part of

Plate 18   The inscription to the emperor Hadrian from the forum at Wroxeter *(W. Rogers, by courtesy of Shrewsbury Museums)*

Britain invaded the Roman province so that when Scapula arrived he had first to regain control of some of the frontier districts. Having done this and even disarmed some of Rome's British allies, he attacked a tribe recorded by Tacitus as the 'Decangi'. The identification of this tribe and its territory affects our opinions on both the course of the Roman conquest and the pre-Roman tribal division of the Marches. Several regions may be eliminated on the strength of inscriptional

Plate 19   A Deceanglian inscribed lead pig (*Grosvenor Museum*)

evidence for other tribes (*fig 27*). To the south-east, on the Cotswolds, was Corinium Dobunnorum – Cirencester – Roman capital of the Dobunni, while to the south the Silures had their capital at Caerwent – Venta Silurum; to the north the Cornovii are commemorated in an inscription over the forum of their capital at Wroxeter – Viroconium Cornoviorum (*pl 18*). The tribe in Clwyd, although lacking a known Roman capital, are recorded as the 'Deceangli' on numerous pigs of lead found in their territory and further afield (*pl 19*). Because of the similarity of name they are generally assumed to be the people Tacitus called 'Decangi'. We cannot put bounds to any of these territories nor to that of the Ordovices who occupied north-west Wales and possibly extended into central Wales and Powys.

The one major area in the Marches that has not been accounted for is the Herefordshire basin, the land of densely populated hillforts centred on Credenhill Camp. The only inscription from Herefordshire that is relevant here is on a milestone of Numerian's reign discovered in the foundations of the Roman town wall at Kenchester. This is inscribed with a much eroded 'RPCD', normally assumed to stand for *Res Publica Civitatis Dobunnorum*, and to indicate that in the third century AD Herefordshire was within the territory of the Dobunni.

Because of the considerable archaeological differences between Herefordshire, where no coins or wheel-turned pottery were used before the Roman conquest, and the Cotswolds territory of the Dobunni with its own coins, wheel-turned pottery and new-style valley settlements like Bagendon, it is difficult to accept that the

Herefordshire area was one with the Cotswolds before the Roman conquest. Accordingly there have been suggestions that it came within the purview of the Silures. But there are considerable archaeological difficulties in the way of this assumption too, – differences in hillfort density and size as well as pottery.

If Herefordshire was neither Dobunnic nor Silurian it would appear strange that, as an area of attested wealth and population, it should be unnoticed in the account of the Roman conquest, despite the clear archaeological evidence that many of its huts were burnt at that time. It seems simpler to assume that the people of Herefordshire were indeed the Decangi of whom Tacitus wrote, whether or not the area was still organized as a separate unit under the Romans, and whether the D on the Kenchester milestone stood for Decangi or Dobunni.

The similarity of Decangi to Deceangli has biased the interpretation of the Roman conquest of the Marches. Since we know that Scapula conducted a campaign against the Deceangli it was for long assumed that a legion was at Wroxeter by about this time. This latter view became increasingly unlikely with the accumulation of further archaeological evidence, and the legionary occupation of that site is now known to have been not earlier than the 60s. It is possible that the legionary fortress of the 50s was at or near Wall in Staffordshire, a rather greater distance from Clwyd.

With the legionary occupation of Wroxeter thus postponed, the case for locating the Decangi rests upon the archaeological identification of the tribes of the border. According to Tacitus the campaign against the Decangi resulted in the Romans acquiring quantities of loot, so the tribe in question should be numerous, powerful and wealthy. The area in the Marches where the field and excavation evidence points unequivocally to a well established densely populated tribal area with agricultural and trading potential to provide it with such wealth is, with no possible rival, the Herefordshire basin. By comparison the few hillforts of Clwyd must represent a far smaller population even if they were all still occupied by the time of the Roman conquest. Their poverty in finds is notorious and they have yet to be shown, despite the great amount of work that has been undertaken at Moel Hiraddug and Moel y Gaer, to have been occupied permanently over long periods of time. Furthermore, we have no knowledge of any contemporary open settlements in that area.

While the equation of Decangi with Deceangli is archaeologically unsubstantiated, the fate of the Herefordshire hillforts fits better with that to be expected of the tribe that was the object of Scapula's campaign, surely a punitive one to show that Rome's enemies could expect no quarter. Most of the final huts excavated at Croft Ambrey and Midsummer Hill had been burnt and the general absence of Roman material makes it clear that they were not re-occupied in the Roman period. At Credenhill Camp the buildings appear to have been dismantled before the excavated area was given over to some shallow pits dated to the early years of the Roman period. It would seem that on all three sites the passage of Scapula's troops was marked by the destruction of settlements, the wrecking of communities that had been in place for something like 500 or 600 years. Following such treatment it is not surprising that the record of Herefordshire in the Roman period is not a particularly magnificent one, and that the only town in the territory is so small.

Scapula's success against a Herefordshire Decangi would explain too why in the next episode of this story Caratacus did not raise his standard at Credenhill, but was with the Silures instead. The next event in the west, following the movement of Legio XX to a forward position from Colchester, was that Scapula entered the territory of the Silures. He can hardly have done this directly from Gloucester, where the legion is thought to have been stationed, unless Herefordshire had already been conquered in 48. Only then could he have moved safely into Silurian territory, crossing wherever he chose the long frontier that ran from near Monmouth to Hay. The chances are that it was from somewhere close to Hay, possibly Clyro, that he advanced south into the northern part of Silurian territory around Brecon, for without a contest Caratacus left the Silures and moved north to the Ordovices. A retreat before engagement would seem uncharacteristic of the man unless his position in South Wales was irretrievably threatened either by the vacillation of the Silures themselves or by the threat of encirclement from the north.

The Silures went on fighting until the 70s, so it is unlikely that they turned against Caratacus now. On the other hand a glance at a relief map of Wales reveals the control that would have been exercised by a Roman force in the Brecon lowlands. From here the Usk valley to the west and the Wye valley to the north-west would have provided easy routes by which to outmanoeuvre British forces in South Wales. Caratacus must have recognized the threat of encirclement and moved accordingly.

If this interpretation is accepted it follows too that the British retreat through Wales must have been well to the west and the final encounter with the Britons under Caratacus in 51 would have been north of the upper waters of the Severn. This reasoning has of course shifted the battle area west and north-west from the border hillforts, on so many of which earlier antiquaries have imagined the final encounter taking place; but even apart from matters of geography it is clear that no force large enough to oppose the Roman army would have trapped itself inside hillforts like some that have been championed – such as the Herefordshire Beacon and Coxall Knoll. The case for Cefn Carnedd hillfort in the upper Severn valley, restated by St Joseph, is no stronger, though the area around would have been a likely setting for the final battle. A site within the Welsh mountains, possibly in the upper Severn valley, seems now more likely than one on the west bank of the Severn between Welshpool and Newtown as once advocated by Webster and Dudley; the attraction of that area was primarily that it formed a suitable target for a force operating from Wroxeter. It is also more likely that the Britons, who chose the ground for the battle, would have preferred to meet the Romans in the mountains rather than on the edge of the plain. Furthermore, the British leader's escape from the disastrous battlefield to the Brigantes in the Pennines is more readily understood if the Roman forces had been to the south rather than east of his position.

The archaeological traces of such campaigns are the temporary marching camps of the Roman army. These were rectangular, single-ditched enclosures with rounded corners and gates towards the middle of all four sides. They were prepared as overnight camps by legionary forces on campaign and as more are discovered it may be possible to conjecture the course of Scapula's battle group. Unfortunately, few of these sites are yet known, for in the lowlands the small banks thrown up from their shallow ditches were ploughed flat long ago. Moreover, the Welsh Marches and Wales were subjected to numerous campaigns of which Scapula's was but the first. We may expect to find marching camps built by the army under Gallus in 52–57, Veranius in 57–58, Paulinus in 59–61 and Frontinus in 74–75; and there were occasions much later too when Roman control of the west was temporarily weakened and fresh campaigns had to be undertaken. When the scope of these historical considerations is set alongside the unlikely loss of much equipment, coins or pottery by a force on campaign, it will be appreciated that the likelihood of dating Welsh border marching camps is remote.

Five key areas are known to have temporary camps which may have been used by Scapula. The most southerly is Clyro, Powys, where a camp of more than six hectares is set about the site of the later fort and commands the Wye valley where it emerges from Wales on to the Hereford plain. A second one is near Leintwardine, where the north-south route used by the Watling Street West is met by the Teme valley route from Wales; large marching camps occur at Walford, enclosing ten hectares, and Brampton Bryan, 25.6 hectares. At Brompton, twenty-four kilometres further north near Montgomery, a fort site is accompanied by three large overlapping marching camps, showing involvement in more than one campaign. The fourth key area is on the Severn plain west of the Wrekin, with marching camps at Eaton Constantine, Cound and Wroxeter. A fifth area at Rhyn Park, east of Chirk, contains a 17.5 hectare campaign base and a presumably earlier fort of at least six hectares. Aerial photography has also recorded large marching camps at Whittington near Oswestry, Stretford Bridge near Craven Arms and Bromfield. There must be many more not yet discovered.

The outcome of Scapula's campaigns was the establishment of new forts further west than before. Anything like precise dating is lacking, but it is probable that elements in this frontier were the legionary fortress at Usk; the ten-hectare fort at Clyro – probably replacing the 6.5-hectare fort at Clifford; the more common two-hectare auxiliary forts at Wroxeter and Jay Lane, Leintwardine; and possibly others at Canon Frome and Hindwell. Like most other Roman military works of the first century these forts had an earth rampart revetted with turf and one or two ditches outside. The excavation of Jay Lane (fig 30) revealed timber gate towers at the entrances as well as corner and interval towers constructed with timber 220 millimetres square, set in post-holes about 0.9 metres square. The uniform size of the post sockets reminds us that the stockpiling of timber was an important preliminary to the permanent extension of the province. No internal buildings were excavated at Jay Lane, but at Usk several timber granaries have been excavated.

Following the defeat of Caratacus there was continued trouble in western Britain, and the Silures seem to have been the mainspring of it. Our knowledge of the events between AD 51 and the campaign of Frontinus in 74–5 is limited, but by 78 the tribes of Wales had been subdued and relative stability established. Legio XIV, whose barracks have been exposed by Webster deep below the remains of the later town baths at Wroxeter, was stationed there in the early 60s but withdrawn from Britain in 66 and replaced at Wroxeter by Legio XX from Gloucester. In the later 70s Legio II Augusta, replacing Legio XX, built its permanent fortress at Caerleon, and about AD 79 Legio II Adiutrix built a fortress at Chester. When Legio XX returned from campaigning in Scotland in 86 the Wroxeter fortress was dismantled and it moved into Chester in place of Legio II Adiutrix which was withdrawn from Britain.

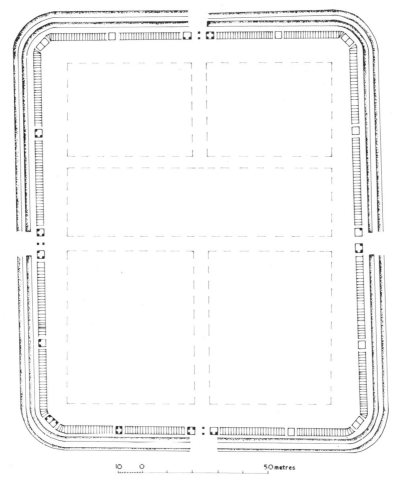

Fig 30 Jay Lane fort: restored plan of defences with the presumed line of the
rampart (shaded) and the conjectured road system (After Stanford
1968b, fig 5)

Caerleon and Chester each held a legion of about 5000 men and
were the corner-stones of the Roman defensive system in the west.
They controlled movement out of Wales along the northern and
southern coastal plains and were on tidal water which facilitated the
supply of the large quantities of stores required for their own garrisons
and those of the outlying auxiliary forts. For the rest, a network of
forts was set up to cover Wales with rearward members in the Welsh
Marches. A fort was built at Usk over the site of the old fortress, and
others were established at Abergavenny and Pen y Gaer. The role of

125

the former fortress at Clyro was taken over by a new auxiliary fort at Brecon. There may have been other forts that were still occupied as late as this in the eastern part of the border, like Walltown, Shropshire.

To this period as well belongs Jay Lane's successor at Buckton, west of Leintwardine. Here, as at Jay Lane, aerial photography and excavation combine to provide a fairly detailed picture of the fort defences. When first constructed, perhaps around AD 80, Buckton had a turf rampart and timber gateway towers and was little larger than its predecessor. It may therefore have been built by the Jay Lane garrison when transferred from the hilltop position which had been appropriate in the Scapulan frontier zone, to a riverside site where a good water supply could be enjoyed and a bath-house constructed. Past claims for forts at Bicton near Clun and Lydham near Bishop's Castle have not been substantiated, and northwards the next fort known to belong to this period is Forden Gaer, Powys, which may have replaced an earlier fort at Brompton.

It is remarkable how few military sites are recorded north of the Severn in the Marches, although north-west Wales has a relative abundance of them. Apart from the legionary fortress at Chester and the works depot at Holt, the only site with proven military occupation after 80 is Whitchurch. Most of the territory of the Cornovii in Shropshire and the Deceangli in Clwyd was apparently either friendly to the Romans or too thinly populated to require sizeable garrisons, underlining the weakness of the assumption that a Clwydian tribe was Scapula's target in 48.

Highland Wales was to remain a constant source of problems; and the army's difficulties there were heightened by the even greater problems associated with the northern frontier in Scotland. As a result it was necessary from time to time to reinforce or remove garrisons from the auxiliary forts so that the Marches, which had served as a springboard for the conquest of Wales, was to be used in later years as a backline for the defence of lowland England. The development of this policy is best understood by considering first the period AD 80–160, and secondly the period after 160.

The Roman frontier AD 80–160

During this period the forts along the Usk above Caerleon were maintained, including Usk, Abergavenny, Pen y Gaer and Brecon. The occupation of Pen y Gaer and Usk, however, probably did not outlast the end of the first century by many years, so that only Abergavenny remained until the mid-second century between Caer-

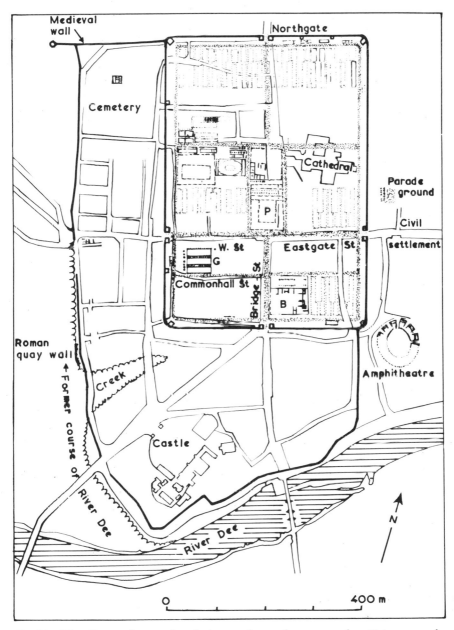

Fig 31 The Chester fortress in relation to the modern street plan. Fortress roads
are stippled
B–Baths G–Granaries P–Principia W St–Watergate Street
(After Thompson 1959 and Petch 1969)

leon and Brecon. In the central Marches the forts at Buckton, Walltown and Forden Gaer remained occupied into the second century, reflecting the special problem created by the protrusion of the Welsh hills across the middle of the border.

The Chester fortress, named Deva after the Celtic name for the Dee, which meant 'goddess', was placed on the north bank where the river flowed round the end of a low sandstone plateau (*fig 31*). It was thus provided with a dry, elevated, level building site near the head of a sheltered estuary, well placed to service both North Wales and north-west England. The line of the east and north walls of the fortress was re-used for the medieval walls, and parts can still be seen; but to the south and west the medieval defences were pushed out to the very bank of the river and the demolished Roman walls on these two sides were left behind to be covered by later buildings. A section of the Roman quay survives below the medieval wall, about 200 metres from the fortress, but the river course used by the Romans is now filled and the only existing channel is 400 metres to the west. Despite the changes in fortune during and since the Roman period the outline of the fortress still shows through the plan of modern Chester. Eastgate and Watergate Streets follow the line of Deva's *via principalis*, the main street across the fortress in front of its headquarters. At right angles to them, Bridge Street perpetuates the Roman *via praetoria* and Northgate Street the *via decumana*. Minor east-west roads are followed by Commonhall Street and Princess Street.

The fortress was unusually large, enclosing 24.3 hectares compared with the normal twenty hectares, but the reason for this is not known. Tombstones show that it was originally occupied, and presumably built, by Legio II Adiutrix, although by AD 90 it had been taken over by Legio XX Valeria Victrix. There had possibly been some pre-legionary activity but the earliest intensive occupation appears to relate to the fortress, with turf and timber defences and timber buildings, constructed in the late 70s. Some of the buildings were twice altered before stone foundations were put in as part of the Trajanic reconstruction, probably soon after 102. A stone wall was then added to the front of the rampart and stone gate-towers were built. The plan generally followed that of the timber fortress with only minor changes.

Although so much of the detail is inaccessible, enough is known to show the magnificence of second-century Deva. Stone buildings so far identified include barracks, granaries and workshops as well as a great headquarters building, *principia*, that is at least 101 by 74 metres, and an intra-mural bath building with a covered exercise hall that together cover a space 80 metres square. Outside the fortress to the east the parade ground has been located and near the south-east angle was an amphitheatre, which was originally wooden but was subsequently reconstructed in stone; it is open to visitors.

Some of the stone buildings were probably rebuilt at the very end of the third century when Constantius Chlorus recovered the province after it had suffered depredation at the hands of invaders from the north. It is uncertain when the legionary occupation ended, certainly not before the disasters of 368–9, and perhaps in 383 when Magnus Maximus took most of the British garrison over to Gaul in his bid for the Imperial throne.

Most Roman military sites in the lowlands attracted civilians too, but there is so far little sign of Deva's civilian suburbs except for structures of a low standard along Foregate Street outside the east gate and some others to the west of the fortress. About two kilometres south at Heronbridge there was a small settlement with stores and workshops along the Watling Street, and twelve kilometres away on the Dee at Holt a legionary works-depot was established in Trajan's time which produced pottery and tiles for the army into the early fourth century (though activity was on a small scale after 250).

The other fortress, Isca at Caerleon, was named, like Chester, after the river on which it stood, being placed where a spur of higher ground narrowed the valley of the tidal Usk and probably afforded a crossing place for a bridge (*fig 32*). The defences, enclosing 20.5 hectares, were first constructed in the late 70s, the clay and turf rampart being placed, as at Chester, on a foundation of logs laid at right angles to the rampart. A stone building inscription, originally prepared to commemorate work in the second consulship of Trajan, shows that the conversion of the fortress to stone was under way by 99 although some of the barracks were still of timber until the late second century at least. The 1.7-metre stone wall that was inserted in the front of the rampart is exposed in the north-west quarter of the fortress along with the foundations of square corner and interval towers and buildings of later periods, including several stone barracks, arranged in pairs, each with twelve two-roomed compartments for the legionaries and a more complex unit against the road for officers.

The headquarters lies under the churchyard, and behind it part of the plan of the *praetorium*, the palace of the legate who commanded the legion, has been recovered. Other buildings in this central area include the barracks of the first cohort and the elaborate houses of their centurions, *primi ordines*, as well as barracks appropriate to an ordinary cohort. Next to the *praetorium* on the south-west side was an exercise

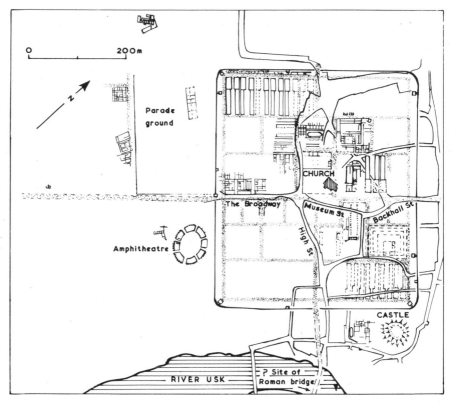

Fig 32 The Caerleon fortress in relation to the modern street plan. Roman roads are stippled. (After Boon 1962 and 1972)

hall and a large magazine, while to the north-east was a workshop and stores. At the south-east end across the full width of the fortress a row of twenty-four barracks matched those at the north-west end. Although little excavation has been possible between these and the *via principalis* it is known that there was a bath building and a hospital there.

During the first half of the second century detachments of Legio II Augusta were away from Caerleon helping to build the northern frontier works, first Hadrian's Wall around AD 122–8, and later the Antonine Wall in the 140s. Nevertheless, there was no general diminution of activity at Caerleon through the second half of the century. The fortress may have suffered damage from local insurgents after 196 when Albinus took the legion to Gaul, for an inscription of 198–209 from the churchyard records the restoration of a building, presumably the headquarters, and there are stamped tiles of the period 213–22 that are indicative of rebuilding. Most of the legion seems to have remained at Caerleon until the end of the third century. The baths and hospital were among the buildings dismantled then, so the fortress was probably not occupied by the legion after 293 when it was probably taken to Gaul by the usurper Carausius.

Although occupation of part of the site continued, the reduction of so much of it at this time explains the lack of correspondence between the modern roads and the streets of the fortress. With so much probably levelled during the Roman period there was more opportunity here than at Chester for post-Roman streets to cut across old building plots and diverge from the Roman alignments to avoid rubble from collapsed buildings. So although the Broadway conforms to the line of the south-west end of the *via principalis*, beyond the churchyard Museum Street and Backhall Street have meandered south of the *via principalis* and over the levelled baths before regaining the Roman line to pass through the north-east gate. The north-west and south-west gates carry modern roads but the High Street crosses the

Plate 20   Caerleon amphitheatre from the north-west entrance (*David Hibbert*)

defences ten metres from the south-east gate. Most of its sinuous course is aside from the *via praetoria* but north-west of Museum Street it follows the Roman street beside the headquarters, indicating perhaps that the south-west side of this building remained a substantial mass of masonry to a very late date.

Just outside the south-west wall of the fortress can be seen the well-preserved remains of the amphitheatre (*pl 20*). One of the major upstanding monuments of Roman Britain, its oval arena measures fifty-six by forty-two metres and the whole structure eighty-one by sixty-three metres. It probably had seating for more than 6000, the nominal strength of a full legion, and could have been used for combat-training and weapon-drill as well as gladiatorial shows. Eight vaulted entrances permitted the rapid assembly and dispersal of even a capacity audience in a building that typifies the professionalism of the Roman army.

The amphitheatre probably lay within the same walled annexe that accommodated the parade ground found north of the Broadway and four bath buildings, including a large one beneath the medieval castle bailey between the south-east defences and the river. Outside the annexe wall was a civil settlement, a *vicus*, traversed by the road from the south-west gate to wharves on the Usk. A large building, about thirty metres square, stood alongside a major street that runs at right angles to the Broadway and was possibly the *mansio*, or official guest-house for travellers. It was built in the middle of the second century and may have marked official approval of the *vicus* development. Here there would also have been houses, shops, warehouses and baths; and inscriptions indicate the presence somewhere of temples of Diana and Mithras.

The Trajanic enthusiasm for reconstruction in stone at Chester and Caerleon was echoed in some of the auxiliary forts, and Buckton, which may have come under the Chester command, was probably one of them (*fig 33, pl 21*). It enclosed 2.3 hectares and, like its timber predecessor on the site, and its earlier equivalent at Jay Lane, probably held a cavalry unit. In the early second century a stone wall was constructed at the front of the old turf rampart and the ditch was cleaned. Impressive stone gate towers, flanking twin portal entrances, were also built. The over-all dimensions of the east gate were 22.3 by 6.1 metres, larger than any other auxiliary fort gatehouse known in Britain (*fig 34*). The remarkable size is to be explained by the unusual provision of stone staircases within the towers, an amenity sometimes used on legionary fortresses but rarely on auxiliary forts. Within the defences the fort was set out with gravel roads, and some of the central

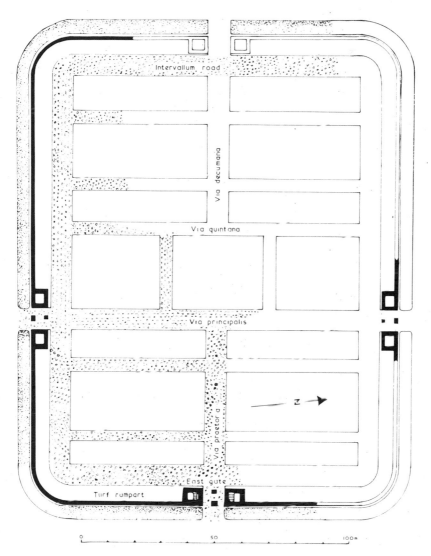

Fig 33 Buckton fort, showing stone defences and roads, shaded where revealed by aerial photographs or excavation (After Stanford 1968b, fig 10)

buildings, including the granaries and headquarters, were also built of stone, although most of the area was still occupied by timber structures.

By about 140 the Romans must have felt that it would be safe to reduce the garrison in the Welsh Marches even more and Buckton was dismantled. The stonework was demolished to the foundations,

133

Plate 21 Aerial view of Buckton fort showing as a crop mark in ripening corn (*W. A. Baker*)

presumably to be utilized elsewhere. Similar sandstone, showing signs of previous use, was found in primary contexts in a bath-house built at Leintwardine in the second half of the second century. Since such stone is not to be found in situ on the Leintwardine side of the river, it is possible that it was taken from the demolished Buckton fort.

Buckton is unlikely to have stood alone in this area during the late first century, and among the possible candidates for its contemporaries, twelve kilometres to the south-west, is Discoed, Powys, where the earthworks indicate a fort about 140 metres wide, the same as Buckton, located to control movement along the upper Lugg valley and presumably replacing the Hindwell fort.

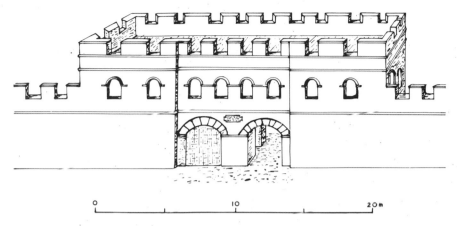

Fig 34   Reconstruction of Buckton's east gate (*porta praetoria*) adapted from Richmond and Child's reconstruction of Housestead's West Gate (1942)

There must be other forts yet to be identified in the hills between Buckton and Forden Gaer; and there is a gap of thirty kilometres between Buckton and the contemporary Walltown fort near Cleobury Mortimer; one might have expected a fort near Ludlow but none is known. At Walltown the first-century rampart was constructed of turf with timber lacing and a stone front was added some time after about 120. The fort is almost square, covering 1.9 hectare, but the rampart is only well preserved south of the road, the northern half of the fort being occupied by farm buildings. The auxiliary fort at Usk was probably not garrisoned after about 110, and the military occupation of Abergavenny probably ended about the middle of the second century.

The Roman frontier after 160

There was a general reduction of garrisons in Wales after 140, although perhaps not as great as was once imagined. It is particularly interesting that the Romans maintained their forces in the centre of the frontier with a quadrilateral of forts at Caersws, Castell Collen, Forden Gaer and Leintwardine, spaced about twenty-eight kilometres apart. All four were occupied through the second century and into the third, with evidence for some occupation in the fourth. Strategically placed to control central Wales and the Marches between the bastions afforded by Caerleon and Chester, they may have represented a new answer to the problems of Wales – possibly employing cavalry, since three of the four are unusually large for auxiliary forts.

135

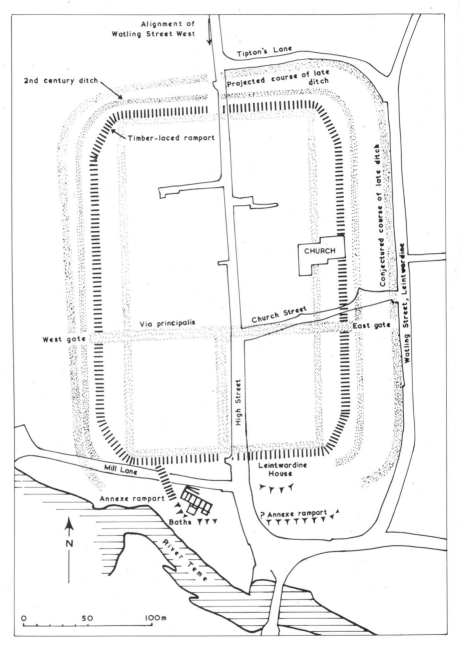

Fig 35 Leintwardine Village fort showing defences and conjectural plan of the main fort roads

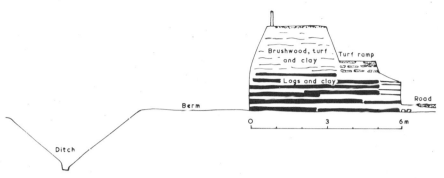

Fig 36   Reconstructed section of Leintwardine's second-century defences (based on a section close to the north-west angle. After Stanford 1968b, fig 24)

The two sites of the quadrilateral which are in the Marches, Forden Gaer and Leintwardine, have much in common. The fort at Leintwardine village (*fig 35*) was constructed after 160, perhaps as late as the 170s, and some time after the fort at Buckton had been demolished. It was constructed on the rising ground north of the Teme and had a small annexe holding a bath-house between the fort and the river. The area along Watling Street West that was taken over by the military had previously been a civil settlement which must have served in turn the garrisons of the Jay Lane and Buckton forts as well as travellers along this frontier road between Chester and Caerleon.

The character of the internal buildings, other than the baths, of either the civilian or military occupation, is uncertain, for Roman levels have been badly eroded except in the lee of the rampart which can still be discerned for most of the circuit but is best seen along the north and west sides. The parish church stands just inside the rampart on the east side. The fort area, measured over the rampart, is 4.5 hectares, about twice as large as Buckton. Since the bath-house must have been quite small it seems likely that Leintwardine was a supply depot for the central Marches, held by a single cohort of 500 men.

The large area enclosed at Leintwardine is unusual for a fort, but there is no evidence of a specifically civilian occupation after about 160; whereas the defences have several features that to judge from surface or excavated remains are indicative of a military site. These include its rectangular form, with four gateways positioned as appropriate to a fort, and an unusual shaping of all four angles of the defences giving symmetry that would be unlikely on a civil site. Moreover the ramparts of the fort and its annexe were both made up of alternate layers of logs and clay, with no form of revetting, either

137

back or front. The fort rampart was six metres wide and separated from the defensive ditch by a berm five metres wide (*fig 36*).

The same construction and dimensions were used for the rampart at Forden Gaer when that fort was reconditioned some time after 160 enclosing 3.1 hectares. Forden Gaer is unusual in showing no superficial evidence of gates in its long sides, but it is difficult to accept a recent suggestion that the road goes straight through the site from north to south gates when the excavated evidence shows the *principia* in the normal position across this course. As at Leintwardine there was third and mid-fourth-century activity, but no stone wall was ever added to the rampart.

Other sites that reflect recurrent difficulties in the central hills are the fortlets of Tedstone Wafer and Clifton-on-Teme (*fig 37*), four kilometres apart, on the high ground north of Bromyard. The former is oblong and double-ditched, enclosing 0.5 hectare on High Lane, a road that is probably of Roman origin. Clifton Camp is less regular in shape but squarish, enclosing 0.6 hectare originally, though later reduced to 0.4 hectare. The modern road that passes the camp may be on a Roman ridgeway alignment. The few pieces of pottery from the two sites suggest occupation after 150, and their ridge-top positions on probable Roman roads argues for their being military rather than civil sites. They are perhaps best regarded as police posts, perhaps manned intermittently by small units of irregular troops. They command very broken country, with the hillforts of Wall Hills Thornbury and Garmsley Camp six kilometres to the west, and Berrow Camp and Woodbury Hill Camp the same distance to the east. If they were police posts it would show that the native inhabitants remained in the area, whether or not they stayed in the hillforts.

Tedstone Wafer and Clifton raise some interesting questions for further research. Their precise date and function is not known; and only extensive internal excavation is likely to answer such questions. Meanwhile, it is apparent that such rectangular hilltop enclosures are probably fairly common in the hills of the Marches. North of Clyro, and just in Powys, Little Mountain Camp encloses 0.2 hectare and may be a similar station. Rennell has traced a road branching from the presumed Mortimer's Cross – Clyro road into Little Mountain Camp's only entrance. Earthworks of such a police post or signal station survive on Linley Hill, near Bishop's Castle. Baker has photographed crop-marks of comparable sites at Rowton and Woolston near Craven Arms and the writer has seen others from the air at Sheet near Ludlow and Yarkhill near Canon Frome.

★

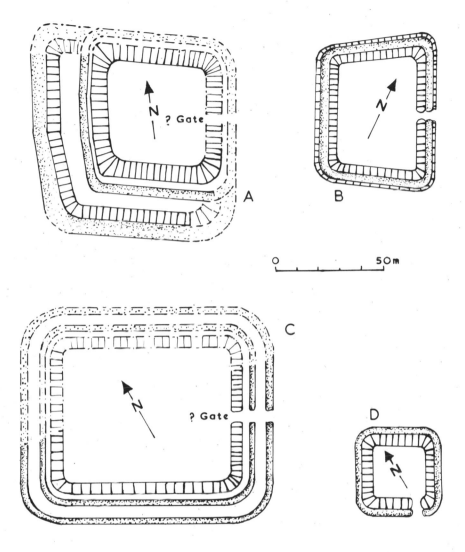

Fig 37 Roman outposts.
    A Clifton (Stanford 1959)
    B Little Mountain (based on measurements in Rennel 1979)
    C Tedstone Wafer (based on measurements and section in Webster 1954)
    D Linley Hill (based on measurements and section in Webster 1955–6)

In summary, the military history of the Marches falls into three periods. In the earliest, from 48 till 74, the Romans gained control first of the Herefordshire – north Gwent region, and somehow extended from this base to control the whole of the Marches. In the second period, following the establishment of Caerleon and Chester in the 70s and the development of a fort network over Wales, several forts in the Marches were abandoned but others were maintained, notably along the Usk and in the central hills at Buckton, Forden Gaer and Walltown. Finally, from about 160, a new policy led to the reconstruction of large forts at Leintwardine and Forden Gaer, alone in the border between Caerleon and Chester. Like Chester these seem to have remained in use until the late fourth century, whereas Caerleon was probably evacuated about the end of the third century. Clearly enough, the threat to the Roman province had shifted. Instead of the Silures being the persistent enemies, by the fourth century barbarians from the north were ready to move in should the Roman hold relax.

Civilian developments (fig 38)

The exploitation of the Marches by the new rulers was of course modified by the military necessity of keeping erstwhile enemies divided and weak. Comparison of the Ordnance Survey *Map of Roman Britain* with the *Map of Southern Britain during the Iron Age* shows a profound difference in the evidence of settlement. The Roman period saw a striking reduction of large settlements of hillfort size, and there is little evidence of lesser nucleations replacing them. Let us consider first the fate of the hillforts.

In the northern part of the border there have been excavations in the interiors of nine out of about thirty hillforts – Eddisbury, Maiden Castle, Moel y Gaer, Old Oswestry, the Berth, the Breidden, Oliver's Point, Ebury, and the Wrekin; and only at the Berth, the Breidden and Oliver's Point has Roman pottery been found. There is little doubt that on the other five sites intensive occupation ceased at or before the Roman conquest. A fire dated to this period in the outer camp of the Wrekin may indicate compulsory evacuation of that hillfort, and it is likely that the detachment that fired the village went from one of the nearby marching camps at Eaton Constantine.

In the Severn valley the Romans may have been content to remove the natives from their most strongly entrenched or naturally fortified sites like Old Oswestry and the Wrekin, allowing occupation to continue in some of the more vulnerable lowland hillforts. The second part of this hypothesis leans heavily on the evidence from Oliver's

Fig 38   The Roman Marches
Civil sites and the legionary fortresses. Although all major sites are
shown, only those minor ones mentioned in the text are plotted.
List of deserted hillforts:

1	Moel y Gaer, Rhosesmor	9	Titterstone Clee
2	Eddisbury	10	Caynham
3	Maiden Castle, Bickerton	11	Croft Ambrey
4	Old Oswestry	12	Credenhill
5	Ebury	13	Midsummer Hill
6	The Wrekin	14	Twyn y Gaer
7	Ffridd Faldwyn	15	Coed y Bwnydd
8	The Roveries	16	Llanmelin Wood

Sites shown by initials only: Ca Caldicott   Cr Cruckton
G Goldcliff   M Magor   R Redwick   W Whitley   WV Whitchurch
Vagas

141

Point, and until a weakly defended hillfort in the plains is extensively excavated an alternative explanation should be kept in mind – that all the hillforts of the northern border were evacuated at the conquest and that there was only sporadic activity on any of them thereafter. The sherds from the Berth and the Breidden are late third- or fourth-century, while Oliver's Point has only second-century pottery. In the absence of excavated Romano-British structures on these sites it cannot be assumed that any of them were re-occupied as villages, let alone defended as hillforts, at any stage after the conquest. It is more likely that they were visited from time to time. As Croft Ambrey shows us, Romano-British religious activity sometimes re-focused on hillforts, resulting in restricted deposits of sherds, unlikely to be recovered by random excavation. The structures associated with such religious ceremonies might be in stone like the Romano-Celtic temples at Lydney Park Camp, Gloucestershire and Maiden Castle, Dorset, both of them dated to the latter half of the fourth century. It is more likely, however, that any Shropshire hillfort temples were of timber, or that the ceremonies were conducted on open terraces as at Croft Ambrey.

The desolation of the hillforts marked the end of a distinct settlement period when the hillfort dominated its environs and the communities were large and closely knit within their defences. Life along these lines had demanded a complex code of behaviour, with acceptance of duties that supported the community through the stress of raids and more serious conflict. It may be that the hillfort experiment had died a natural death in the extreme north of the Marches even before the Romans arrived; but there is no knowing where or in what numbers the population from them had resettled. Without hillfort communities the northern border would have fallen readily before the Roman army even as the non-hillfort south-east of England did in 43. It may be significant that one of the few Roman forts known in southern England is actually built inside the hillfort of Hod Hill, Dorset. Hillfort defences themselves could not be held for long against Roman siege tactics, but a zone of hillforts gave time for the organization of defence in depth and, above all, the concentration of population in a few villages made the tribal chain of command much more effective than it could be in a land of scattered farms. The Romans had to destroy the unifying social and political influence of enemy hillforts by dispersing the population, reducing once proud strongholds to deserted villages. Those leaders who were not seduced to the Roman cause and yet were spared to continue farming did so in fragmented communities, shorn of authority first by defeat and then by isolation. At least, that seems a likely interpretation of what evidence we have; it

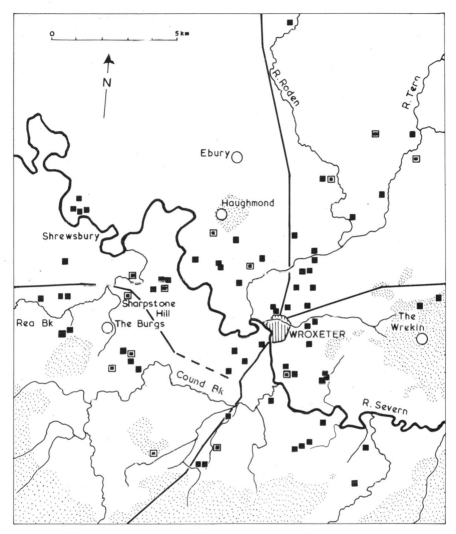

Fig 39   Rectangular enclosures in the Severn valley revealed by aerial
photographs with hillforts shown by circles and land over 122 metres
stippled (Extracted from a map by G. S. G. Toms, 1973)

may be pondered against the facts that follow.

    In the Severn valley, where the double-ditched enclosures of prob-
able pre-Roman farms are not yet correlated with hillfort chrono-
logies, it is possible that some hillforts were already breaking up before
the Romans arrived; although there is good reason to believe that most
were still occupied, including Old Oswestry, the Breidden and the

143

Wrekin. With their evacuation at the conquest there would have arisen the problem of large-scale resettlement. From the Shropshire and nearby Powys sites within or overlooking the valley of the Severn would have come something like 12,000 inhabitants – if they were all as closely occupied as their Herefordshire counterparts.

Just outside the Breidden hillfort is a weakly-positioned univallate enclosure known as New Pieces. Within it were found second-century sherds; and it is likely that the site was established as a farmstead by survivors from the Breidden following the Roman conquest. There is a rarity of other dated sites in the middle Severn valley to house the hillfort refugees, but more and more rectangular single- and double-ditched enclosures are being discovered on the plains. In an area of 320 square kilometres between Ironbridge and Montford, eighty such sites have been mapped by Toms from aerial photographs (fig 39). They are mostly undated but probably Roman, although some may have been founded before the conquest. One of those at Sharpstone Hill measured thirty-five by forty metres, enclosing 0.1 hectare within its ditch, and contained a four-post structure, 4.4 metres square, within a penannular eaves drip gully ten metres in diameter. Pottery in the native Iron Age tradition could be of the same date as the Romano-British first- and second-century sherds from the site, for the Malvern potters who sometimes reached this area in the Iron Age continued their business into the Roman period, supplying the forts as well as the towns and farmsteads.

A double-ditched enclosure on Sharpstone Hill is strikingly similar internally, with semicircular eaves drip gullies enclosing posts that could represent elements of four-post buildings about three metres square. But detailed consideration of the implications of these most interesting sites must await their full publication. It is also apparent that such enclosures would have held little more than a family unit, perhaps ten persons, giving a population for the eighty known sites of 800 persons, few more than might be expected in the two hillforts of Haughmond Castle and the Burgs that are within the area where most of the enclosures have been photographed. They amount to 3.2 hectares together; but on the fringes of the area Ebury Hill, the Wrekin and Wall hillforts enclose in all another fourteen hectares.

From these considerations it appears that we are a long way from accounting for the probable dispersed hillfort population, and that unless massive deportation took place, there must be many more enclosures – perhaps another 200 – to be found. Many may lie on sandstones and clays away from the gravel areas and will prove more difficult to discover from the air.

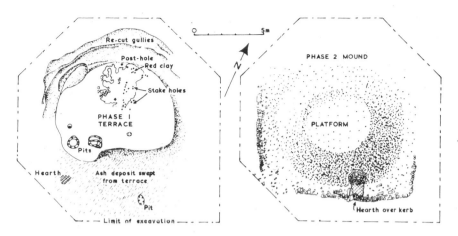

Fig 40   The successive forms of the Croft Ambrey Romano-British sanctuary
(Based on Stanford 1974a, figs 64 and 65)

It is, however, already clear that in the Roman period the large
hillfort nucleations had been mostly broken up and numerous small
units substituted. Most of the new farms were presumably carved out
of the old fields which would have extended for two or three
kilometres from the hillforts; but others must represent the new intake
of land not previously used. This is especially likely to be the case
around Wroxeter, itself established at a distance from any hillfort and
possibly attracting new farmers who left behind neglected sheep
pastures around their old hillfort villages. Perhaps the Cornovian
farms close to Wroxeter included newcomers from further afield,
possibly from the hillforts of the central Marches; for in that difficult
terrain, where Roman military activity continued throughout the
occupation, there is no evidence for the permanent occupation of any
hillforts after the conquest, despite excavations on Ffridd Faldwyn,
the Roveries, Titterstone Clee, Caynham and Croft Ambrey.

Only at Croft Ambrey have even a few Romano-British sherds
been found within the main enclosure; but there can be no doubt that
occupation of the site as a village terminated with the conquest.
Nevertheless, the inhabitants seem to have continued to worship in
front of their old rampart, for on the sloping ground within the low
bivallate defences of the hillfort annexe they prepared a terrace for
ceremonies that probably involved animal sacrifices supported on
stakes (*fig 40*). The red clay floor of the terrace seems to have been kept
clean, for the rubbish from these ceremonies was nearly all found on
the slope immediately below, and consisted of charcoal, numerous

Plate 22   Croft Ambrey mound from the south-west in the course of excavation

sherds of Romano–British pottery, some burnt bones of sheep, pig and cattle, and a number of bronze brooches. The use of this terrace sanctuary extended from the first century into at least the mid–second. It was then covered by a flat-topped mound nearly twelve metres square at the base and one metre high (*pl 22*). A rough drystone kerb with rounded corners survived on three sides. Just to the south of the sanctuary the annexe defences had been breached in Roman times, as though to enable worshippers to reach it more easily from outside the hillfort, where presumably their new dwellings lay.

Since there are many hillforts in the central hills, the displaced population must have been considerable, and we have already noted that some in the north may have moved into new land around Wroxeter. Others may have gone to new farms in the Severn valley downstream to Worcester, and many may have been resettled in the valleys around their traditional strongholds, where there are already a few enclosures known that are not unlike the Cornovian farmsteads of the Severn valley. Baker has photographed five within five kilometres of

146

Leintwardine, and there are several in the Ludlow-Bromfield area. There would have been considerable changes in the landscape. Whereas the hillfort communities would have cleared most of the hilltops around their villages and probably much of the more distant land in the valleys, if only for rough grazing with glade pastures, the change in settlement pattern would have led to the clearance of valleyward sites around the new homesteads and the reversion of old fields around the abandoned hillforts to scrub and then forest.

Further south, a more selective policy was probably employed by the invaders. The huts of Croft Ambrey and Midsummer Hill, around the edge of the Herefordshire basin, were burnt and no villages were re-established on them. By contrast there was a long continued Roman occupation of Sutton Walls and Poston Camp, and Roman sherds have been found inside Dinedor, Aconbury, Wall Hills Ledbury and Uphampton Camps. It looks as though the natives stayed on in most of the hillforts in the middle of Herefordshire; but not in all, for the Romano-British finds over the top of the dismantled huts at Credenhill Camp were few indeed and none need be later than the 60s. This may indicate that early in the occupation, if not in Scapula's time, the policy of evacuation was extended to all the more powerfully placed hillforts, sites like Credenhill, Chase Wood, Little Doward, Symonds Yat and Capler Camp.

One way and another, something like half of the hillfort population of Herefordshire was probably displaced – about 13,000 people, an enormous number to locate. If we suppose they were re-settled in farms of ten persons each, there will be more than a thousand such farmsteads. The problem may be reduced by making some allowance for those attracted to the towns and other Romanized settlements like villas, but the most generous allocation to known sites of this kind would hardly reduce the total to less than 8000 people, requiring 800 farms. At present we have the most shadowy impression of perhaps a score of possible farmsteads in Herefordshire, none of them excavated.

The abandonment of hillforts that characterized south Herefordshire, more particularly along the Wye, probably extended southwards to the coastal plain of the Severn. Twyn y Gaer, our viewpoint on the Black Mountains, was abandoned, not surprisingly in view of its altitude. But no Roman pottery or structures was found in Coed y Bwnydd either, at only 198 metres. Along the southern edge of the Marches, free from the tangle of hills and narrow valleys, the treatment of hillforts varied. East of the Wye, the hillfort in Lydney Park was probably abandoned at the conquest; but in the second century

147

iron ore mining brought renewed activity there until the fourth century, when an imposing temple was built and dedicated to Nodens, probably a Celtic god, who combined concern for healing, hunting and the sea (*fig 41*). This could not have been built just for local use, but was rather a massive investment in the profitable field of piety, equipped to cater for pilgrims from a wide area. The centre of a healing cult, it was provided with an unusual long cubicled building, the *abaton*, in which invalids might rest assured of being visited by the benevolent Nodens in their sleep. For their further comfort during their stay there was a large courtyard-plan guest-house and a suite of baths. Lydney may have succeeded a native temple or have been sited to benefit from the hallowed aura enjoyed by many ancient earthworks, including Neolithic long barrows, in the Roman period.

First-century samian pottery at Llanmelin Wood Camp may indicate less intensive occupation continuing for a decade or two after the conquest, as at Credenhill; but late third- and fourth-century pottery echoes the revival of interest in hillforts seen elsewhere at that time. At Sudbrook Camp there is abundant pottery to show continued occupation, probably into the early second century, and some less intensive use through the rest of the Roman period.

With the exception of Sudbrook, the larger hillforts of Gwent, like those in the hilly margins of Herefordshire and west Gloucestershire,

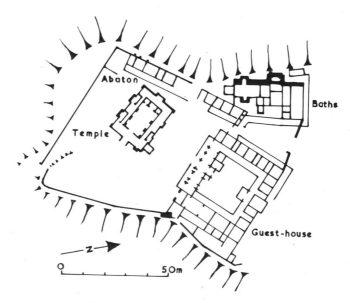

Fig 41   The Lydney Park temple complex (After Lewis 1966 fig 119)

148

were probably abandoned and the population dispersed. There is little published evidence on this question, but Romano-British sherds from the Camp at Bryngwyn in Llanarth Fawr parish show occupation of this small univallate enclosure which is on a low ridge at ninety-one metres. Chance finds of Roman material from buried sites along the coastal plain at Uskmouth, Goldcliff, Redwick and Magor reflect dispersal, and probably also show that the plain was inundated about the end of the second century, so that a second major movement of population would have ensued within 150 years of the first.

The Romanized Britons

For those Britons who were permitted to continue their self-sufficient farming, whether from hillfort or farmstead, the Roman occupation involved important changes in their way of life. The tribute probably demanded more corn from this area just behind the hungry garrisons in Wales, so there may have been an increase in arable land. Some technological improvements came along too, like the stone corn-drier inside Sutton Walls hillfort. The VCP field stoves (or salt containers) of the Iron Age (*p 108*) are rare in Roman contexts; larger ovens (or other vessels) had probably replaced them. In these and other ways a Romano-British culture was permeating even the villages; and the old pottery firms, presumed to be based near the Malverns, turned to large-scale production of wheel-turned vessels.

There were of course the more romanized elements of settlement and industry in the Marches – the towns, villas, potteries and mines, linked by a road system that was quite new for Britain both in style and concept. The straight metalled roads must have been quite unlike any pre-Roman tracks, and although on occasion they possibly coincided with parts of prehistoric routes, evidence of precise superimposition is lacking. Watkins' theory of an extensive system of straight tracks in pre-Roman times lacks proof.

The new Roman roads (*fig 29, p 118*) were not, after all, designed in the first place to serve the native communities but to communicate with the forts – whose disposition was dictated by wider considerations as well as local factors. Military needs required a north-south road from Chester to Caerleon which connected Whitchurch, Wroxeter, Leintwardine, Kenchester, Abergavenny and Usk. North of Hereford an eastern route branched from this to cross the Wye at Hereford and proceed, it is thought, due south to Monmouth and Caerwent. Feeders to the Welsh forts ran from Chester to North Wales and the upper Dee valley, from Wroxeter to Forden Gaer and the upper Severn, from Leintwardine along the Teme valley towards Castell Collen, from Kenchester westwards along the Wye valley, from Abergavenny along the valley of the Usk and from Caerleon along the Vale of Glamorgan to Neath and Carmarthen. This network served, along with subsidiary roads as yet inadequately explored, to distribute men and materials along the Welsh frontier. For reinforcement from further afield there were two main and obvious routes of entry to the Marches: in the north from Penkridge to Wroxeter via Redhill and to Chester via Whitchurch; and in the south from Gloucester north-west into the middle Wye valley and south-west to Caerleon. In between these a third road must have reached Canon Frome from Worcester, and another from Greensforge passed along Corve Dale to Craven Arms and thence to Forden Gaer.

Three walled towns grew up in the Marches, at Wroxeter, Kenchester and Caerwent, one for each of the main tribes, the Cornovii, Decangi and Silures. They differ greatly in form and history, and between them show many of the diverse facets of Romano-British towns, the creation of which was an important part of imperial policy, following hard on the heels of the army. The town provided the necessary centre for government, including the administration of justice and taxation, and also houses and shops for the merchants and other professionals who sought more wealth in the newly acquired markets. Such immigrants would look for the provision of the usual Roman amenities of streets and water-supply; and the promise at least of temples and baths. A vehicle for the transmission of Roman culture into distant lands, the effect, if not the purpose, of the town was to wean the more ambitious and co-operative of the natives from their traditional way of life and graft them on to the imperial system.

Wroxeter, known as Viroconium Cornoviorum, was the capital of the Cornovii, but started life as a legionary fortress (fig 42). When this was demolished about AD 86, army detachments may have stayed on to assist in planning the new town and constructing public buildings on the same alignments as the military plan. Work on a bath-house west of Watling Street, whether intended for the army's or city's use, was unfinished when the army left, and it is not known for certain what buildings, if any, were started on the other side of the road. The extent of the fortress remains unknown, although the discovery of a military-style rampart just east of Watling Street on the later baths' insula in 1975 led Webster to speculate that it extended from here to the line of the later town defences to the east where they overlie two shallow first-century ditches. A problem with this interpretation is that it requires almost completely different street

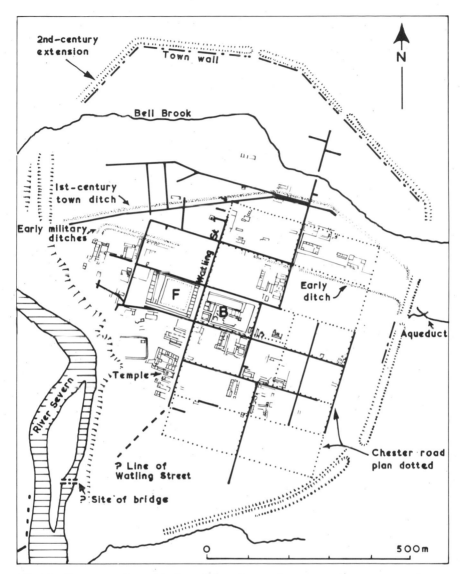

Fig 42 Wroxeter plan with that of the Chester fortress roads superimposed.
(Wroxeter details, mostly from aerial photographs, taken from Baker
1968 and 1970)   F-forum; B-baths

plans for fortress and town, as too would Baker's attribution of the
'Early Ditch' in fig 42 to the fortress. Possibly both rampart and ditch
have some other context.

The arguments formerly proposed for the re-use of one or two of

151

the fortress roads are equally valid for the others, and it is worth considering the possibility that virtually all the military roads were re-used and that they defined subsequent building areas. Aerial photographs have removed some of the uniformity assumed for the town grid by earlier workers, and in particular have disproved the conjectured connection between two roads that enter the town grid from north and south on a common alignment 190 metres east of Watling Street but do not cross the central insulae. Instead, they stop against cross streets, as do the longitudinal main streets of a fortress. With this recognized, the symmetry of the rest of the plan is obvious. Known roads, with their centres 190 metres east and west of the axis just described, may indicate the longitudinal intervallum roads of the emergent fortress, while the overall measurement of 380 metres almost matches the same dimensions at Caerleon and Chester, where they are 385 and 373 metres respectively. The long axis of the fortress would thus be confirmed north-south, but conclusions regarding its aspect depend upon comparison of the position of the cross roads. The identification of most roads is obtained when the plan of Chester is superimposed on the Wroxeter grid with the fortress facing south as on fig 22. The Chester plan is that of the stone fortress which follows in general the lines of its timber predecessor, although there are thought to be indications of a shift of 23 metres in the position of the *via principalis*. It is interesting that if the assumed position of the earlier Chester *via principalis* is used, the fit with the Wroxeter plan is even better. The cross streets of Caerleon's plan do not match Wroxeter's at all closely either way round.

These observations, if confirmed, would help to explain the enigma of Wroxeter, though far away in the north-west of the province, being the fourth largest town in Roman Britain. Given a legionary fortress of twenty-four hectares and nine hectares of extramural buildings, *canabae*, for traders and other camp-followers under military jurisdiction, between Watling Street and the Severn, the new town was already provided with a street plan covering thirty-three hectares. When the first-century town was enclosed with a rampart and ditch these would have been set out to reach the corners of the street grid but to bring in as well any ribbon development along the roads to north and south. The larger circuit held fifty-two hectares, already large enough to rank fifth in the walled towns of Roman Britain, but it did not necessarily relate closely to the built-up area.

In the late second century the earthwork defences were taken north across the Bell Brook to enclose another twenty-eight hectares, making the defended area about eighty hectares. There are few signs of buildings or roads in the added area and it is possible that the construction of these defences reflected some new policy either of anticipating growth that never came or providing space for some other purpose. Richmond conjectured that the northward extension might have brought in a holy area, and Wacher that it was farmland.

The extension of Wroxeter beyond its military legacy may have resulted, as Richmond argued, from the immigration of the native landowning class, seeking the protection and amenities of the town rather than face continued difficulty and possible danger in a countryside that had been disrupted by the conquest. From excavation and aerial photographs a dozen large houses – suitable residences for wealthy merchants or landowners, retired officers and officials – are known within the defences, and there were at least two temples. These hardly provide an adequate explanation for the size of the walled area, and only the recovery of more information from the suburbs can be expected to do so. Meanwhile, almost all our knowledge of Wroxeter comes from the very centre of the town where the Museum and exposed remains are to be seen today.

The wall known as the 'Old Work' (*pl 23*) which still towers eight metres high in the town centre is part of the south wall of an enormous exercise hall, alongside the public bath-house, the exposed foundations of which date from later than 160. The facilities included cold plunge baths as well as warm and hot rooms with either dry or humid

Plate 23 Wroxeter baths, the Old Work

153

conditions. A magnificent covered swimming pool in the south-west corner went out of use by about 210, when there was a major reorganization involving some new rooms and the encasement of the original bath block within a new wall to counteract settlement and cracking of the barrel vault over the main rooms. The late construction of the baths suggests there was not a large population initially, and indeed the town had to wait until 130 for the completion of its forum and basilica, dedicated to Hadrian (*fig 43*). This was bigger than Silchester's and should imply that the town was relatively wealthy. The basilica was a long aisled hall flanked by offices. To the east was the forum, a courtyard with colonnades around its other three sides. Across the far end of this was another range of offices pierced by the main entrance. The hall served for gatherings of the tribal council, while the offices provided rooms for government officials, lawyers, and other professionals. The courtyard would have served as the main market-place for the town.

The military-style bath-house over whose unfinished foundations the forum had been built was the first of the Wroxeter failures, and the forum continued the town's history of disaster and misdirected endeavour. About 165–185 it was burned, and a century later destroyed again and not rebuilt, so the town had no forum in the fourth century. The first fire had involved the buildings in the neighbouring insula to the south, but did not affect the baths opposite, so it may have been simply a local fire. However, the baths may not have been finished at this time – so would have had no superstructure to burn. The Wroxeter fire coincides roughly with the construction of the timber-laced defences of Forden Gaer and Leintwardine, and while there need be no connection between these events, the possibility remains that there was serious trouble in the Welsh border in the 160s. Perhaps the earlier withdrawal of troops from Wales had been followed by rebellion. Richmond saw the privilege of having their militia enrolled as a regular unit – Cohors I Cornoviorum – as a legacy of the long-standing necessity for encouraging the Cornovii to defend themselves against attack by brigands from the hills of Wales and south Shropshire.

Turning to the countryside, it is no easier to see a ready explanation for Wroxeter's size. In the whole of the border, villas are rare and smaller urban centres almost unknown. In the territory of the Cornovii only about eight villa sites are known, and three of these, at Cruckton, Lea Cross and Whitley, are grouped together in the middle Severn valley, where too the unimproved native farms proliferate. These are all old records and the absence of stone buildings on the innumerable aerial photographs taken in the past twenty years is a formidable piece of negative evidence against any large number of stone villas materializing in the future. The outlying villas at Yarchester, Acton Scott, Rushbury, Stanton Lacy and Stowe, and the establishment at Linley, do little to change the impression of poverty that

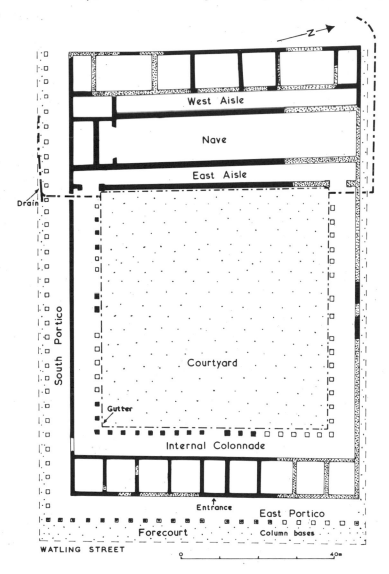

Fig 43 The Wroxeter forum (based on Atkinson 1942 p. 173)

155

surrounds everything but the capital of the Cornovii.

Mention of Linley, however, introduces other Cornovian resources. The western edge of the territory lay along the metalliferous zone of the Shelve district, and Linley may have been the headquarters for processing lead. Mining started at least as early as Hadrian's reign, as inscriptions reading 'IMP HADRIANI AVG' on five of the lead pigs found around Minsterley testify, but the enterprise is not thought to have lasted very long. This may have been due to the absence of a rich silver content, which encouraged persistence with many lead deposits elsewhere, or to the decline in demand for lead once the initial needs of Wroxeter's water conduits and baths had been met. Copper was probably obtained from veins around Habberley and was taken in larger quantities from mines on Llanymynech Hill. To the north, exploitation of lead from the Deceanglian mines on Halkyn Mountain in Clwyd started as early as 74. The frequency of lead pigs from this source around the Mersey suggests that much of it was shipped from the Mersey or Dee.

The resources of the northern border, the land of the Cornovii and Deceangli, are seen to have been relatively few and scattered, whether we look to the modernized villa as a sign of progress or to the mines as an indication of exportable wealth. The administrative centre for this region was Wroxeter, but although the political heart of the region from Roman to modern times has been in the Severn valley, it does not necessarily follow that the pre-Roman capital was there too. If it was, then Bury Walls, enclosing eight hectares, and where Camden wrote that Roman bricks and coins had been found, is a more likely candidate than the Wrekin; but the dispersal of hillfort communities which we have discussed above may have been accompanied by a shift of capital too, perhaps from the central hills where Titterstone Clee Camp encloses twenty-eight hectares, or from the west on Llanymynech Hill, where the known defences mark off fifty-six hectares.

The Wye basin

In the lands to the south, conjecturally occupied by the Decangi, the price exacted for the tribe's earlier assault on the infant Roman province was heavy indeed. The only walled settlement of which we have knowledge is a roadside agglomeration at Kenchester, Magnis, on the road to Clyro (fig 44). Its early timber-built nucleus may have been at the junction of that road and the Watling Street West, but most of the lateral development of side roads took place west of the junction; and

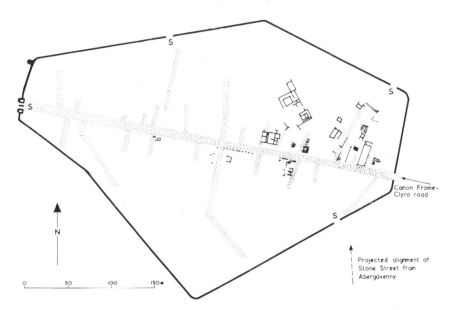

Fig 14 Plan of Kenchester, showing excavated west gate and bastion (Heys and Thomas 1962) internal foundations (Jack and Hayter 1926) and roads showing on aerial photographs (Baker 1966). Gates marked on Stukeley's plan of 1721 are labelled 'S'.

when the settlement was fortified, the junction itself was left outside the kite-shaped enclosure. Inside the defences were several substantial structures, though no public buildings have been identified. The street plan shows well on aerial photographs, but there are large areas without evidence of stone buildings, just as at Wroxeter. Like Wroxeter, too, Magnis bears the signs of a troubled history. Beneath the stone buildings Jack and Hayter found a thick charcoal layer as though a timber-built settlement had been burned to the ground. We may surmise that this was linked to the Sutton Walls hillfort massacre, and took place probably between the rebellion of Boudicca in 60–61 and the late second century.

It is possible that the rebuilding introduced the first of several changes of building alignment, the understanding of which would surely unravel the town's history. The axial east-west road is along the line of the Canon Frome-Clyro road and the other east-west and north-south alignments are presumably related to this primary axis. There are also roads and walls adjacent to the main road which are set at 105° to it, and so approximately parallel to the course of the road from Credenhill to Kenchester; and one large building is at an angle of

157

Plate 24   Kenchester, bastion foundations on the west wall of the town

50° to the road.

Although the roadside development of Magnis extended east of the defences, its lateral growth was small. Nevertheless, it was eventually fortified and bastions were added to the stone wall that was inserted in its second-century rampart, probably in the late fourth century (*pl 24*). Another indication of troubled times at the end of its history was the blocking of one of the portals of the west gate.

Its small size has led Wacher to list Magnis as a village; but its acquisition of bastions places it in an unusual category – one of only six bastioned villages. Four of the others are grouped in eastern England, the only other outlier being Mildenhall in Wiltshire. This unusual treatment for such a small town that is also distinguished by being central to the Hereford basin and the territory of an Iron Age tribe that I have argued was the Decangi, leads us to suspect that it fulfilled some administrative functions. There is, however, no evidence from inscriptions, literary references or buildings for its ever being a regional capital, and it is commonly assumed that the whole of Herefordshire was administered from Cirencester as part of the canton of the

Dobunni. The basis for this view is the milestone found at Kenchester inscribed *RPCD*, generally read as *Res Publica Civitatis Dobunnorum*, to which reference has been made on p 120. The *D* could equally well refer to the Decangi; and if this tribe still enjoyed a separate existence in the Roman period their capital must have been at Kenchester. The walled area of the town, at nine hectares, is remarkably small for a tribal capital, though the Icenian capital of Caister-by-Norwich enclosed only fourteen hectares, and Moridunum, Roman Carmarthen, which is thought to have been the capital of the Demetae, extends over only six hectares. The very locations of the capitals, if any, of tribes like the Deceangli of Clwyd and the Parisii of east Yorkshire are unknown or uncertain.

Magnis offered little accommodation for the displaced tribesmen of the region, and could only have taken a few of the four thousand evicted from Credenhill Camp, two kilometres away. Many others must have been resettled on farms around the town, and a mosaic pavement at Bishopstone is a sign of someone's wealth. A similarly favoured agricultural area was probably in the lower Frome valley, west of the settlement of Epocessa at Canon Frome. The nucleus of this settlement, west of the early fort, probably originated as a posting station at the junction of the east-west Kenchester road with the north-south one from Gloucester, but spread along the latter road, thereby giving rise to the discovery of many objects on the site of the canal aqueduct south of Stretton Grandison. The full extent of the place is unknown and the only defences are those of the nearby fort.

Herefordshire's other named settlement, Ariconium, is a problem. Building debris and pottery have come from a wide area around Bury Hill, east of Ross-on-Wye, but despite the name which often indicates defended sites, as in Aconbury and Risbury, no sign of defences has been recorded. It is tempting therefore to regard it as an open settlement and to ascribe its considerable extent to industrial activity that required plenty of space and spread its waste widely. Over the fields to the north of the Bromsash road there is much iron slag, and Bridgewater's excavations revealed primitive furnaces and working hollows, the ore presumably coming from the Forest of Dean.

Excavations by Jack and Hayter located a building but there is inadequate structural evidence elsewhere to know whether we are dealing with a small town or an extensive but amorphous spread of industrial sites about an administrative nucleus. Its inclusion in the Antonine Itinerary and the survival of the name as that of the post-Roman district of Erging, or Archenfield, across the Wye show that it was of some significance. It was occupied early in the Roman period and may have developed on a pre-Roman industrial centre. An iron-working site has also been excavated at Whitchurch, in the Wye valley.

The most completely excavated border villa lies on the southern edge of Decangian territory at Huntsham in a splendid loop of the Wye at the foot of the Carboniferous Limestone hills of the Forest of Dean. Here an extensive villa development has been photographed from the air, and among the buildings excavated are the main corridor-house, a minor dwelling and an aisled barn. The house area itself was enclosed by a thick precinct wall, a necessary precaution on the edge of the Forest of Dean. The site covers in all about eight hectares and was occupied from at least the second century until the late fourth.

The total of surface finds in the Herefordshire basin is too small to allow any clear impression of the intensity of agricultural exploitation under the Romans. There is some evidence of a bias in favour of well-drained soils, particularly the river gravels of the Wye, Lugg and Frome valleys, and we know that the scene probably included village communities in some of the hillforts, like Sutton Walls, Poston and Uphampton Camp. There is no evidence of expansion into previously undeveloped areas, and the chances are that there was something of an agricultural retreat from the margins due to depopulation in the wake of the conquest.

The Dean-Trelleck uplands

The territory between the Decangi and Silures was but thinly occupied. Roads linked the nodal settlements that grew around the sites of the early forts at Abergavenny (Gobannium), Usk (Burrio) and probably Monmouth – the site of Blestium, but their extent and status is unknown. Quantities of iron slag at Monmouth show that it had an interest in smelting; and the working of blackband ore from the Coal Measures was pursued in the vicinity of Abergavenny which was named after the 'river of the blacksmiths' on which it stands. An iron furnace was found too in the post-military levels at Usk. The high grade haematite ores of the Crease Limestone of the Forest of Dean were especially important for a technologically primitive industry, and that area was widely exploited. Most of the ore would have been obtained by quarrying the outcrop of the productive beds, but there was also some mining, as the shallow shaft and gallery inside the Lydney Park hillfort indicates. The forests would have been exten-sively felled for charcoal production, but were probably allowed to recover as coppice rather than provide extra agricultural opportunities.

The location of the Lydney Park temple on the forest edge must have been especially attractive for those whose wealth to pay for these amenities had been won in the large villas across the Severn or in public service in the towns of Britain. The improvement of the enclosing hillfort rampart was an understandable precaution probably undertaken in the fourth century rather than later, for with a naturally wild environment on their doorstep, priests and guests may sometimes have needed such a safeguard against brigands.

Across south Gwent several Roman locations are known but many more must be covered by silt. Roman pottery kilns at Caldicot are just north of a presumed villa site, and there was some form of settlement at Chepstow. Reference had already been made to the extramural settlement beside Isca Silurum which may have extended over twenty hectares, and would have acquired important functions as a port for civilian requirements as well as military needs. In this way it might have enjoyed continued prosperity even after the withdrawal of the garrison at the end of the third century.

With the Caerleon fortress established on the Usk, more than three-quarters of Silurian territory lay to the west under close military control well into the second century. It is not surprising therefore that the only town in the territory, Caerwent – Venta Silurum – should be established behind the front and close to the eastern boundary of the tribe's territory (fig 45). There is no evidence that its location reflects the former presence of a pre-Roman native capital in the vicinity. Llanmelin Wood Camp, only two kilometres to the north, recalls the spatial relationship of Credenhill to Kenchester, but the Gwent fort is small, enclosing only two hectares. If we are to look for a local reason for the siting of Caerwent it may be that it took over the role of Sudbrook Camp, less than five kilometres to the south-east. As a port Sudbrook would have been better placed than Llanmelin to maintain contact with the far-flung Silurian lands along the northern shore of the Severn, but the chances are that the pre-Roman Silurian capital was further west, somewhere in the Vale of Glamorgan. The shift to the east probably arose because the rest of the territory remained for so long under military control.

This argument is in harmony with the view that Caerwent was established without defences early in the Roman period before the second-century reduction of tension in South Wales made a western Silurian capital feasible. There is however an alternative hypothesis that the town was built on the site of an earlier undefined fort and that the first-century pottery belongs to this. The rectangular layout of defences and streets for the eighteen-hectare town certainly gives the impression that army surveyors were in charge, and the similarity of

Fig 45   Plan of Caerwent, somewhat simplified from plans by V. E. Nash-Williams (1930 and 1968); north-east bastions added from D.o.E. handbook 1976 (Crown Copyright—reproduced with permission of the Controller of Her Majesty's Stationery Office)

plan with that of the Icenian capital at Caister-by-Norwich encourages the view that both reflect the desperate poverty and lack of potential for spontaneous development of two tribes that had been hammered by Rome for hostility and rebellion.

Extensive excavation, mostly in the earlier decades of this century, has revealed a detailed plan of the stone buildings of about three-fifths of the interior. Despite its frontier location Caerwent displays most of the characteristics of Romano-British towns. As at Kenchester and elsewhere, the main street – here the road from Gloucester to Caerleon – traverses the settlement between opposing gates. Beside this, in the centre of the town, the forum and basilica dominated the urban scene. Although the composite structure covered an area eighty by fifty-six metres, it was small by comparison with the same buildings in other towns, less than half the size of the Wroxeter forum and three-fifths the size of Cirencester's.

Other public buildings took up twice as much space again as the forum and basilica, so that the recognized public buildings account for about a quarter of the excavated area. They included a bath-house complex south of the forum and a temple across the road to the east. The latter was of a common Romano-Celtic plan with a central *cella* six metres square, surrounded by an ambulatory two metres wide. The whole was enclosed within its own boundary wall, giving a temenos almost rectangular in plan and measuring thirty-four by twenty metres. Just outside the east wall of Caerwent was another, unusual, temple with an octagonal cella central to a circular temenos forty metres in diameter.

A large building just inside the town's south gate is usually thought to be a *mansio,* the official guest-house and inn; its ground floor plan shows some twenty rooms around three sides of a courtyard, the fourth being closed by the town wall. An unusual elliptical structure with diameters of forty-four and thirty-seven metres lies north of the forum and may be an amphitheatre with only its outer wall in stone and the seating unidentified because it was carried out in timber; or it may have served some other purpose like a cattle market. Apart from its public buildings, Caerwent contains more than its share of large courtyard houses, upwards of thirty metres square, of a style appropriate to the curial class recruited from the tribal aristocracy. In their final form they were splendidly furnished, several having mosaic floors. They enjoyed a piped water supply and at least one had its own bath suite.

It hardly needs emphasizing that such houses represent in unequivocal terms the physical and cultural estrangement of the tribal

163

leaders from the communities with whom their forebears had shared common danger and toil before the conquest. With the gardens and orchards that were probably beside many of these properties, the ground taken up by the houses, offices and amenities of the state and its ruling class accounted for a very large part of Venta Silurum. There was little room for the poorer classes, except as necessary to serve the needs of the wealthier residents and officials. Within the excavated areas some twenty narrow buildings of simple rectangular plan, most of them end-on to the main street, were probably occupied by shop-keepers and craftsmen.

If Caerwent, like Kenchester and Wroxeter, started its urban life in the first century without defences it might be interpreted as a reflection of confidence that the army would quickly subdue the natives and peaceful commercial development would promptly follow. The eventual need to fortify the towns of Roman Britain marks, in part, the failure of this programme. At Caerwent an earth rampart was put round the town some time after 130, probably a reaction to increasing local unrest following the removal of most of the auxiliary troops from South Wales. Local brigands, finding cover in the wooded valleys to the north, may have threatened the safety of the town-dwelling aristocracy. In the second half of the third century a massive stone wall was inserted in the front of the rampart, three metres wide at the base and standing five metres high in places; the surviving stretch along the south side is still a most impressive sight (*pl 25*). The almost rectangular town plan was pierced by four gates, one on each side, towards the middle, the main entrances being at the east and west ends on the main road. Of the minor gates on the other sides the single-portal North Gate is well preserved and restored. What evidence there is suggests that the stone gateways were first constructed when the earth rampart was built.

At a late stage in its history Venta Silurum too was provided with bastions, the north-western one being dated not earlier than 350. The bastions are upstanding or recorded about fifty metres apart along the south and north walls of the town; but none is known along the east and west sides. Such fortifications represent a resort to new tactics against enemies who before the end of the fourth century were arriving in groups numbered in hundreds rather than tens. The bastions could have carried large catapults capable of dispersing such forces before they could reach the town's defences.

Whenever they were in sufficient strength the brigands from the hills and the raiders from the sea would have sought the special prizes that lay in the towns, which were virtually the only repositories for

Plate 25   The south wall and bastions of Caerwent (*David Hibbert*)

civil wealth in the Marches, for there were few villas. Such wealth may partly reflect their own commercial success but is more likely to have resulted from the concentration of what little surplus was produced over a wide area around. Later on, when raiders in larger numbers sought land as well as loot, the attacks on towns would have had the military objective, too, of knocking out the local militia.

The origins and influence of the new terrorists are better considered in the next chapter, for by the late fourth century Rome's interest in, and control of, the remoter parts of Britain was waning. The legions, which had been temporarily withdrawn on previous occasions, were taken over to the continent again in 383 by Magnus Maximus to bolster his own attempt to gain command of the empire. It is unlikely that there was any permanent military occupation of the forts in Wales and the border thereafter.

CHAPTER EIGHT

A New Frontier

Between the withdrawal of the legions and the Norman Conquest the historical evidence relating to the Welsh Marches is sparse, and particularly so before the construction of Offa's Dyke soon after 784. With the exception of this and related dykes the archaeological scraps that can be confidently ascribed to this period are tantalizingly few. In these circumstances a detailed regional treatment is impracticable, and it seems better to treat the Marches as a whole, as already done for the Roman phase of frontier definition.

The period began, and mostly continued, in a state of flux and uncertainty. It was a protracted period in which the changing fortunes of invading English settlers, and the shifting alliances between them and the surviving or emergent British kingdoms, culminated in the political supremacy of the Anglo-Saxons in what is now England and the sharper definition of Welsh culture in what came to be Wales. The things we do not know about the period are numerous and sometimes quite basic. For example to what extent was the British population replaced by the English? And did large numbers of refugees flood westwards from the battlefields of the north and east? Certainly the facility with which British kings and English princes occasionally allied in common cause suggests that much of the conquest took place in the interests of personal aggrandisement rather than as a search for new farmlands for land-hungry followers. We might in general perhaps expect that political acquisition rather than large-scale colonizing activities became increasingly important once the early flush of settlers was absorbed in south and east England; and that by the time the tide approached the Welsh border there was possibly only a small replacement of population in many areas. Certainly today the physical characteristics of the border population are virtually indistinguishable from those in neighbouring parts of Wales, and although this may be the result of more recent peaceful migrations we may suspect that it has its origin in a substantial survival of the Romano-British population.

Among the important questions for this period is the obvious one of the legacy left by the Romans. Normally we seek the positive aspects of this legacy, the extent to which the roads and towns formed the framework for later communications and settlements, but we should also have regard for the negative aspects, and see how far the Roman neglect of certain areas influenced later events. For this we need to know the rate and process of decline of the Romano-British settlements and how to recognize their survival, if any, in the medieval settlement pattern. There is information in greater quantity about the influence of early Celtic saints, based on church dedications and place-names, but the contemporary archaeological evidence for them is minimal. Later in this period there is considerable evidence of the frontier works between the English and Welsh, foremost amongst them Offa's Dyke; and investigations into the early history of town plans and defences have gathered momentum in recent years.

In a period of such uncertainty it would be unwise to attach more significance to particular dates, but it may be useful to think of the period as falling into four phases. In the first of these, from 383 until about 430, Britain was learning to live without the legions. In the second phase, when all hope of assistance from Rome was dead, the English came in larger numbers and by the early seventh century had conquered the English lowlands. The third phase, the struggle for supremacy in the Marches, lasted until the construction of Offa's Dyke soon after 784 concluded the period of maximum movement in the border. The fourth phase is the remaining three centuries before the Norman Conquest.

Without the legions: AD 383–430

While ruled by Rome, Britain had relied for its defence upon the professional soldiers; indeed, in the later Empire it was illegal for civilians to wear arms. When the legions were withdrawn it was natural enough that the citizens of Britain should expect them to return. There were, after all, some troops left in the north of Britain and it is possible that some remained in the big forts of the central border after 383; almost certainly others would have been left to man the town defences. In these conditions some senior citizens may have anticipated the difficulties yet to come and have acquired control over local garrisons. Apart from anything else, the loss of imperial interest in the fate of Britain and the small amount of coinage brought into the country in the last decades of the fourth century would have made the soldiers attentive to the requests of anyone prepared to pay them.

Disgust with the failure of the central government to provide for the defence of the province is thought to have led the Britons to reject the Roman officials and take over government themselves no later than 410 when, in response to their plea for military support against the Picts, they were told by the emperor Honorius to look to their own defence. We have noted above the construction of town bastions – generally thought to date later than the Anglo-Saxon and Pictish raids of 367, although their variety of form and irregular spacing may indicate construction over a fairly long period, the outcome of local rather than imperial decree. It is therefore interesting to notice that Kenchester and Caerwent have similarly disposed bastions of pentagonal outline, which contrast with the rectangular forms found, for example, at Cirencester and the semicircular forms which at Caister-by-Norwich appear alongside rectangular bastions. It is possible that some were constructed as late as the beginning of the fifth century, and if further excuse were needed by then, the advice of Honorius should have been sufficient to have encouraged any laggardly community to improve its defences. No bastions, however, are known at Wroxeter, although aerial photographs show that the late wide ditch around the town diverges from the defences at the corners as though to accommodate bastions. Was the construction of the bastions too costly for a small community lumbered with such a long perimeter? Were the fourth-century defences unfinished, like the first-century baths?

The investigation of bastions, as much as any other features of the period, is hampered by the inadequacy of dating evidence. The conservatism of local potteries is a commonplace in pre-Roman archaeology and even in the Roman period, once the variety of imported samian ware gave way in the late second century to locally manufactured fine wares, the chances of dating sites by pottery decreased. Thus it is not easy to recognize from small collections the difference between third- and fourth-century deposits, particularly in remoter areas like the Welsh border. With the withdrawal of the legions and the breakdown of regular contact with the continent there would have been a further loss of stimulus to innovation, and so the forms current in the middle of the fourth century could have continued for a century or two. It has not so far proved possible to recognize any distinctly native, non-commercial products in the west to compare with some of the hand-made vessels found in late Roman or sub-Roman contexts in eastern Britain. There, Frere has estimated that the large potteries came to an end by about 420 through the loss of security for goods in transit and the escape of slaves once imperial law collapsed It is not known whether the same was the case in the west or whether the

Severn valley potteries continued to operate through changes of government, but it is unlikely that they continued for long on a large scale, for the shortage of coins became so acute that by 430 they were no longer in use as a general medium of exchange. Britain went back to bartering, and there must have been other changes in the commercial system including a reduction in the size of producer units.

Without coins or distinctive pottery, there is only structural evidence such as Frere has unravelled at Verulamium, Hertfordshire, to carry us into the fifth century. This will involve the detail of repairs to timber structures like the barns of villas or minor buildings in towns where such repairs can be found above dated fourth-century contexts.

Only at Wroxeter, of the border towns, has there been extensive recent excavation aimed specifically at the recovery of late and post-Roman structures. Here, on the site of the demolished basilica of the baths, in an area widely explored and planned by Wright in the middle of the nineteenth century, Barker has put forward for interim consideration an interpretation of post-Roman levels which involves rectangular timber buildings, some on a massive scale and others like small cells built against remnants of the basilica. These are held to represent a survival of the classical building tradition after the knowledge and skills of constructing stone buildings had been lost. They have been distinguished mainly by variations in wear and materials in the rubble surface on which they were constructed. They lack any consistent occurrence of foundation features normally associated with Roman or pre-Roman structures, such as big post-holes, sleeper trenches or regular stone sills, so that the interpretation is inevitably extremely speculative. The interim presentation of the evidence invokes too many unusual explanations to prove the occupation of Wroxeter in the Dark Ages.

This is not of course to say that continued occupation of the city into the fifth century is unlikely. The Romans seem to have paid some special regard to its defence since some six lead-weighted darts, *plumbatae,* have been found there, mostly around the baths' basilica. Such darts were in use in the fourth century by some legions and it has been suggested that these may have been lost by members of Theodosius' force, perhaps billeted in the basilica when they were here to recover the province following the raids of 367. For the late fourth-century occupation of the town centre there are coins of the house of Valentinian, 364–83, found in occupation soil over the robbed market hall colonnade, but so far no coin later than 367 has come from the basilica site. In all the published finds from Wroxeter there are only three coins which must have been minted after 394, coins of Arcadius, emperor of the Eastern Empire, 395–408.

We are equally at a loss to document the last years of Kenchester and Caerwent. On both of these, as elsewhere in Roman Britain, late fourth-century coins are uncommon and at Kenchester Jack and Hayter recovered no coins minted later than 383. From Caerwent however there are coins of Arcadius and Honorius, 393–423. Other evidence for the end of Roman life in these towns is rare and its significance disputed. The occasional skeletons found within the towns, for example beside the roads at Wroxeter and Caerwent, may have been the victims of disease left unburied by a community that had lost its civic sense of responsibility, but are more probably late burials put in graves cut from a post-Roman surface that has been rendered unrecognizable by root or plough action. Disease may have played a part in rendering the towns unattractive and ungovernable; but to place too much importance on this factor is to overlook the undoubted resistance of the Britons to the English advance. It did, after all, take the newcomers some 200 years to reach the Severn; and almost the same time again was to pass before an agreed line was established by King Offa.

Frere has stressed the likelihood that the resistance to the English was probably directed from the west, from the border and Wales, a view based on the traditional association of the two best known Britons of the early fifth century with the Marches. Though equally opposed to the incoming English, these two probably had very different political ideas for the government of what remained of the province. The northern border and North Wales is thought to be the homeland of Vortigern, probably self-appointed as a leader around 425. He has been seen as the head of the groups accepting the Pelagian heresy, insisting on the right of individuals to decide their own fate, which in a political context meant without the aid of Roman officials. The other, Ambrosius Aurelianus, was a Roman noble linked by name to the family of the Catholic Bishop of Milan, and a supporter of the old regime and its system of patronage. He is thought to have had his special field of influence, if not kingdom, in the lands of the Severn estuary, in modern Gwent, Gloucestershire and Somerset.

Vortigern, himself the son-in-law of Magnus Maximus, must have had special reason to be grateful for the victory won by St Germanus over the Picts and Saxons in 429, probably somewhere in North Wales. Following this, and in order to remove the threat of Irish settlers in north-west Wales, Vortigern brought in frontier folk from south Scotland, from the territory of the Votadini under the command of Cunedda. It is possible that they used Chester as a base for the attack on the Irish in North Wales, and Cunedda was certainly successful in

171

establishing his own authority. This is about the time when it is now considered that, in an attempt to keep the Picts at bay in the east and prevent their sea-raiding, Vortigern invited Saxon mercenaries under Hengist and Horsa to establish themselves in Kent on the Isle of Thanet.

The Saxons advance to the Severn

The south-east had suffered the problems of North Sea raiders for some time and now was experiencing settlement by these foreigners. In the west more friendly relations had been developing with the Irish who had settled in Wales in the late fourth and early fifth centuries; now, with Cunedda's help in the north, a *modus vivendi* had been established, permitting the Celtic west to maintain its traditional links with western Gaul and by that route with the church in Rome. A rare find near Wroxeter throws some light upon this state of affairs in the later fifth century. A re-used tombstone carries the crudely cut inscription CUNORIX MACUS MAQUI COLINE, translated as 'The Hound King (or Great King) Son of the Son of the Holly', an Irish name with a style that suggests a leader, perhaps of a group of mercenaries employed for the defence of Wroxeter. The date suggested on linguistic grounds is 460–75 and it suggests that Wroxeter still fulfilled a capital role, attracting important persons.

This is in accord with our understanding of towns elsewhere. At Verulamium new water pipes were being laid after about 450, though Frere has concluded that organized town life there probably ended about 500. By now of course Vortigern's rule had ended. He had probably been succeeded as first war-lord in Britain some time after 443 by Ambrosius Aurelianus. Aurelianus in turn is thought to have been succeeded by a hero like the legendary King Arthur, whose medieval fictional exploits and chivalrous attributes appear to have been attached to a British war-leader, rather than king, of this period, probably the one who defeated the Saxons at Mount Badon about the period 500–516.

There is so far no comparable evidence for such late urban survival at Kenchester or Caerwent. The basilica at Caerwent was destroyed by fire, though this would not preclude the continuation of life without the trappings of the Roman *civitas*. The town also lacks the late fifth-century Mediterranean pottery which is well known in the south-west peninsula and Somerset, and appears in Wales on the fortified camps of Dinas Powys, Glamorgan, Coygan Camp, Dyfed and Dinas Emrys, Gwynedd. However, it is nowhere plentiful enough to justify relying upon its absence as a dating criterion.

It needs to be noted here that the crude earthenware found on the Breidden, Old Oswestry and Eddisbury Camps and once thought to be Dark Age domestic pottery is now regarded as Iron Age: either ordinary coarse ware as at Eddisbury, or VCP from field ovens or salt containers at Old Oswestry and the Breidden. With these removed, the only pottery from the border that should belong to the fifth or sixth century is a small sherd from near Goodrich, which resembles the imported Mediterranean class Aii wares.

The small southern border towns of Caerwent and Kenchester would have had little attraction or vitality once the Roman officials had been ousted at the end of the fourth century. Nevertheless there is every reason to suppose that the regional units in the Welsh border, which had been focused on the three Roman towns, survived the fifth century and were sufficiently distinct in the minds of the inhabitants for the town names to be given to kingdoms and peoples in the seventh and later centuries. Thus Caerwent gave us the Kingdom of Gwent, Magnis probably perpetuated the name of the district, *Mage*, adopted by the Magonsaeta who inhabited Herefordshire and south Shropshire, while Viroconium – Wroxeter – rather than the Wrekin, is the probable source for the tribal group known as the Wrocensaetna. Between Magnis and Caerwent the Kingdom of Erging derived its name from Ariconium. Whatever may have been the eventual balance of Celt and Saxon, and however the pattern of settlement was rearranged, these names themselves are sufficient to show that the slate was not wiped clean, but rather that some form of accommodation was achieved between the invaders and the resident Britons.

The Celtic saints

Although Christianity received official recognition in 313 the old gods remained popular, as the Romano-Celtic temple boom of the late fourth century proves. The conversion of the mass of the population to Christian ideas came after the Roman withdrawal, and was stimulated by a new generation of priests whose origins were partly Romano-British but who were also influenced by ideas reintroduced to Britain via the western sea-routes from southern Gaul, or derived from the Celtic church in Ireland and west Wales. Many churches and chapels were founded by members of this church during the sixth and seventh centuries, but the full extent of their activity can never be known, for, in the border north of the Wye, where the English impress was firm, the churches were mostly rededicated. Although dedications may indicate some regional cult preferences it is not possible to use most of them to illustrate the Dark Age scene, since, away from certain original sites founded by the saints in question, dedications may even post-date the arrival of the English.

The archaeological evidence regarding the activities of these Celtic saints in the border is nil. It is not even clear whether we should anticipate any particular form of settlement accompanying or developing upon the site of a Celtic church. Nor do we know from any local examples what these early churches were like, for we assume that they are buried beneath, or cut away by, the foundations of the later Norman churches that had probably succeeded most of them on the same ground. Archaeology may again find here a fruitful field of research as and when excavation is possible on the site of ruined churches that have an early dedication. Again, we do not know whether these churches were grafted on to existing Romano-British settlements. Certainly, a distinction is to be drawn between the mother churches with many monks, likely themselves to focus settlement, and the anchorite cells that sought seclusion in remote valleys and moors. On such physical matters archaeology should at some time have something to say.

One effect of this evangelical period was to emphasize the separateness of certain parts of the border from the pagan English lowland and from other Celtic Christian regions to the west. There was considerable Romano-British survival which may be instanced by dedications to Saint Elen, Helena wife of Magnus Maximus, at Llanellen near Abergavenny and to her son Constantine, or Cystennin ap Maxen Wledig, at Welsh Bicknor, formerly known as Llangystennin. In the same general area, in Erging, was the main field of activity for Saint Dubricius, or Dyfrig, one of the earliest Welsh saints, who is given the attributes of a Roman priest and seems to be the embodiment of the respect for the Empire that was earlier shown in the political field by Ambrosius Aurelianus. The only dedications to St Dubricius outside this area are one near Builth and another at Porlock. In Herefordshire dedications to him survive at Hentland and Ballingham; and the churches at Moccas, Madley, Wormbridge and Llanwarne were also formerly dedicated to him. There was also a chapel of Dubricius just opposite Ballingham in Woolhope parish, perhaps near Buckenhill Farm where a piscina was recovered in the 1950s. This is the saint's only dedication east of the Wye. Before the arrival of the English Erging may have extended beyond the river to include Woolhope and Ariconium. Dedications to other Celtic saints in Erging include Dewi, or David, at Dewchurch and Kilpeck, and to St

Plate 26   Memorial stones of the tenth or eleventh century in Llanveynoe
Church. The inscriptions at the top of the right-hand stone read XPC,
M (?Ω) and IHC; and at the side HAEFDUR FECIT CRUCEM, IHC
A Ω

Beuno at Llanveynoe, in which church is an early Christian memorial
stone similar to several found around St David's, Dyfed. The Llanveynoe example is thought to date from the tenth or eleventh century,
like the crucifixion stone now beside it (*pl 26*).

 Gwent was not similarly distinguished by having such a peculiarly
localized cult area, although Cadog, its most popular early saint, was,
like St Dubricius, steeped in Roman tradition. He founded churches

175

widely in South Wales and Brittany, and has a cluster of dedications in north Gwent rather like that of Dubricius in Erging. He was remembered at Llangattock nigh Usk, Llangattock Vibon Abel and Llangattock Lingoed, and also at Monmouth, Penrhôs, Raglan, Clytha and Caerleon. From the west emanated an enthusiasm for dedicating churches to St Teilo, who is commemorated at Llantilio Pertholey, Llantilio Crossenny and Llanarth in north-west Gwent; and also to St Dewi, patron saint of Llanddewi Skyrrid and Llanddewi Rhydderch.

An early evangelist in Gwent was St Tathan, thought possibly to have come from Gwynedd and, with his Irish name, to have been a refugee from the Sons of Cunedda. It was he who founded a church at Caerwent, though not the apsidal building found in earlier excavations and thought to have been a church; current opinion is that this was the remains of a post-medieval cottage with attached oven.

These dedications, and what can be learned of the activities of these saints from their lives, show that a considerable Romano-British population survived in the southern half of the border. Saints like Dubricius not only sprang from this population but set up churches to serve it. Here, if anywhere, one might expect continuity from the Romano-British scene. Here, where there had been a pottery tradition back to the early years of the local Iron Age, there is likely to have been some attempt to maintain a supply of pottery. If it was impracticable to keep the factory production going we might expect domestic manufacture based on fourth-century models; and the looting of military cemeteries for vessels of any period. Either way, the pots in use around the early churches will be difficult to distinguish from those deposited in Roman times; and where grave vessels were re-employed they could be centuries earlier than the Dark Age deposits in which they are found. Nevertheless, this reasoning provides a stimulus for investigating the vicinity of churches with Celtic saint dedications and nearby finds of Romano-British sherds. It is interesting to notice that recent excavations just south of St Dubricius' church at Hentland found timber structures and ditches, as well as a few Romano-British sherds, below the level of medieval and later buildings.

North of the Wye, the rivers retain their British names like Frome and Lugg, Severn and Teme, and Welsh elements are sometimes found in place-names, but there are few dedications to Celtic saints. Signs of this earlier religious background are, however, provided by the Welsh name for Leominster, Llanllieni, where the church was founded by Dewi, and by the former dedication of Kenchester's church to the Celtic saint Keyna. There is a notable cluster of dedications to St Tysilio in northern Powys against the national boundary; the church of Llandysilio itself is almost on Offa's Dyke, although its parish extends either side. A similar juxtaposition of early Celtic dedications and the boundary occurs in the upper Severn valley between Berriew and Guilsfield, where dedications to St Beuno and his associated saints all lie immediately west of the Severn and the Dyke. The impression given by these two groups is that they have been reduced by the English advance, and that the Celtic dedications once extended eastwards into the lowlands, as is still the case further north where the descendants of Coel Godebog and Cunedda appear in half a dozen dedications in the middle valley of the Dee from Llangollen downstream to Bangor-on-Dee. The English were less successful in the north-west, and St Beuno, along with his associated saints, is well represented in the area around Whitford between the Clwyds and the Dee estuary.

The struggle for the border: to AD 800

While the pressure on the southern border was from the West Saxons, the threat in the north was from Northumbria. In the late sixth century the northern border enjoyed the protection of Urien of Rheged, who was fighting against the Northumbrians in the 570s. With the English victory of Chester in 614 and the subsequent march of Edwin into North Wales the security of the Severn valley and the farmlands around Wroxeter was placed in jeopardy. This may have been the occasion for the abandonment of Wroxeter in favour of a smaller, more easily defended site, perhaps the Berth hillfort near Baschurch, or the nucleus of Shrewsbury, where the Severn offers defence on three sides. The only dating evidence to support either of these is a bronze cauldron pierced for use as a waterclock and dug up in the marsh that formerly surrounded the Berth. Such cauldrons are currently thought to be peculiar to the Dark Ages, but the device is widespread and the date of particular examples uncertain. There is ceramic evidence that the Berth was occupied in the Iron Age and Roman periods.

The issue of the successor to Wroxeter dogs the discussion of ensuing events in the Severn valley. The response to the Northumbrian invasion was an alliance between Penda of Mercia and Cadwallon of Gwynedd resulting in the defeat of Edwin in 632. But ten years later the northerners under Oswald were again campaigning in Shropshire. Again they were defeated, and Oswald killed, at Maserfelth, uncertainly located in Shropshire and argued to be an earlier name for

Oswestry which itself means 'Oswald's tree (or cross)'. In 654 Penda was defeated and killed in battle near Leeds and there followed the disruption of the Mercian Kingdom. While the English Magonsaeta were settling the border from the Wrekin to the Wye there was a resurgence of British resistance north of the Severn.

Among the sources for this period are the poems of Llywarch Hen. a late-sixth-century king of Lancashire who fled to Powys when the English conquered his land. He tells of the exploits of a seventh-century hero Cynddylan, son of Cyndrwyn, who raided the English and lived in a great hall at Pengwern in the white town by the woods. Tempted by the clues provided in the poems, various scholars have sought to identify Cynddylan's abode. Morris suggested Viroconium, the plastered buildings of which would have befitted the 'white town' of the poems. Richards has argued for the Wrekin, which is mentioned as 'Dinlleu Vreconn', but the windswept hill is hardly appropriate for the 'head of the alder grove', which is what Pengwern means. In the thirteenth century Giraldus Cambrensis equated Pengwern with Shrewsbury, but the latter had its own British name, Amwythig. We have already noted that the water clock found at the Berth could belong to this period. The edge of the marsh at the Berth would have been a suitable habitat for alder, and only a mile from Baschurch, where Cynddylan was buried. The poet's description of Cynddylan's home being between 'Tren and Trodwydd', thought to be Tern and Roden, has raised the further possibility that Pengwern was Bury Walls, a large hillfort between these two rivers. With such a diversity of possibilities it seems likely that the poet himself was confused or was writing of times already long past, as Wright believed, or of places that have not survived in historical documents.

What is certain is that the seventh century saw further English settlements in the border. Archaeology had long been silent on the processes and locations, but in 1978 an Anglo-Saxon Christian cemetery was excavated at Bromfield within the ancient farmstead enclosure (fig 11, p 68). Twenty-three graves were found, orientated east-west and all but three devoid of grave-goods. Two burials with Anglo Saxon scramasax-type knives point to a hang-over of pagan English customs and remind us that there is likely to be an earlier, truly pagan cemetery nearby. This we seem to have at the east end of the same field where the ring-ditch of a ploughed-out barrow (pl 27) is most reasonably to be interpreted as later than the Roman marching camp ditch that is tangential to it. It is probably therefore one element of an Anglo-Saxon pagan cemetery, dating to the conquest period in the early seventh century. The pattern of the two cemeteries recalls those

Plate 27   Aerial view of the Roman marching camp ditch and contiguous
Anglo-Saxon barrow ditch at Bromfield showing as crop marks in corn

of this period in southern and eastern England, and we may expect that the Christian cemetery at Bromfield was in use somewhere between the late seventh and the tenth century or whenever burial became the prerogative of the local church, presumably the priory church at Bromfield village across the river.

Place-name evidence for pagan Saxons in the border is scarce but not unknown, as evidenced by Wolferlow in north Herefordshire, meaning 'Wulfhere's burial mound'. Other English place-names, however, dominate the modern map, eloquent of the way in which Anglo-Saxon culture replaced the British from the Mersey to the Wye and overspilled into Erging or Archenfield. It even penetrated the central hills and reached into the Vale of Radnor.

In recent years many earlier conclusions regarding the significance and relative dating of English place-name types have been overturned. There is now an emphasis on the importance of surviving Romano-British villages as focuses for the earliest English settlements with their pagan cemeteries and names in '-ham' notably the Wickhams, or 'vicus hāms', settlements by Roman villages. It is also widely thought that such early names will eventually be seen to include not only many containing earlier, British, place-names but also many topographical names in '-ley' and '-field', for example, which had previously been

179

allocated exclusively to a secondary phase of settlement. Names in
'-ingham' are now regarded as normally secondary to the '-hams',
while later still come the group-names in '-ing' from '-ingas', an
element of great antiquity in folk-names but now thought to be
applied to place-names only in a secondary phase of colonization.

There has been no modern detailed publication of place-names in
the Marches so it is too early to see how the new understanding of
place-naming processes worked out for eastern England will affect the
significance of names here. Names ending in '-ham' from 'hām' seem
to be rare south of Cheshire, where Dodgson regards them as indicative of the earliest stage of English settlement in the seventh century –
in contrast to the fifth or sixth century date argued for such names in
south-east England. Away from Cheshire the virtual absence of the
now later '-ing' place-names is at least one pointer to differences in the
settlement processes, and consequent place-naming, from that of
eastern England. By the time the English entered the Marches their
full range of place-name types was already established, to be drawn
upon at will. Furthermore the social and military organization of the
settlers and their relationship with the Welsh will have been modified
since the days of the mercenary war-bands, brought in originally to
protect the residual Romano-British way of life. For such reasons it
may never be possible to use place-names alone to discern the progress
of the English settlement of the border, but they will nevertheless still
provide an invaluable commentary on the contemporary geography
of the area.

In particular place-names reflect the continuing importance of the
Roman roads and the survival of certain empty forested areas from the
Iron Age. Thus there is a concentration of names in '-ley' and '-field'
on the west Herefordshire lowlands, a land that was undeveloped in
the Iron Age. Almeley, Eardisley, Kinnersley, Weobley and
Sarnesfield show that it was still mostly forest when the English
arrived. Across it, following the gravel terrace of the Wye, went the
Roman road to Clyro, and along the road occur places with names in
'-ton' like Winforton, Staunton, Letton and Monnington that were
probably exploiting land that had been broken in by re-settled hillfort
people during the Roman period. Along such roads there were also of
course some forested areas, as Willersley indicates. Taking over the
clearances that survived from Roman times, the English planted their
'tons' along the road from Gloucester at Preston, Aylton, Ashperton
and Stretton Grandison, but there too was a mixed landscape, with
woodland increasing away from the road and recalled by names like
Putley and Pixley, Munsley and the Marcles.

A further area where '-ton' names predominate is around Leint-wardine, where too there was intensive Iron Age and Roman activity. Here, names like Letton, Burrington, Adforton, Buckton and Brampton Bryan are grouped closely in the vale near the Teme-Clun confluence.

Apart from such limited areas where particular place-name types are concentrated, there is over most of Herefordshire a mixture of types including many topographical names in '-hope' meaning valley, and '-ford'; and others that used British river and district names. Thus the several Fromes carried the British name of the local river, and Marden and Maund in the Lugg valley perpetuated the name of a district 'Mage', a name related to the Welsh *maen* or stone, which also had an original and more appropriate meaning of 'plain'. Across the Lugg, Roman Magnis is thought to have derived its name from a similar source, *magni*, the rocks. Around Leominster – Welsh Llanl-lieni – village names terminating in '-land', like Eardisland and Kings-land, show the partial extent of the pre-Domesday hundred of Lene that may have coincided with a former British district; it is assumed that a lost Welsh word *llion*, meaning stream, or its plural *llieni*, would have been the original form of the name.

Survivals like this show that there must have been a period when English-dominated and Welsh-dominated communities lived side by side, and the establishment of the eventual political map need not have involved conflict between English and Welsh neighbours, but rather a common acknowledgement of an outside political power based in Mercia. The original groups of English adventurers like the Magon-saeta and the Hwicce, who moved into east Herefordshire across the Malverns, established their own enclaves in the late sixth and early seventh centuries; but by 693 the Diocese of Hereford had been founded and the region was brought under Mercian control. What was left of an independent British culture was mostly blanketed by the uniformity of an alien language and separate religious organization; but the Domesday recognition of Welsh custom in parts of Hereford-shire, and the presence of Welshmen even north of the Wye, hints that below the political and religious veneer some British communities survived to integrate slowly and form the border's own culture, neither lowland English nor upland Welsh. This of course is a specula-tive assessment for archaeology to test by exploring the material culture of these early English and Welsh neighbours.

The broken terrain of south Shropshire was even less amenable than Herefordshire for settlement in broad successive zones. The invaders had perforce to feel their way between the hills and between their settlements there was inevitably much marginal land left for secondary colonization. The range of place-names is broadly the same as in Herefordshire, and only detailed work can hope to elucidate greater significance from them. Nevertheless, just as we have seen further south, there are occasional glimpses of nuclear areas where names in '-ton' predominate. One such is on the watershed south of Much Wenlock where are found Bourton, Acton Round and Monkhopton; and similar names spill south-west into Corve Dale focusing attention on the Roman road close to which stand Shipton and Stanton Long. Whereas their Herefordshire equivalents include many Anglo-Saxon personal names, these are comparatively rare in Shropshire, though among them are Dorrington – 'the village of Dodda's people' – Cardington and Woolstaston near Church Stretton, and Chetton near Bridgnorth.

North of the Severn the mixture of place-name types is much the same. Albrighton near Shrewsbury includes the personal name Eadbeorht; but beyond the riverside gravels '-ton' names are much less common and names in '-ley' and '-field' show that much of the Ellesmere moraine and its margins was still wooded. Beyond the moraine the place-names of Cheshire show a different balance and suggest a different process of settlement. West of the Weaver there are no fewer than eleven names in '-ington', and one in '-ingham' which include personal name elements; together with the names in 'ton' these far outnumber the topographical names in '-ley' etc.

The impression of early and intensive English settlement of this area, which extends for a few miles west of the Dee between Wrexham and Hawarden, is in accord with the historical record of the Northumbrian capture of Chester, opening the area to English settlers during the first decades of the seventh century. For a while the infertile lands of the Ellesmere moraine saved the British communities in the Severn valley from coming under pressure, although to their south the English had by now probably moved into Herefordshire. So, for a generation or two, Celtic and English provinces alternated along the border. Gwent and Erging remained Welsh, though English conquests across the Wye reduced the size and viability of the latter as a separate kingdom. Herefordshire was under English control and the vanguard was ready to push into the Vale of Radnor. With the northern plains under English control too, Shropshire may have been the scene of a rearguard action for British survival involving places

Fig 46 The Dark Ages—principal locations mentioned in the text and Roman roads. U.S.D. and L.S.D. are the Upper and Lower Short Ditches in Powys.

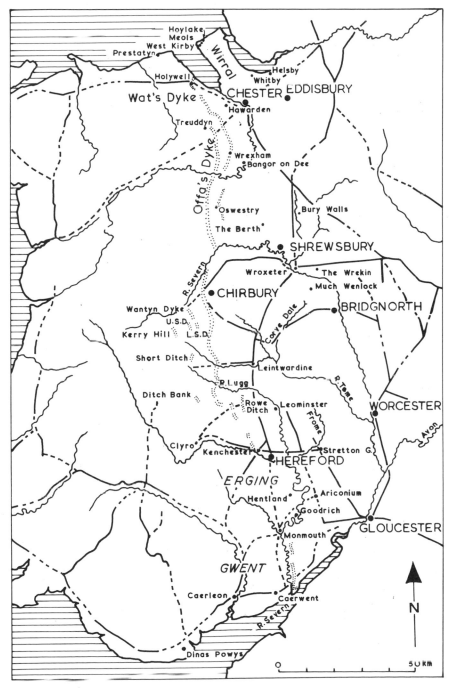

Hoylake
Meols
West Kirby
Prestatyn
Wirral
Holywell
Helsby
Whitby
CHESTER
EDDISBURY
Wat's Dyke
Hawarden
Treuddyn
Offa's Dyke
Wrexham
Bangor on Dee
Oswestry
The Berth
Bury Walls
R.Severn
SHREWSBURY
Wroxeter
The Wrekin
CHIRBURY
Much Wenlock
Wantyn Dyke
U.S.D.
Kerry Hill
L.S.D.
BRIDGNORTH
Corve Dale
Short Ditch
Leintwardine
R.Teme
R.Lugg
Ditch Bank
Rowe
Ditch
Leominster
WORCESTER
Frome
Avon
Clyro
Kenchester
Stretton G.
HEREFORD
ERGING
Hentland
Ariconium
Goodrich
Monmouth
GLOUCESTER
GWENT
Caerleon
Caerwent
N
R.Severn
Dinas Powys
0   50 km

like Oswestry, the Berth, Shrewsbury and Wroxeter. One of the probable results of this laggardly submission to the new warlords was that Shrewsbury acquired no cathedral and Shropshire came to be divided between the dioceses of Hereford and Lichfield.

Archaeological evidence is lacking for the conflict of these years, whether military or cultural. Nor is it certain that it is to be found at or close to the villages or hamlets that bear pre-Domesday names, for there has been plenty of time for changes in the pattern of settlement. If there was anything here like the movement of farms and cottages that Wade-Martins has demonstrated for some East Anglian parishes the area within which a pioneer settlement could occur is large indeed, though it is likely to be adjacent to the church as the most stable element in the parish. Unfortunately, the large farms and houses of the modern village are also often close to the church and the surface is deeply eroded into hollow ways and stockyards. In such circumstances the chances of discovering Dark Age traces are remote. We therefore need to look for sites with early names that were abandoned as villages long ago – sites on which the destructive forces of agricultural erosion and building have had less opportunity to proceed.

The earthworks of a deserted village beside an isolated church would be a better bet than the stockyard of a modern farm in an existing village centre, but we really need sites that were abandoned before the late Middle Ages, settlements of which all record has gone since their entry in Domesday Book in 1087. This may mean dispensing with the churches as guide-posts, and searching on the basis of earthworks alone; and the normal scarcity of pottery in this part of the world will render the task all the more difficult. Furthermore, the reason for the desertion of many villages is that they lie on marginal land, difficult to cultivate and most sensitive to adverse fluctuations of climate because of their altitude or poor drainage. Such locations are not likely to have been among the first to be seized by the incoming English, so their excavation is unlikely to reveal the habits of seventh-century pioneers. Nor would we expect at that early date the dispersal of a viable village community as a result of independent enclosure of open-field holdings. The best hope may lie somewhere in the Domesday lists of parishes that were said to be waste, probably as a result of raids, but which were still recorded later. In such cases there must be a chance that the medieval rebuilding took place on fresh ground, though probably close to the original, destroyed, settlement. Towards such parishes, though not with undue optimism for quick answers, we might look for information on the material culture of our Dark Age farmers.

Among the questions are: what were the origins of the medieval . timber-framed buildings found in the border and what relationship, if any, had they with the rectangular timber houses of the hillforts? Single-cell structures no larger than the 3.74 by three metres of the hillfort dwellings are still to be found in the border (*pl 28*), though usually enlarged by the addition of extra modules. Two obvious

Plate 28 A single cell timber-framed house behind the Boot Inn, Orleton (*David Hibbert*)

185

differences are that the surviving post-medieval buildings have stone chimneys and are based on sleeper beams instead of ground-fast posts; however, there remain enough hints to prompt questions of continuity of architectural tradition. The question of population replacement might just possibly be settled by an abandoned cemetery with bones still preserved. This means choosing a wasted manor with a soil as alkaline as possible, perhaps a site somewhere near the limestone of Wenlock Edge, or the hills around Wigmore.

The Mercian boundary dykes

The expansion of English power during the seventh and eighth centuries brought the new settlers to the banks of the Wye in the south and the front of the Cambrian Massif elsewhere. The consolidation of these acquisitions by powerful kings led to the definition of boundaries between English and Welsh, in order to avoid border disputes in areas where previously a man had been able to cultivate what he could hold, and to serve as a forward defence against Welsh resurgence. There are several frontier dykes involved and their development is generally considered to have taken place over a long period.

The most extensive system of linear earthworks in Britain is named after Offa, King of Mercia, 757–96, whose frontier, using a combination of rivers and artificial dykes, ran from the mouth of the Wye to the estuary of the Dee. This marked the culmination of boundary-making in the west and is thought to have followed the use of other dykes to the east like Wat's Dyke, attributed to Aethelbald, 716–57, and the Rowe Ditch. It is difficult to guess the date of a number of other shorter, cross-ridge and cross-valley dykes west of Offa's frontier. They are generally thought to belong to the early years of Mercian expansion, perhaps to the reigns of Penda, 626–55, or Wulfhere, 656–75, though some might have served, if only temporarily, as outworks of Offa's system.

Wat's Dyke (fig 47)

This earthwork forms, with a number of streams, a line between the Afon Vyrnwy and the estuary of the Dee. Like the other boundary dykes it consists of a single bank thrown up from a western ditch, set where possible on a west-facing slope, and clearly an English construction against the Welsh. There are two particular features about its character and course which support the view that it is of a different period and probably earlier than Offa's Dyke, which lies on a roughly

parallel course between one and six kilometres to the west. First, an
eastern quarry trench with the spoil thrown downhill to form the
dyke, was not used even when the dyke was placed on quite a steep
slope, whereas this technique is found occasionally on Offa's Dyke.
Secondly, the Wat's Dyke frontier incorporates as many miles as
possible of the deep ravines that trench the northern plains, thereby

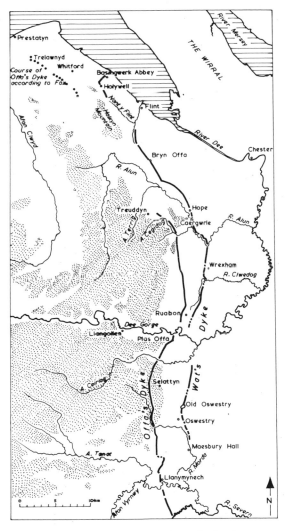

Fig 47   Offa's Dyke and Wat's Dyke in the
northern Marches (Sources Fox 1955
and Hill 1974). Land over 250m stippled.

acquiring the strong positions appropriate to a newly formed frontier at the limit of colonization. Today, it lies regularly along the divide between English and Welsh names, but the apparently Welsh names that are found between Wat's Dyke and Offa's Dyke to the west include many, like Selattyn and Brogyntyn, that are English names modified by subsequent Welsh re-occupation. Offa's frontier was only extended in this sector as far as the English settlement had proceeded since the time of Wat's Dyke.

The total frontier of Wat's Dyke, as interpreted by Fox, ran from Holywell to the river Morda, a tributary of the Vyrnwy, which in turn joins the Severn near the Breidden. The whole frontier is some sixty-one kilometres long with at least thirty-three kilometres of dyke known, an uncertain amount of destroyed dyke, and many lengths of ravine. Fox's detailed study showed this frontier to have been unitary in conception and method, composed of numbers of straight alignments and achieving a notably direct, though locally sinuous, course. In one form or another it is clearly and continuously defined northwards as far as the Nant y Flint, the stream which flows into the Dee at Flint. Fox regarded the latter town, surely correctly, as the natural termination for this frontier, but nevertheless proposed that the dyke continued, although most intermittently, another six kilometres to Holywell and the Abbey of Basingwerk, thereby taking in an uncomfortable finger of coastal plain beyond the area of predominantly English place-names. In making this suggestion he rejected the local place-name evidence for the frontier here being known as Clawdd Offa, and a fourteenth-century reference to Basingwerk as the end of Offa's Dyke.

Fox was clearly influenced by his belief that Offa's Dyke itself was to be traced, though with difficulty, along the uplands to the west, to terminate near Prestatyn. The evidence in this sector was always very slight and Hill's excavations at Trelawnyd and west of Whitford have failed to find Offa's Dyke along the course proposed by Fox. The whole of this northern extension of Offa's system has therefore come into question and it looks as though the historical evidence for Offa's Dyke ending near Basingwerk Abbey by Holywell should be allowed to stand. The Offan earthwork would be presumed to have come down to the plain to adopt the existing Wat's Dyke between the Terrig-Alun confluence and the Nant y Flint, where the earlier frontier will be presumed to have closed with the sea. By extending the frontier north-westwards to Holywell, Offa would have brought extra Welsh land under his rule, just as he did in those other sectors where his frontier was separate from that of his predecessor.

The frontier defined by Wat's Dyke bounds the territory of the northern plains and by way of Old Oswestry closes with the left-bank tributaries of the Severn, the Morda and Vyrnwy. As with Offa's Dyke, relatively few parish boundaries follow it, only coinciding with about 13% of the constructed work and leaving it an open question whether the dyke was earlier or later than the drawing of such boundaries. Noting that straight alignments occur in potentially cultivable areas, while sinuous stretches are located especially on hill slopes that are likely to have been wooded, Fox argued that the former represented work across cleared country. The proportion of straight to sinuous alignment led him to suggest that about 50% of the dyke south of Caergwrle had been built across agricultural land, whereas north of this to Holywell only some 20% was straight and arguably across cleared country. He concluded that the northern sector was less densely populated and included much uncleared forest. If the argument is sound it shows that when Wat's Dyke was built no more than about half of the available lowland had been reclaimed close to the frontier; extensive areas, particularly on the slopes, still awaited clearance.

Plate 29 The Rowe Ditch at the Leen, Pembridge

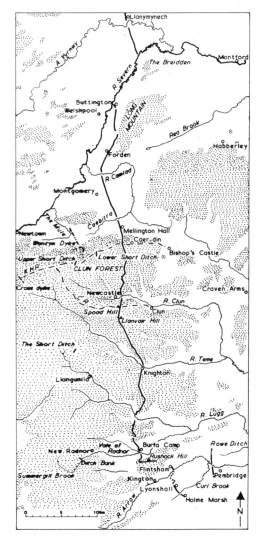

Fig 48 Offa's Dyke and the short dykes
in the central Marches
C.R.   Clun Ridgeway
K.H.R.   Kerry Hill Ridgeway
Land over 250m stippled (Source
Fox 1955)

The Rowe Ditch (fig 48)

This earthwork is in the same longitudinal position as Wat's Dyke, but its construction across a broad valley is more reminiscent of some of the western cross-dykes. Furthermore, English place-names predominate far to the west of the Rowe Ditch in marked contrast to their absence west of Wat's Dyke. The two earthworks may not therefore be of the same date.

The Rowe Ditch (pl 29) crosses the flood plain of the river Arrow near Pembridge, twelve kilometres west of Leominster. It lies some five kilometres east of Offa's Dyke and is about four kilometres long. Fox interpreted it as a barrier across the cleared valley land, closing the gap between a forested area to the south and the hills to the north. It consists of a single bank, up to fifteen metres wide, thrown up from a ditch on its west side. Like Wat's Dyke it has an obvious defensive capability and provided a protected causeway across the often flooded valley, a useful asset for the deployment of troops. To the south the place-names indicate the late survival of forest, making further boundary definition unnecessary.

Offa's frontier

In the ninth century Bishop Asser described Offa as the king who 'ordered the construction of a large rampart the whole way from sea to sea between Britain and Mercia'. The conventional date for the start of this work is shortly after 784. The length of the frontier (fig 46) defined by Fox from the Severn estuary to Prestatyn is 240 kilometres; termination at Holywell would make it about 226 kilometres. Whichever of these is used there was still 120 kilometres of earthwork south of Treuddyn, a project equivalent to constructing the ramparts of about seventy-five Midsummer Hill camps. Such a massive undertaking must have taken some considerable time and it is not surprising that it appears to be incomplete, the victim of a changing political climate or dwindling economic support. It will be appreciated too that although it was the boundary between Welsh and English and to that extent a unitary scheme, it takes in several very different sectors of frontier, each with its own topographical, economic and political problems. Some of these differences had their origins earlier in the post-Roman period, when the Romanized south had special links with the Irish Church whereas northerners were brought into the Dee basin to check the Irish incursions. The mixture of cultures along the Wye contrasted with the imposition of a powerful Anglian supremacy in Cheshire. The situations confronting politicians and frontier

191

engineers were thus different and so consequently were their solutions.

North of Herefordshire, Offa's Dyke lies on the edge of the highlands (*fig 47*), claiming the whole of the lowlands for Mercia including a strip in the north with many Welsh place-names. The English must have been in a strong position to negotiate this line. Whether the frontier terminated at Prestatyn or Basingwerk there are many gaps in it north of Treuddyn, although the dyke has recently been found in some of these. They may have been due, as Fox thought, to lack of labour in a thinly populated region, but it is also clear that more has been ploughed down than he appreciated.

No such ambiguity attends the recognition of Offa's frontier from Treuddyn southwards. Here it becomes the massive bank with accompanying western ditch that characterizes the frontier rampart for most of its course. Constructed across broken ground west of Wrexham it runs via Ruabon to the lower end of the Dee gorge. Striking across hill and valley to the high ground north-west of Selattyn, it is brought downhill west of Oswestry and then follows the sides of Llanymynech Hill to the plain of the Vyrnwy. On the far side of this valley it is laid across an extensive tract of lowland to the Severn.

Along the whole sector from Treuddyn to Llanymynech the dyke lies roughly parallel to Wat's Dyke, and has a similarly forthright course involving comparatively few alignments. It leaves little ground below 250 metres to the west, and has roughly marked out the western limit of intensive arable farming. Thus the land on the eastern slopes of Wales which was now part of Mercia was tributary to the lowlands instead of the uplands, and it was made more difficult for the communities of the truncated Welsh valleys to communicate with one another. As a result both the economic and military potential of the Welsh in this sector was further reduced.

At the end of this stretch, in Powys, the whole situation is different, for the Cambrian front is neither so abrupt nor high, and an extensive area of cultivable land remained Welsh. Just here in fact, where one might expect the population to have been considerable on both sides of the frontier, the Offan frontier makes little military sense (*fig 48*). For a start the Severn itself, a meandering and fluctuating stream in these reaches, served as the boundary for eight kilometres from near the Breidden to the vicinity of Buttington near Welshpool. Thence a frontier dyke climbs obliquely towards the top of the south-west corner of Long Mountain, acquiring a fine view of Wales but leaving the Welsh in occupation of both banks of the Severn. From the top of Long Mountain the dyke descends to the plain again near Forden on an alignment as though heading for Powys and the hills, but instead curves southward across the Camlad to stay in the middle of the plain until reaching the south Shropshire hills at Mellington Hall. The dyke's weak position here was probably a compromise, protecting some of the English communities in the Camlad valley, but relinquishing more westerly settlements like Hopton, which until then had probably been shielded by the westward-facing Wantyn Dyke, six kilometres to the west, at the foot of Clun Forest between the rivers Mule and Caebitra.

Offa's Dyke now enters its mountain zone on the uplands of Clun Forest, where it reaches its highest points, between 360 and 426 metres in an almost empty land, with sheep farms strung along tight valleys which make it a most difficult region to cross. Pursuing a southward course it makes as much use as possible of westward facing slopes and diverges to gain suitable hills from which new alignments can be laid. Its course does not follow the wandering edge of any pioneer settlement; it was clearly set out as an agreed frontier, probably giving up certain hills in order to gain the advantage on others. Nowhere is it more splendidly constructed or more brilliantly conceived than in this long stretch from the Powys border to Herefordshire. Crossing the Kerry Hill ridgeway route, it demonstrates that one of its functions was to prevent ridge-top movement, whether of soldiers or cattle rustlers. No sector is neglected. Though locally-based enemies may have been few the danger lay further afield in the heart of Wales; and that way, south-west along the ridge, lie short cross-dykes at points where the approach of steep tributary dingles creates easily defended waists along the route. The first, the Lower Short Ditch, lies some four kilometres west of Offa's Dyke at about 457 metres; it is 730 metres long with a western ditch. Three kilometres further west at the next waist is the Upper Short Ditch, at the same height and about as long, commanding the junction of the ridgeway from Clun with the Kerry Hill ridgeway. Just west of this the present Shropshire boundary marks the limit of English interest in the mountain zone; indeed, the prevalence of Welsh names between Offa's Dyke and this western salient suggests that the English element here was never numerous.

Eight kilometres west again, and now fifteen kilometres from Offa's Dyke, lies a third cross-ridge dyke at the western end of Kerry Hill. It is difficult to regard a work as far west as this as constructed by early English settlers, but equally it is difficult to divorce it in function from the other two cross-ridge dykes. All three may have served as customs barriers but could belong to brief episodes of conflict, thrown up by an English army against the threat of pursuit from Wales. In connection with them Fox drew attention to Caer-din, a univallate rectilinear earthwork with rounded corners, enclosing about 0.8 hectare, on the Kerry Hill ridge rather more than a kilometre east of Offa's Dyke. This, he thought, might be Dark Age, but it could equally well be Iron Age or Romano-British.

Leading southward over this dissected plateau the dyke crosses the Clun valley below Newcastle, climbs over Spoad Hill and Llanvair Hill, and reaches the Teme gorge at Knighton. Taking an awkward course across lowland and hill it enters an English salient in the Vale of Radnor, where it zigzags around the eastern rim of the Vale to leave a large area of English place-names to the west. Soon, on Rushock Hill, it turns its back on upland Wales and looks out over Herefordshire.

It is likely that the English settlement in the Vale of Radnor was another pioneer area left on the Welsh side of the negotiated boundary, helping to balance the Welsh territory recently acquired in Clwyd. Support for this view may be seen in another valley dyke, Ditch Bank, across the valley of the Summergill Brook less than two kilometres south-west of New Radnor and about ten kilometres west of Offa's Dyke on Burfa Hill. A last ridge-dyke in this sector, the Short Ditch, crosses an important route north-west of Llangunllo, spanning the ridge between the heads of deeply incised dingles. Like the other short dykes, especially on the ridges, it probably had a localized function, perhaps to prevent interference with work on Offa's Dyke itself.

On Rushock Hill, on a south-facing slope, there is no forward ditch, only a pronounced quarry-ditch behind the dyke. From here to the Wye at Bridge Sollers there are only short sectors preserved across the main valleys. First, that of the Arrow is crossed between Flintsham Farm and the river cliffs on the far side. These latter continue the frontier. Then, starting near Lyonshall, a large earthwork crosses the valley of the Curl Brook (pl 30).

There is then a considerable gap before the Yazor Brook section is reached, a gap where a reasonably straight alignment could have been obtained along the watershed of the Lugg and Wye drainage and where Fox concluded that the area was forested and so did not require a dyke (fig 49). He put his emphasis however on the richness of the Old Red Sandstone soils in giving rise to a dense and impenetrable undergrowth in oak forests. It was probably more significant that these poorly drained plains had never been extensively cultivated. No Roman settlements occur there, nor are there any hillforts. This was therefore a desert, and it was presumably the consequent lack of Welsh pressure that enabled the English to dispense with Offa's Dyke. The

Plate 30 Offa's Dyke, crowned by oaks, on the east side of the Curl Brook valley in Herefordshire

English settlement of Herefordshire had pressed along the valleys, where extensive spreads of sand and gravel offered better drained soils, and the dyke had only to cover these intakes as far west as they had gone to date. Beyond the valley dykes, place-names in '-ley' and '-wood' confirm the forested nature of the area.

Short stretches of dyke occur on either side of the Yazor Brook, and the last stretch before the Wye crosses the plain where it is narrowest, south of Garnons Hill, a choice that emphasizes its military purpose. Fox and Jack failed to find the Roman road from Kenchester where it was expected to approach the dyke and so assumed that it was diverted a little northwards, probably on the course of the modern A438 by the Steps.

For ninety-six kilometres, from Bridge Sollers to the highest limit of tide, near Redbrook, the Wye was probably used as the frontier, although Fox allowed for half a kilometre of broken dyke on the south side of the river in English Bicknor, coupled with half a kilometre of river cliff. The only other short ditches invoked in discussion of this

195

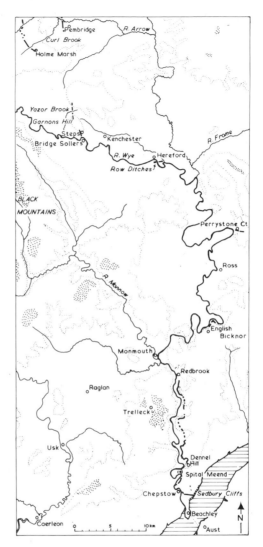

Fig 49 Offa's Dyke in Herefordshire and
Gloucestershire. Land over 250m
stippled and 120m contour dotted
(Source Fox 1955)

frontier are the Row Ditches at Hereford and a bank and ditches at Perrystone Court, Foy. The latter is an uncertain earthwork, suggested by Fox as a possible pre–Offan Magonsaetan boundary facing south. The Hereford Row Ditches, one to the south of the city protecting the bridgehead, the other north of the river protecting arable land in Portfield, are thought to be medieval and certainly not part of Offa's Dyke; nor are they attributable to the Scots army in 1645 as shown on the Ordnance Survey map.

On the south-west side of this long frontier, marked solely by a river that is fordable in several places, English place-names are mixed with Welsh ones, and were thought by Fox to represent post-Offan settlements. In the absence of a strong difference of place-name pattern between the two sides of the river these settlements may equally prove to be earlier than Offa's frontier, and, if the Wye was the frontier all the way to the Forest of Dean, they may have been yielded by Offa.

South of Redbrook the dyke reappears, high on the eastern cliffs of the Wye, only occasionally descending to cross re-entrant valleys. A certain amount of labour was saved by utilizing sections of cliff, and where the dyke was constructed it was often built by throwing material downhill from an eastern quarry-ditch. From Dennel Hill in Tidenham parish the river cliffs were followed for three kilometres before a short stretch of dyke brought the frontier down with the cliff to the river bank just north of Chepstow. In this sector, where a triangular promontory is occupied by Spital Meend Camp, the frontier presumably utilized the hillfort defences just as Wat's Dyke used the west side of Old Oswestry. From the vicinity of Chepstow the cliffs must have served as the boundary to its end half a kilometre below the railway bridge. Here a cliff-top earthwork holding about 0.2 hectare was thought by Fox to be possibly associated with the dyke, but it is perhaps more likely to be Iron Age; the iron lance-head socket found at the bottom of the natural hollow forming the west end of the fort's ditch is not closely datable. The silted creek on the south side of the fort presumably served as the boundary for the first 250 metres across the Beachley peninsula; but the remaining kilometre was defined by a dyke running straight to the south end of Sedbury Cliffs where the great frontier terminated.

The construction of dykes to connect lengths of river cliff downstream from Redbrook instead of using the river as a frontier is of special interest and invites consideration. In the first place, leaving the Beachley peninsula in Welsh hands was probably an acknowledgement of Welsh interest in Beachley port, which was the northern terminus of the old ferry from Aust. Welsh insistence on navigation rights may be further reflected by their retention of the full width and both banks of the Wye as far upstream as the limits of even the highest tides, for no other physical reason is apparent for terminating Offa's Dyke at Redbrook. There would also have been very important fishing interests, in salmon and eels, that may have concerned the Welsh particularly. Whatever the reason, the Welsh were able to safeguard their local interests. Perhaps, in this wide gorge, Offa was doing no more than recognizing his inability to change an established frontier, for Gloucestershire on the east is distinctly English whereas little but Welsh influence is apparent on the west bank.

Offa's Dyke had finally defined the frontier in a manner not previously attempted and put an end to any possibility of regional independence for the people of the Marches. Whereas in earlier years the border had its own character, distinct from the territories to east and west, it was now to be forever tributary to its neighbours. North of the Wye it was declared to be part of Mercia, whereas south of that river it remained in the Welsh kingdom of Gwent. As a frontier district it was to be the battleground where the rivalries of English and Welsh princes would be settled, a buffer against Welsh attacks, a springboard for English assaults. With most of it subsidiary to the lowlands it became an obvious target for raiders from the highlands. It is appropriate that such an important political and cultural watershed should now be used for a national footpath, the Offa's Dyke path, originally designated in 1955 but only coming fully into use as a result of the energetic advocacy of Noble and others in the 1960s. The walk from Sedbury Cliffs to Prestatyn offers a fine introduction to the border, though it should be noted that the path does not follow Offa's frontier between Monmouth and Kington, nor between the Vale of Llangollen and Prestatyn. In these two areas, where the dyke is in any case an intermittent work, the footpath climbs westwards on to the more exciting ground of the Black Mountains and the Clwydian Range.

While English and Welsh struggled to extend their power at each other's expense, the Vikings threw in their contribution to the chaos of the late ninth and tenth centuries. Their raids in the Severn estuary have left no recognizable monuments, nor is much known about the fortified settlements, known as *burhs*, established against them. Along the Severn the main bridgepoints at Gloucester, Worcester, Bridgnorth and Shrewsbury were guarded by *burhs* (*fig 46*). The one at Shrewsbury was in existence as early as 901, when it was recorded in the Charter of Ethelred and Ethelfleda. There was a mint at Shrewsbury, as indicated by its mark on issues of Athelstan, 925–939, and his successors until the Norman Conquest, so the town must have remained fortified (mints were only allowed to operate in defended places, ports or *burhs*, from the tenth century onwards). The Shrewsbury *burh* probably occupied the highest part of the town and the few sherds of late Saxon pottery known as Chester ware, found in 1968 on the site of 2A St Alkmund's Place, may derive from it. The presence of Saxon houses in the castle area is indicated by the recorded destruction of fifty-one of them to make way for the outer bailey when that was added by Earl Roger of Montgomery between 1074 and 1086.

In 914 Ethelfleda built a *burh* at Eddisbury, presumably reoccupying the hillfort, and in 915 another at 'Cyricbyrig', thought to be Chirbury, east of Montgomery. Chirbury Castle, a rectangular enclosure in the north-west corner of the village, may have been the site of this *burh*, but excavations there in 1958 revealed no palisade nor defensive ditch, nor any sign of internal occupation.

At Hereford, the centre of the bishopric since the late seventh century, Mercia faced the Welsh in Erging, or Archenfield, over the Wye and the two powers were locked in battle there in 760. The city's earliest rampart may belong to this period, but has only been observed on the west side of the town beneath later ramparts beside Victoria Street (*fig 50*). It is thought to have followed West Street and East Street as far as Offa Street, before, conjecturally, turning south to close with the river east of the later cathedral, the Saxon minster probably being beside the river. The earliest town would then have been almost square, disposed either side of an east-west High Street along the line perpetuated by King Street and Castle Street, and would have enclosed nearly thirteen hectares, not much larger than Roman Kenchester.

This rampart was subsequently enlarged and provided with a timber front revetment possibly in the early tenth century, the equivalent of the *burh* defences erected elsewhere. Certainly Hereford had the status of a *burh* in 914 when the Danes were raiding Archenfield. The town by now extended east of Castle Green to the line of the later city wall beside Mill Street, and enclosed about twenty hectares. Later in the Saxon period the rampart was given a stone face – perhaps when defences were restored by Earl Harold following the sack of the city in 1055 by the north Welsh under Gruffydd ap Llywelyn, aided by the Mercian Aelfgar. Suburbs were probably already developing in the eleventh century to the north of the town wall, and when the defences were next reconstructed the new rampart was set out to enclose these, establishing the line along New Market Street, Blue School Street and

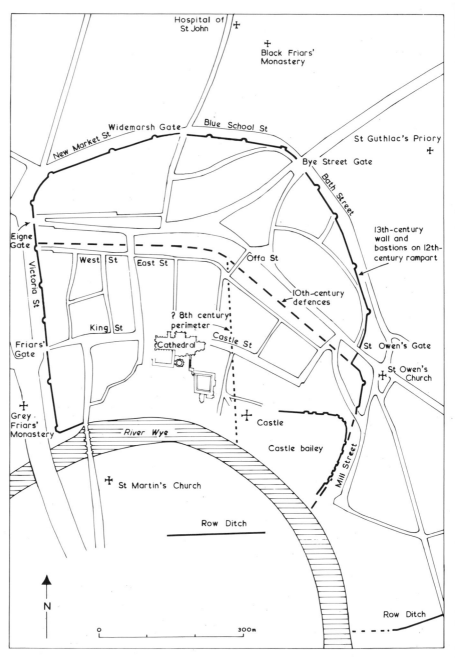

Fig 50   The successive defences of Hereford (Sources Taylor 1757 and
Shoesmith 1975)

roughly parallel to Bath Street. Two cooking pot sherds found in the Bath Street section are of twelfth-century form and make it likely that the extension followed the 1189 Charter for the fortification of the city, although the view has also been published that the extension dates back to 1055. Whatever its date this is the maximum extent of the defended area, thirty-seven hectares.

In the thirteenth century a stone wall was inserted in front of the rampart. The latter had probably been set out on a curve, but the wall builders preferred working in straight sectors and produced a segmental enclosure matching the curve as best they could. Since the original curve was not regular the angles formed by the changes of wall alignment were not equally spaced along it and as a result neither were the semicircular bastions which were placed at these angles and probably built at the same time. The Rowe Ditches, whose possible functions have been discussed on p 191, are most likely to belong to a late Saxon phase in this sequence but need not be contemporary with each other.

The emerging history of Hereford's defences may serve to underline the complex pattern of Viking raids and Welsh pressure that lies behind the development of town fortifications. Slowly the archaeological record of this story is being recovered from new building sites in Hereford, Shrewsbury and Chester. If anything, the record from the ground is even more eventful than that given by the documents, for the present assessment of Hereford's defences postulates no fewer than five major phases of fortification between the eighth and thirteenth centuries.

Through most of the border there was no permanent legacy of the Danish raids. In the north, however, raids from Viking bases in Ireland and the Isle of Man were accompanied by the settlement of the Wirral peninsula and Merseyside, distinguished by Norse place-names like West Kirby, Whitby and Helsby, and accompanied by missionary activity that is commemorated by Anglo-Norse wheel-shaped crosses evolved from the Norse crosses of Ireland and the Isle of Man. They are found as far south as Chester; but over the rest of Cheshire Mercian round-shaft crosses predominate.

The northern extremity of Wirral attracted seafarers and traders throughout the Dark Ages as it had done in prehistory. This at least is the impression given by numerous finds that, while not individually amenable to very close dating, seem best explained as the accumulation of centuries. They include belt fittings, annular brooches, a pottery flask of Mediterranean origin from the immediate post-Roman centuries and two Mercian coins of the late seventh or early

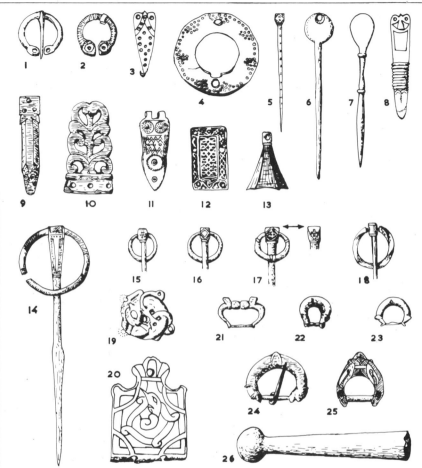

Fig 51 Dark Age bronze objects from Meols, Wirral (After Bu'lock 1960) All x½.

1 & 2 Sub-Roman penannular brooches
3 Belt hook, probably eighth century
4 Anglo-Saxon annular brooch
5 Faceted pin, seventh–ninth century
6 & 7 Disc-headed pins eighth–tenth century
8–10 Strap ends, ninth–eleventh century
11 Buckle plate
12 Mount, eighth–ninth century
13 Six-sided bell
14–18 Ring-headed pins, seventh–eleventh century
19 Mount with intertwining animals, eighth–ninth century
20 Mount, tenth–eleventh century
21–25 Zoomorphic buckles, ninth–twelfth century
26 Viking drinking-horn mount terminal

eighth century. Late Saxon faceted and disc-headed pins, bronze mounts and strap ends attest the continued importance of the peninsula, particularly of Whitby monastery and the port area of Meols, Hoylake and West Kirby. Among the objects belonging to the Viking period in the later ninth and tenth centuries are long ring-headed pins and zoomorphic buckles (*fig 51*). It seems there was a gradual increase of Irish and then Norse influence as a result of trading and missionary activities over a long period, rather than a sudden displacement of the native population by large-scale Viking invasion. Most of the finds have come from along the coast where marine erosion has bitten into old settlements and redistributed the land-spits which until the nineteenth century defined the Hoyle Lake lagoon. Hitherto this had served as a harbour at the seaward end of the peninsula.

One effect of Viking pressure on North Wales had been to restrain the ambition of Rhodri Mawr, 844–78, King of Gwynedd, Powys and Seisyllwg, against the kings of South Wales, but on his death the threat posed by his sons Anarawd and Cadell to the kingdoms of Gwent, Brycheiniog, Morgannwg, Rhwng Gwy a Hafren and Dyfed, caused their rulers to seek the help of Alfred, King of Wessex. South Wales thus turned, of geographical necessity, across the Severn for help, demonstrating anew the tendency for unity in the Bristol Channel region and giving later English kings a precedent for their subsequent claims to be overlords in Wales. Though the country was briefly unified under Gruffydd ap Llywelyn (1039–63) it fell into separate kingdoms again following his defeat and death as a result of Earl Harold's invasion of North Wales in 1062–3. Gruffydd had raided as far as Chester and Leominster, but at his death the frontier was again close to that set out by Offa.

The scene was now set for the Norman invasion that was to alter the course and character of English social and political history.

CHAPTER NINE

Castles in the Marches

The Norman feudal system was based on military service; and the Welsh border country, more than most other areas, came under the heavy imprint of the professional soldier and his paid troops. Castles sprang up on every hand, from the major strategic centres of the king to the mottes that mushroomed in almost every western parish. The region had known before the defence-works of its hillfort farmers and the forts built to hold Roman imperial garrisons. It had known something too, of the *burhs*, constructed by Anglo-Saxon princes for the benefit of the whole community. It was now to see the proliferation of strongholds designed as part of a professional war game to be carried on against any rebellious English and, more importantly, the neighbouring Welsh, for the prime object of increasing personal and family wealth and prestige. Just as the social developments prompted or accelerated by the Conqueror's accession were to result in an increasing gulf between the governors and the governed, so too were the defence works of the military to impress a character of conflict and a memory of bitterness upon the lands of the border and the valleys of Wales. The Marches castles survive as frequent and cruel monuments to that phase in our history when the Anglo-Norman east became indelibly distinct from the Celtic west.

The stage for later conflict was already being prepared about 1050 with Edward the Confessor's infusion of Normans into the border. His nephew Ralph built the first castle at Hereford, while the Norman Osbern established the Lordship of Ewyas Harold in the Black Mountains and another Norman built a castle at 'Auretone' – Richard's Castle. Despite these preparations, Hereford was destroyed in 1055 and its defences had to be rebuilt by Harold Godwinson, Earl of Wessex, when he became Earl of Hereford. In view of Harold's great influence in the Marches it is not surprising that a Herefordshire thegn, Eadric the Wild, with Welsh princes as his allies, was one who rebelled against King William in 1069, nor that the Conqueror should make rather special dispositions of his most trusted soldiers along the Welsh border.

In 1071 arrangements were made for the administration of the lowlands of the Dee, Severn and Wye as three earldoms, of Chester, Shrewsbury and Hereford respectively. These three great resource territories were to be defended by castles both within their own territory and, where possible, westwards in Wales (fig 52). In the north Hugh d'Avranches was made Earl of Chester with a forward defence against the Welsh at Rhuddlan which was under the control of his cousin Robert. In the centre Robert of Montgomery became Earl of Shrewsbury with an outpost on the Welsh side of the dyke at Montgomery or, as Barker has argued, at Hen Domen, a small motte and bailey two kilometres to the north-west. In the south the Normans, headed by William FitzOsbern, Earl of Hereford, defended the Wye basin with castles at Wigmore, Clifford and Ewyas Harold, and invaded Gwent, establishing the Lordship of Striguil around Chepstow. By 1086 the Normans held Caerleon and the line of the Usk, and in 1093, following the defeat of Rhys ap Tewdwr, they extended their control of South Wales with the establishment of the Lordships of Brecon and Glamorgan. The sequence was that of the Roman conquest all over again.

From Montgomery, or Hen Domen, the Earl of Shrewsbury attacked Wales along the Severn valley to gain control of the Cantrefs of Cydewain and Arwystli, thus imposing border power on the waist of Wales in a manner reminiscent of the protrusion of hillforts from the Marches to Aberystwyth. From Oswestry the Normans pressed north-westwards into Welsh lands beyond Offa's Dyke, and in the far north, moved quickly along the coastal plain, establishing castles at Deganwy, Conway and Caernarvon.

The ensuing Norman campaigns, the Welsh resistance and successive rebellions, produced a long sequence of castle building with the expenditure of much energy and wealth to render the new constructions secure against improving methods of attack. The process continued with little abatement for three hundred years, and some quite elaborate works were still being undertaken four centuries after the first Norman infiltration of the border.

Most stone castles therefore underwent a long history and even apparently simple works often saw more than one phase of construction. The most important sources for dating castles are documents; but the documentary record is frequently incomplete, and too often inadequately specific. There may be a reference to the building or repair of a particular castle, but the record of itself does not normally

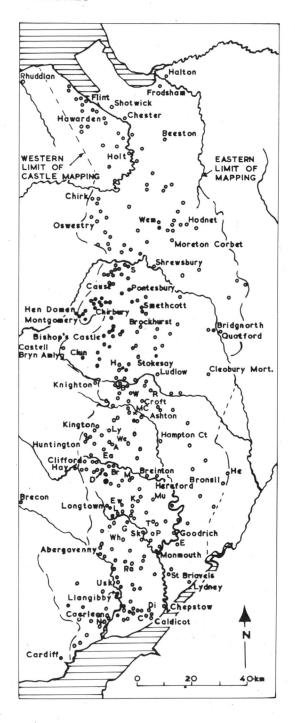

permit us to know to which part of the surviving remains the reference relates. The documents must therefore be interpreted with regard to architectural detail and historical probability. Excavation will normally permit the elucidation of the building sequence, allowing the several parts of the structure to be placed in a relative chronology, but datable finds are likely to be few, for the close dating of medieval pottery in the Marches still eludes us. The position is therefore difficult enough for large castles, but even worse for the minor motte and bailey castles that often have no medieval record at all. Most of these were occupied by the minor vassals of the border barons, and although they proliferated during the anarchy of Stephen's reign, 1134–54, the majority probably go back to the eleventh century. There was, moreover, a pre-Conquest tradition of unlicensed castle building in Normandy itself; and in view of the trouble King William had in England from some of his own Normans it is likely that some unlicensed castles, especially in the remote west, date from the early years of the Conquest.

It is generally thought that the idea of the motte and bailey castle was brought here from the continent in the mid–eleventh century, although Davison has argued that the castle mound, or motte, was invented by the Normans after the Conquest. Certainly in the early years English castles were built both with and without mottes and the latter may have contained timber towers, possibly close-boarded to resist penetration by firebrands. It would have been an obvious step to cover the lower part with turf for further protection, and even to fill in the bottom with earth, so giving rise to a motte surmounted by a tower.

Fig 52   The Norman border —castles within the chosen area with the addition of those at Halton, Hen Domen, Montgomery, Knighton, Brecon and Cardiff (Based on Hogg and King's lists 1963, 1967 and 1970 and Ordnance maps for the few east of the longitude of English Bicknor)

A Almeley	H Hopton	P Pembridge
B Brampton Bryan	He Herefordshire	R Richard's Castle
Br Bredwardine	Beacon	Ra Raglan
C Caerwent	K Kilpeck	S Shrawardine
D Dorstone	L Llancillo	Sk Skenfrith
Di Dinham	Ly Lyonshall	T Treago
E English Bicknor	M Madley	W Wigmore
Ea Eardisley	MC Mortimer's Cross	We Weobley
Ew Ewyas Harold	Mu Much Dewchurch	Wh White Castle
G Grosmont	N Newport, Gwent	

Plate 31   Richard's Castle motte

Recognition of the probable frequency of castles without mottes in Norman England is of special significance for the pre-Conquest castles of the Welsh Marches, where it was formerly expected that the earliest phases of the mottes at Richard's Castle, Ewyas Harold and Hereford would belong to pre-Conquest castles. Curnow and Thompson have shown, however, that the huge motte at Richard's Castle (*pl 31*) belonged to the twelfth-century castle rather than a pre-Conquest structure. If the pre-Conquest castle of Auretone was on the same site as that later fortified by Richard FitzOsbern, and known thereafter as Richard's Castle, its remains will lie under the later motte. The one-time hope of distinguishing the plan of a pre-Conquest tower at the top of its contemporary motte is thus probably false; only with the removal of the existing motte and its stone keep could such a plan be recovered.

Chepstow is an early post-Conquest castle without a motte (*fig 53*). Built by William FitzOsbern probably between 1067 and 1070, it has been described by Taylor as 'historically and architectur-

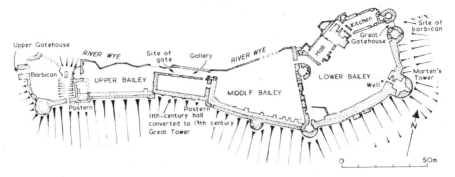

Fig 53   Plan of Chepstow Castle (After Ministry of Works Official Guide 1955). Crown Copyright—reproduced with permission of the Controller of Her Majesty's Stationery Office.

ally one of the most important castles in the Welsh March'. Instead of a motte, the first castle had a remarkable stone hall which was converted in the thirteenth century to a three-storey tower. The hall is held to derive from the same ancestry as the stone hall of 994, or a decade or two later, at Langeais on the Loire. It measures thirty-two by twelve metres and indicates the kind of central building that may have been present in stone or timber in the earliest phases of other important castles. At Skenfrith, excavation has shown surface appearances to be deceptive, for the thirteenth-century keep is not built on an earlier motte and it would seem that the eleventh-century castle here too lacked a motte. Ludlow Castle, built like Chepstow on a limestone hill, had no motte or other earthworks and was stone-built from the beginning. The royal castle at Brockhurst near Church Stretton, which is first recorded in 1154, similarly lacked a motte and is thought to have been rendered in stone from the start.

The early castles would have been surrounded where necessary by a ditch, the upcast of which was used to form an internal bank as a foundation for the palisade. One of the most spectacularly sited of such ring-works is on the highest point of the Herefordshire Beacon hillfort, and known as the Citadel. The nineteenth-century excavations resulted in much internal destruction and little useful record, although some twelfth-century pottery has since been identified among the few finds. On other sites some of the ditch spoil was disposed outside to make a counterscarp bank as seen on the Bayeux tapestry round the castles at Dol, Dinan and Bayeux. The motte at Pontesbury, a circular mound about three metres high and between thirty-seven and forty-six metres in diameter, probably started as a ring-work with a simple dump rampart and had a stone tower added

209

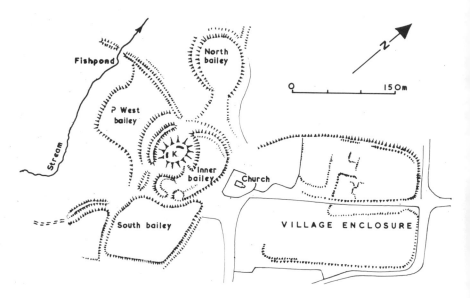

Fig 54 Plan of Kilpeck Castle and village earthworks.
K remains of keep on motte (After RCHM Herefordshire I, 159)

in the twelfth century. At Castell Bryn Amlwg a ring-work formed the first defence and a circular stone keep was added in the thirteenth century. This pattern of development was probably common, the added tower being in timber or stone as resources permitted.

Once the earth motte had been developed it was likely to be used by those who could not afford the skilled labour required for a masonry tower. The spoil from a circular ditch provided a flat-topped hillock which might be about thirty-seven metres in diameter, diminishing to fifteen metres at the top. This was sometimes constructed around a newly-built wooden tower but in other cases the tower posts may have been set in the top of an existing motte, and almost certainly so if the timber tower rotted and had to be rebuilt. A motte with the post-holes of a tower coming through its top has been excavated at Smethcott; but the report is not yet published. In many cases stone towers were afterwards built into mounds that had presumably once held timber towers. At Hen Domen Barker's interim reports of a continuing excavation show that an all-timber motte and bailey castle may, nevertheless, have seen many phases of reconstruction.

Whether a hall or motte was used as the central feature, it was normally accompanied by a subsidiary enclosure – a bailey – for ancillary buildings like stables and workshops. Later, baileys were

Plate 32   Hopton Castle keep

sometimes used for spacious residences. There might be more than one; in addition to an inner ward containing the hall, Chepstow had upper and lower baileys from the beginning, protected by their own curtain walls on those sides away from the central enclosure, and at Kilpeck (*fig 54*) there are three outer enclosures as well as an inner bailey. Some of the little mottes in west Herefordshire and Shropshire, known locally as tumps and often labelled as 'tumuli' on old Ordnance Survey maps, have no visible baileys and may have been simple tower mounds for overnight refuge.

The functions of the stone hall as a residence and of the wooden tower as a stronghold came to be combined in the large rectangular keeps, often square, that were built within the castle enclosures or on their mottes. Such keeps were being constructed through the twelfth century and often into the thirteenth. They are the normal form for most masonry castles in the border and particularly fine upstanding ones may be seen at Clun, Hopton (*pl 32*), Goodrich and Monmouth.

211

Plate 33 Longtown Castle keep

In the late eleventh century the French were experimenting with round towers to overcome the several weaknesses of the square keep; and the round form was widely used in the succeeding decades in Germany too. It was possibly as a result of German influence that the round keep was introduced into the southern border in the late twelfth and early thirteenth century; there is a fine example at Longtown

212

Plate 34 Samuel and Nathaniel Buck's engraving of Wigmore Castle in 1732
(*David Hibbert*)

(*pl 33*) with a diameter of fourteen metres overall, dating from about
1190. Others survive at Caldicot, Lyonshall, Monmouth and Skenfrith and are also thought to have existed at Ashton in north Herefordshire, Llancillo and Caerleon. They are occasionally met with further
north in the border, for example at Castell Bryn Amlwg and Hawarden. Most of the advantages of the circular tower could be obtained by
a multangular tower, like the octagonal one exposed by excavation at
Richard's Castle.

Contemporary with central towers were many shell-keeps with
minor towers incorporated in the curtain wall as at Wigmore (*pl 34*).
The rectangular wall-towers of early times were increasingly sup-
planted by semicircular ones, matching the change in keep shapes. As
the thirteenth century wore on the separate keep became less popular
as more defenders were stationed on the bailey wall, and the main
strong-point came to be moved to the perimeter in which elaborate
gatehouses and extra large towers were often incorporated. The gatehouses at St Briavels and Llangibby were virtually self-contained
fortresses capable of being held even when the rest of the castle had
been overrun; and Martin's tower in Chepstow Castle is an example of
a secondary keep-like structure in a bailey wall. Barbicans, as at
Goodrich, were constructed to cover the approach to the drawbridge,
particularly long ones being employed at Abergavenny and Brampton
Bryan. In the outer bailey at Clifford twin circular towers project at
the far end of the gate passage, the whole arrangement of which, with
guard-rooms housed in the thickness of the curtain wall just inside the
portcullis, recalls the out-turned entrances of some hillforts. With

such devices and the provision of machicolations around towers and along battlements the fourteenth-century castle was rendered virtually immune from attack.

Hogg and King have listed and mapped the castles of Wales and the border as far east as grid line 360, the longitude of Ross-on-Wye, and have distinguished between those known or likely to have existed before 1215 including undocumented mottes and ring-works, and later castles including all masonry castles. Allowing for the few east of this line, there are about 260 early castles and more than ninety later castles in the Welsh Marches as we have defined it.

Castles west of the Wye

In Offa's day the Wye was the boundary between English and Welsh, but with the Norman Conquest the land of Gwent was once again a matter of dispute, so important castles came to be built along the river at Clifford, Hay, Bredwardine, Hereford, Goodrich, English Bicknor, Monmouth, St Briavels and Chepstow. Sometimes on the Welsh side, sometimes on the English, according to local tactical or wider strategic requirements, they formed the Norman base line.

Clifford and Hay guarded the exit of the Wye from upland Wales and the frequency of military activity in their neighbourhood is marked by a dozen or more undocumented motte and bailey castles extending to Dorstone in the Golden Valley. A string of mottes south-eastwards along this valley brings us close to a line of mottes from Madley to Much Dewchurch, placed as though to screen Hereford against raids from the south-west; but of their actual purpose history is silent. More mottes along the upper Monnow valley show the fear of eruptions from the valleys of the Black Mountains and hint at the use of this north-eastward trending route which again points directly at Hereford. The lower Monnow valley must have been an important route itself and, moreover, probably remained a cultural boundary between the Anglicized Welsh of Archenfield to the north and the Norman-occupied Welsh district to the south. Three important castles lay along the Monnow at Monmouth, Grosmont and Skenfrith, while a fourth, Whitecastle, controlled the high divide between the Monnow and the Usk. White Castle, Grosmont and Skenfrith are known as the Three Castles and were long held by the Crown although garrisoned by various lords. They formed a triangle of power in a vital area. There are several more mottes on the uplands of central Gwent and more still on the coastal plain. West of Chepstow there were early castles at Caldicot, Caerwent and Dinham, while,

214

towards the Usk, a small group of mottes leads to the early recorded castles at Caerleon and Newport.

The stone castles that were in use in the southern border in the mid-thirteenth century are an indication of the resources that had to be committed to the defence of the southern March as a result of the campaign of Llewellyn the Great. They recur for the most part on sites previously fortified along the Wye and the Monnow but there was an increase in castles on the coastal plain with no fewer than ten between Chepstow and Newport. In the west the old sites at Abergavenny, Usk, Caerleon and Newport were still occupied. With little change this pattern persisted into the mid-fourteenth century, after which the only stone castles to be added were Pembridge, in Welsh Newton parish, and Raglan.

Castles in the central Marches

In Herefordshire and Shropshire between the Wye and Severn there are few early castles east of the longitude of Hereford, Ludlow and Shrewsbury, save for a line along Corve Dale which always offered an easy route from the central border to the Midlands. By contrast, the plains of west Herefordshire are thick with undocumented mottes filling the space between early castles like Weobley, Eardisley, Huntington, Kington and Wigmore. The close pattern extends without break westwards into the lowlands of Powys, creating a strong defensive zone some sixteen kilometres wide, a remarkable contrast with Offa's largely undefended frontier in this sector. Of particular interest in Herefordshire is a group of mottes around Almeley, and another around Wigmore where a castle had been built on waste ground before 1086. The site chosen at Wigmore was away from the main east-west routes, implying that the choice was restricted by ownership of land or by concern to utilize the topographical advantages of that particular site rather than by strategic considerations.

Some of the motte groups in Shropshire look specially interesting. A line of five extends along the north-east front of the Long Mynd southwards from Pontesbury, while another group in the valleys around Bishop's Castle guarded against incursions from the upper Severn. A formidable cluster of mottes is found in the vale of Montgomery between Montgomery and Shrewsbury. King and Spurgeon have noted the considerable uniformity of motte here – tall and narrow-topped, between three and six metres high and about six or seven metres across at the top. Observing that many of the farms on which these mottes stand were held in recognition of the duty of castle

215

guard at Montgomery, King and Spurgeon have concluded that there was a general policy of farmstead fortification consequent on the re-settlement of the area with soldier-farmers after some Welsh raids. The mottes must be later than 1086 since the area was then waste and are thought to date somewhere between then and 1102, during the Earl of Shrewsbury's tenure of the Lordships of Montgomery and Chirbury, for most of them are on land held by the Corbets who were important tenants of the Earl. They were certainly in existence by 1225, when their owners were required to refurbish them. A concentration of mottes around Cause castle may reflect a similar origin, for Cause was also held by the Corbets. Apart from the presumed, but generally unproven, disuse of most of the mottes, the pattern of mid-thirteenth-century castles shows little change. Important castles rendered in stone included Lyonshall, Wigmore, Richard's Castle, Ludlow, Bishop's Castle, and Caus. By the mid-fourteenth century many of these were no longer defensible.

Castles of the northern Marches

North of the Severn there are fewer castles, just as there are fewer hillforts, a reflection of the less populated character of these clay lands. There remains however a network of strongholds dating to the eleventh century, and between the Severn at Shrawardine and the Dee near Chirk a line of motte and bailey castles forms a frontier to thwart access to the Shropshire lowlands from northern Powys. They are a Norman response to the same problem that confronted the Mercians when they chose the line of Wat's Dyke and the river Morda as their frontier just to the west of these mottes. It was an area where the Welsh succeeded in retaking land in the twelfth century, including Oswestry and, south of the Severn, Caus Castle. In contrast to east Herefordshire, where mottes are rare, east Shropshire has many castles including Wem, Hodnet and Moreton Corbet to indicate the persistence of unsettled conditions with these eastern castles remaining in use into the thirteenth and fourteenth centuries.

In the far north most of the castles are along the Dee or west of it. The activity of early years was often followed by abandonment so that in the mid-fourteenth century between the Dee and the Clwyds the record of occupation is certain only at Flint, Hawarden and Holt. In fact there are more castles securely documented at this time east of the Dee, at Chester, Shotwick, Frodsham, Beeston and Halton.

Late castle building

No major campaigns into Wales were undertaken after the suppression of Owen Glyndwr's rebellion in 1403, so most castles became redundant. Furthermore, the devastation effected by the Welsh armies, coming on top of a general agrarian decline in the late fourteenth century, made most landowners look for ways of raising capital rather that disposing of it. They were more likely to sell part of their arable land than add machicolations to the ancestral home. Moreover, the national trend was for more spacious and civilized residences; so those who could afford to change left their draughty castles for new houses, often fortified in a simple way, but outside the old curtain wall and sometimes on new sites at a distance. Where and while the castles were retained they were often given larger windows and additional fireplaces. With such improvements some of them continued in use until the seventeenth century, but when they were recommissioned during the Civil War many had been decayed for long before. Stokesay, Brampton Bryan, Monmouth and Goodrich were among those that changed hands during that war and Raglan holds the distinc-

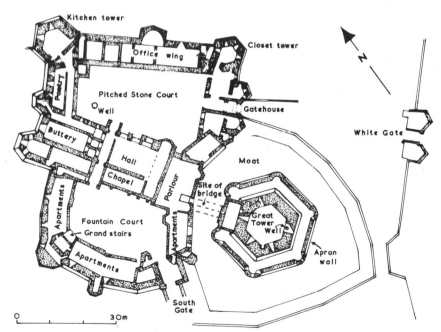

Fig 55   Ground floor plan of Raglan Castle (Somewhat simplified from Ministry of Works Official Guide Plan 1950). Crown Copyright—reproduced with permission of the Controller of Her Majesty's Stationery Office.

217

tion of signalling the effective end of Royalist resistance when it was surrendered in 1646, a fitting distinction for a castle that was only constructed after new castle building had virtually ceased in England and Wales.

It was the improved fortunes of a small landowner, William ap Thomas, that had permitted a start on rebuilding Raglan castle in the 1430s (*fig 55*). When his son William Herbert, later Earl of Pembroke, amassed a wealth of lucrative lands and offices, particularly as a result of supporting Edward IV at the Battle of Mortimer's Cross in 1461, a lavish building programme was undertaken to produce the palatial stronghold seen today, a fortress offering comfort and security appropriate to royal visitors. Herbert's continental experience of the resurgent enthusiasm for keeps led to the building of a magnificently massive hexagonal one, set within its own apron wall and surrounded by a wet moat. The keep was thus outside the main castle enclosure which was itself fortified with closely set multangular towers (*pl 35*). Since the only other major Welsh border castle reconstructed in the fifteenth century was Newport, which the Duke of Buckingham had

Plate 35   Raglan Castle, the Great Gate
seen from the keep

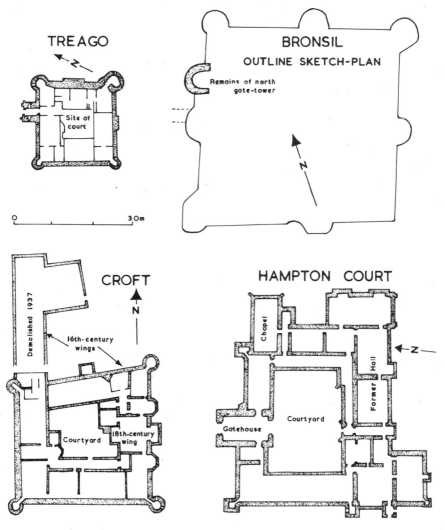

Fig 56   Fortified house plans in Herefordshire: Treago, St Weonards; Bronsil Castle, Eastnor; Croft Castle; and Hampton Court, Hope-under-Dinmore. Drawings simplified from the plans of the Royal Commission on Historical Monuments (England). Bronsil is included for size comparison only.

rebuilt after devastation by Glyndwr's forces, it is easy to see Raglan's special importance.

While Raglan was being admired, less wealthy landowners built more modest fortified houses. The typical form of the finer examples

219

was quadrangular with towers at the corners and suites of rooms arranged about a central courtyard (fig 56). This is well shown at Treago Castle, Croft Castle, and Hampton Court near Leominster, for which a licence to crenellate was granted in 1435. The scale of such buildings varies considerably. Treago is only twenty-one metres square, although its curiously differently sized circular angle towers project widely beyond this; Croft Castle similarly has circular towers projecting from the original courtyard plan with sides thirty-four metres long; and Hampton Court's fifteenth-century plan was even larger, about thirty-nine metres square. The dilapidated remains of a similar castle licensed in 1460 lie within a wet moat at Bronsil in Eastnor parish. Originally provided with corner-, interval-, and gate-towers about a central courtyard, it shows a great concern for an impressive defence, remarkable for a castle that is only fifty metres square.

CHAPTER TEN

Town and Country
in the Middle Ages

It was the royal castles and their baronial neighbours that set the fashion in fortification, providing both strong-points of defence and garrisons to spearhead the assault against Wales. For the further supply of men and provisions the local area was called upon and so settlement and castle came to be closely integrated (*fig 57*). Just as the motte was set beside church and manor farm so was the larger castle associated with a town. At Hereford, Caerleon, Shrewsbury and Chester a castle was placed at the perimeter of the existing town which took on the plan and function of an extensive bailey. Hereford's medieval defences have already been described (*pp 199 201*); its motte and bailey, probably on the site of the pre–Conquest Castle, was within the Saxon defences at the east end of town. It was rebuilt in stone and occupied into the later Middle Ages, but was subsequently demolished in the quest for building stone for a growing city. At Shrewsbury too the medieval town defences took in the castle site (*fig 59*) but stone robbing and encroachment by domestic buildings have sadly mauled and largely eclipsed most of the features of this mighty motte and bailey, seat of the Earl of Shrewsbury. At Chester a massive castle complex evolved on the banks of the Dee estuary just outside the Roman fortress wall.

Where there was not an existing settlement a new borough was often founded to accompany the castle. The building, or 'plantation', of new boroughs, with rectangular street grids, goes back to Saxon times but the Normans extended and accelerated such work and added castles. English plantation towns generally have been discussed by Beresford; and in the central Marches, where there were so many early castles, Noble has discerned four phases of castle and borough establishment between the Norman Conquest and the mid thirteenth century.

221

Fig 57 Medieval boroughs in the Welsh Marches

In the first phase, within a few years of the Conquest, new castles were built at Wigmore and Clifford, and the one at Ewyas Harold was rebuilt. These three were presumably intended as a base from which to attack Wales and boroughs were attached to them; the early castles at Chepstow and Monmouth too may have had boroughs that have escaped documentation. The town defences at Monmouth are Edwardian but the suburb of Over Monnow is protected by a defensive ditch, Clawdd Du, and has a Norman church. At Wigmore the new borough was probably set out on a grid-iron plan parallel to the ridge on which the church stands, and the original castle, without a motte, was probably nearer the church, where minor earthworks may still be seen. For the massive stone castle that was built later, more ground was required and this was found to the west on the wider part of the ridge. The borough at Wigmore only gave rise subsequently to a large village, and at Clifford and Ewyas Harold there was even less development. The founder of these boroughs, William FitzOsbern, probably inherited the pre-Conquest castle borough at Richard's Castle. The trial excavations within the village enclosure there were not extensive enough to reveal any detail of the borough which must have failed at an early stage.

A second phase of borough plantation, from the late eleventh to the late twelfth century, is less clearly documented. It involved the establishment of castles and boroughs by some of the lesser barons who were soon to be known as 'Lords Marcher'. The De Lacys added a castle to Anglo-Saxon Weobley, creating a borough with an irregular street plan and possibly set out a new borough beside the castle at Grosmont. At White Castle there are hints of an unrecorded borough by the castle, and further south, Trelleck village has the grid-iron plan of an undeveloped borough. Although there is no documentation of a borough at Dorstone the lay-out of the village and castle is thought by Noble to suggest a borough plantation. Early in the reign of Henry I a new honour was created for Adam de Port around Kington and the nucleus of the twelfth-century borough should be around Castle Hill and Kington church; but there are few surface indications, and no normal plan of streets or strips representing burgages, to support this expectation.

A third phase of borough building saw the establishment of Huntington, probably between 1174 and 1190, but population and commerce preferred Kington. Huntington never became more than a village, although the ghost of its borough plan extends from the castle south to the chapel. In Powys, Hay was now laid out as castle and borough, set like Huntington against the very edge of the Welsh uplands; and in the Black Mountains at the ridgetop site of Longtown, a castle was under construction between 1185 and 1195. Attached to it is an enclosure of 1.2 hectare protected by a remarkably high embankment, once thought to have been the remains of a Roman fort. The accompanying borough lies to the south with its thirteenth-century chapel overlooking a triangular market place.

By now there were castles enough but anticipation of trade encouraged the founding of more boroughs. In west Herefordshire licences were granted for markets and fairs at Eardisley in 1233 and Pembridge in 1240 (*pl 36*). They were accompanied by only modest village development whilst Ploughfield, described as a borough in 1273, is now but a hamlet in the parish of Preston-on-Wye. Meanwhile in east Herefordshire boroughs which had no castles but enjoyed the patronage of the Bishop of Hereford or the Prior of Leominster flourished at Leominster, Bromyard, Ledbury and Ross.

In Shropshire too there is a similar pattern and history of borough plantation. Ludlow, the finest, was established by the De Lacys. On a

Plate 36   Pembridge, the sixteenth-century market hall of a failed borough
(*David Hibbert*)

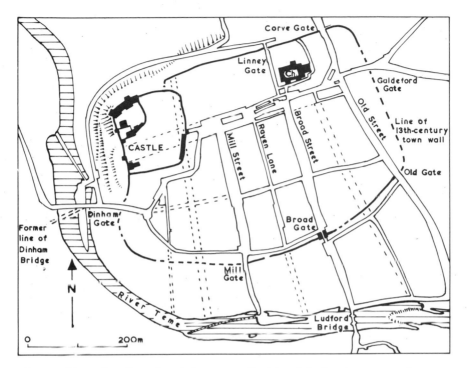

Fig 58 Plan of Ludlow showing town wall with original seven gates and
probable earlier streets as pecked lines

site chosen for its defensive capability, the castle was integral with the
town defences, though the early borough at Dinham is not thought to
have extended as far as Mill Street. The enlarged grid-iron of the
thirteenth-century town plan survives in the modern street plan
(*fig 58*).

Against Wales, new towns were planted to support castles at Clun,
Bishop's Castle, Caus, Oswestry, Ellesmere and Wem, most of them
achieving only moderate success as towns, like their west Herefordshire counterparts. That at Caus had only nine of the thirty-three
burgages in the outer bailey of the castle still occupied in 1540 and they
too have long since been abandoned. Among the eastern plantations
established with an eye on commercial gain, success attended the
boroughs set up at Newport, Market Drayton and Madeley; but
others at Baschurch, Ruyton-eleven-towns and Acton Burnell grew
to nothing more than villages.

The coastal road from North Wales was barred by the Edwardian
castle of Flint and its adjoining borough set out with a symmetrical

225

grid-iron plan on virgin ground in 1277 and completed in less than five years – not with local labour but relying, amongst others, on ditch-diggers from Yorkshire brought thither under armed guard, and carpenters from Derbyshire. Nine hundred and fifty ditch-diggers were employed in the first week's work.

In the boroughs that were successful and became market towns the topographer and local historian have a wealth of material with which to satisfy our curiosity, and in them the opportunities for economic excavation of all save a few salient features will always be rare. It is with those boroughs that were still-born or which fell into disuse prematurely that the archaeologist can be most profitably employed; on such sites he can expect to recover early building plans and arrangements that no historical research could possibly discover.

Later town defences

In the successful boroughs the defences had to be refurbished and extended from time to time as the towns outgrew their original plans; but with their disuse the town-walls were pillaged for stone and the filled ditches became the routes for new streets. Eighteenth-century cartographers have often left us detailed plans of town walls, gates and bastions; but so much has since gone that the average observer may today be totally ignorant of them. Although the course of the walls of Chester is virtually intact, in other towns it is only by excavation and sympathetic development in newly cleared areas that this part of our urban legacy has been recovered. This has happened in Hereford, where parts of the thirteenth-century wall and bastions can now be seen. The limited excavation carried out on the defences of Welsh border towns does not allow confident comparisons to be made between them, but several share a record of wall building in the thirteenth or early fourteenth century, following the earlier construction of earthwork defences. At Chepstow the Port Wall across the neck of the promontory holding the castle and town was probably constructed on a fresh line between 1272 and 1278, for no earlier defences have been found beneath. It had no foundation trench and was fronted by a ditch six metres wide and only a metre deep. Seven of the ten semicircular towers survive, and there is one rectangular tower, resembling the one at Hereford in Blue School Street which was rebuilt in that form during the Civil War.

Abergavenny's town defences are now virtually obliterated but their history is indicated by murage grants of 1241–6, 1259–64, 1295–1301 and 1314–19 which allowed the town to levy taxes or tolls to pay

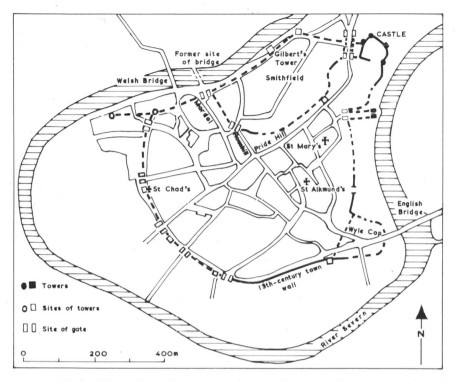

Fig 59 Plan of Shrewsbury showing modern roads and medieval town and castle defences (Based on Carver and Wills 1974, p. 182 and Carver 1974, fig 28)

for town fortifications. A bank discovered in Castle Street is thought to be the defence referred to in the earlier two grants, while the stone wall that had been built into it is regarded as the product of the later grants. As at Hereford the defences were dilapidated by the time of the Civil War and the ditch had to be recut.

The earliest defences so far revealed at Shrewsbury date from about 1220–1242 (*fig 59*). They occupy the top of the slope on the inside of the Severn's meander and are still followed by the curving course of the perimeter road between the Welsh and English bridges. The half-moon of the lower town defences was linked to the castle, which commanded the neck of the meander, by walls which must have followed the river-cliff top in general but are only known intermittently. The castle was derelict by 1443 but in the Civil War the defences were refurbished and in 1645 on Cromwell's orders the riverside district of Smithfield was protected by a new wall linking Gilbert's Tower to the Welsh Bridge.

At Chester the medieval wall followed the line of the Roman

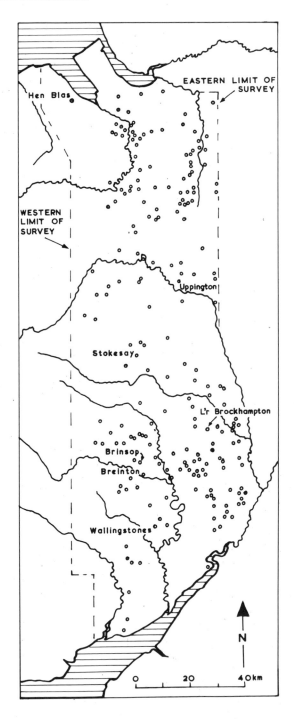

fortress walls on the north and east but also brought in the riverside areas to the south and west which had been used for extramural buildings in Roman times (*fig 31, p 127*). The medieval castle was placed in the south-western corner of the fifty-three-hectare enclosure, where the Dee formerly turned northwards to flow beside the City's west wall. None of the medieval town gates survives but some of the wall towers, and the north-western Spur, built in 1322, are still visible.

Moated sites

Probably throughout the period of castle construction and town fortification the smaller fry among the landowners saw to their personal protection as and when they could afford it by building strong houses or digging moats about their property. The latter are particularly conspicuous and common in the English border counties with more than seventy visible in both Shropshire and Herefordshire (*fig 60*). There are few in north-west Cheshire and they are rare in Gwent and Clwyd as in the rest of Wales. Their frequency in the border does not necessarily reflect the proximity of Wales, for wet moats are even more common in Warwickshire and Suffolk. Nowhere would they have been dug to slow the advance of invading armies but a wet moat would have been a considerable deterrent to robbers and vagrants. It could be stocked with fish and would have kept the house-site dry. The essentially English distribution may be partly explicable geologically since digging in rock was expensive; but it is more likely to reflect different social conditions either side of the boundary. Most moats, in the English Midlands at least, seem to be earlier than the mid-fourteenth century and it is thought unlikely that many were dug after 1500. In Warwickshire they are particularly frequent in areas of late woodland clearance, but in the border, as in Yorkshire, this generalization is not applicable and it would seem that they mainly illustrate the increasing separation of the English land-owning class from the peasantry, of the manor from the village.

Moats are usually about ten metres wide and most frequently enclosed rectangular areas with sides of about thirty to fifty metres, although larger enclosures occur, like the one at Wombridge Priory Grange at Uppington which encloses 1.5 hectare. Their need for water resulted in the majority of moats being found on the bottom clay lands or beside streams in hillier districts. There are few lowland parishes in

Fig 60 Moated sites in the Marches (taken mainly from the OS One-inch map)

Plate 37   Lower Brockhampton manor

Herefordshire and Shropshire that do not have one and in some there are two or three, for moats were dug around granges and hunting lodges as well as around manor houses. At Hen Gwrt in Gwent the fourteenth-century moated site was abandoned in the fifteenth, only to be re-occupied in the sixteenth as a lodge of Raglan Castle Red Deer Park.

The status and function of some moats is still apparent, for their farmhouses survive either in stone, as at Brinsop Court, or timber as at Lower Brockhampton near Bromyard. While there is a *prima facie* case for regarding the moat as roughly contemporary with the building now inside it there is always the possibility, as suggested for Hen Gwrt, that it was dug about an existing building that might have stood for a century or more, and this is especially likely with moats in existing or deserted villages. Lower Brockhampton (*pl 37*) is a case in point, for the adjacent Norman chapel ruin and indistinct nearby earthworks suggest there was once a larger settlement. The fine half-timbered house is judged to be probably late fourteenth century but the moat is crossed through a timber gatehouse of fifteenth-century date, and this may be the structure that really dates the moat itself. On the island here, as on most moated sites, there was room for outbuildings as well as the main residence.

230

It would be interesting to know whether the incidence of moats was encouraged by the dispersal of village communities and so whether one might tentatively date village desertion by ascertaining dates for moat digging. So far no more than about a dozen moated sites have been excavated in the border and only at Hen Blas in Clwyd and Wallingstones, Tre-Essey in south Herefordshire could the work be described as extensive, though still far from complete. Both are in Welsh areas and are hardly likely to be typical of the border.

At Wallingstones were found the remains of a thirteenth-century strong house, a hall with undercroft and garderobe tower. After the addition of another wing on a mound raised to allow it to be on the first-floor level of the original house, the manor was eventually surrounded in the fifteenth century by a curtain wall and may have had a moat too, fed from the adjacent stream. The excavation of Breinton, on a bluff above the Wye near Hereford, showed that it was protected on the landward side by a small ditch and low rampart and was probably abandoned in the thirteenth century. Its cellared building may have been simply the vicarage for the neighbouring church about which today are the indeterminate earthworks of a more extensive settlement. At the other end of the border at Hen Blas near Flint a twelfth-century motte site was used for domestic occupation in the thirteenth and fourteenth centuries.

These examples suffice to show something of the variety of history and function involved on moated sites, the interpretation of which is extremely difficult when their buildings have been reduced to ground level by stone-robbing. To rebuild them in the mind existing farms and residences may serve as models, like Lower Brockhampton, or Stokesay Castle where the late thirteenth-century hall flanked by towers occupied the west side of a courtyard that is now entered through an Elizabethan gatehouse. Such a building is closer to the castle model, but closer still is the contemporary fortified house at Acton Burnell, a keep-like residence with towers at each corner.

Ecclesiastical sites

While the king and his barons built their castles, and the second-tier landowners dug their moats, the third element of the landholding classes, the clergy, were busy too, drawing in money as gifts and tithes to build and rebuild churches and establish abbeys and nunneries in extensive estates. In 1066 there were some thirty-one major religious establishments in the border, the English minsters and their equivalent Welsh 'clas' churches. These were not evenly spread, but placed as the

Plate 38   Llanthony Priory, built between 1175 and 1230;
the nave from the south chapels

accident of benefactor or patron saint dictated. There were only two in Gwent east of the Usk, at Caerwent and Llandogo, whereas in Archenfield there were five, reflecting the early work there of Saints Dubricius, Dewi and others: Dewchurch, Garway, Hentland, Moccas and Welsh Bicknor. There was none in the Welsh lands of the northern border.

Seven of the English minster churches were to be found in the towns of Bromyard, Chester, Hereford, Ledbury, Leominster and Monmouth; while the minster churches of Bromfield and Stanton Lacy were within four kilometres of Ludlow, and Withington and Moreton were within six kilometres of Hereford. Few of the others were far from the relatively rich agricultural areas, and none was in a

232

Plate 39 Buildwas Abbey, built between 1135 and 1200; the nave from the west

remote area.

The Normanizing of the border led to the development of monasteries, many following this early tradition of lowland location. These included St Kynemark's Priory Chepstow, Flanesford Priory Goodrich, Dore Abbey, the monasteries of the Grey Friars and the Black Friars in Hereford, Leominster Priory, Wigmore Abbey, Chirbury and Alberbury Priories, Haughmond Abbey, Wombridge Priory and St Mary's Monastery Vale Royal.

A different setting was sought for the houses of the Cistercians and others in remote and undeveloped woodlands and mountain valleys. First among these is Tintern Abbey, founded in 1131 but mostly rebuilt in the thirteenth century and still magnificently ruinous in the Wye gorge, though dissolved in 1536. By contrast the thirteenth-century Grace Dieu Abbey, Llantilio Crossenny, another Cistercian foundation, has disappeared. In the high valleys of the Black Mountains are Llanthony Abbey (*pl 38*) and Craswall Priory; and in the hills of north-west Herefordshire on the edge of Deerfold Forest there were houses of nuns and monks at Limebrook. At the entrance to the Severn gorge Buildwas Abbey (*pl 39*) was built about 1148 in a

233

situation similar to that at Tintern, on a narrow flood plain bordered by steep, wooded hills.

Many of these monasteries were enormous. Although the church was the dominating architectural feature, the cloisters and kitchens, guest-houses and stables, workshops and farm buildings extended far. The exposed walls alone of Tintern Abbey cover about 1.7 hectare. The recovery of the plan of such complexes is a formidable task and we are in some ways fortunate that the upstanding ruins often encouraged the exposure of other foundations by early antiquaries even though they left much unaccounted for and did little to pursue the sequence of building and repair. The work of establishing the full extent and history of the monasteries has continued since, notably on sites like Tintern and Haughmond that are in the care of the Department of the Environment.

Henry VIII's dissolution of the monasteries meant that most of them became simply convenient quarries for stone, and they were rapidly reduced, leaving problems for the archaeologist to tackle. No such fate befell the parish churches and cathedrals which therefore offer a wealth of extant architectural and documentary evidence for the post-Conquest period. Through them we can see how European culture, as expressed in stone and religion, could be disseminated through the medium of powerful, wealthy landlords. Especially noteworthy are the twelfth-century carvings of the 'Herefordshire School' which was responsible for the decoration of several churches in Herefordshire and neighbouring English counties. Their work, most magnificently displayed on the little church at Kilpeck (*pl 40*), drew its motifs and inspiration from Anglo-Saxon, Continental, Celtic and Viking art. The portrayal of the Celtic goddess of creation and destruction, the Sheila-na-gig, at Kilpeck (*pl 41*), Holdgate, Twyford and Stoke Prior, Droitwich might be used to argue for the survival of Celtic mythology even among the English of the border; but one does not need a Gaelic-speaking grandfather to see that the squatting figure at Kilpeck offers wordless instruction in the art of self-delivery.

As more churches become redundant we can expect more opportunity for excavation within or around them and this could have an important role in guiding the restoration or sympathetic adaptation of these buildings. The archaeologist is, however, more likely to be concerned with locating the lost churches, for redundancy has a long, if intermittent, history in the border. In north Herefordshire, when the churches of Great and Little Collington were united in 1352, Little Collington was chosen to be maintained as being of greater conveni-

Plate 40   The doorway of Kilpeck church (*David Hibbert*)

ence for access and in better repair; but where was Great Collington? – probably not far from the modern church, built to replace Little Collington a kilometre to the north-west.

In 1364 the nearby churches of Whyle and Pudlestone were united and there is now no church at Whyle. Such unions, the result perhaps of a combination of a local epidemic in small parishes over-endowed with churches, and a re-distribution of population, reflected an adjustment to a new economic balance. Other churches suffered from war. In 1406 some twenty-six churches in Herefordshire were exempted from contributing to the King's Aid because they had been 'destroyed'. This did not mean that all had been razed to the ground; far from it, for only Bacton, Hentland and St Weonards in that list exhibit architectural evidence of large-scale rebuilding in the fifteenth or early sixteenth century. Several churches were abandoned in the nineteenth century and rebuilt at more convenient locations, including Collington 1856, Llanwarne 1864, and Little Marcle 1870.

There are many more lost chapels. One at Webton near Madley was recorded in the Bishop's Registers in 1536 but was in ruins when Taylor mapped Herefordshire in 1786. He shows another chapel in the

Plate 41 Kilpeck church: the Sheila-na-gig corbel
(*David Hibbert*)

same parish at Wisteston, and a ruin at Hampton Wafer, possibly the chapel listed in 1536. Old chapel ruins are marked on the deserted village site at Newton, Clifford where a fine motte and bailey is the obvious landmark today; and so are Vowmynd chapel ruins at Mynydd Brith, Dorstone, and those of St Ailworth's chapel at Walterstone, of Coughton chapel near Ross, Glewstone chapel in Llangarron, Glynstone chapel in Llangrove village, the ruins of a religious site at St Wolstan's Farm, Welsh Newton, and a chapel near Trewadoc, Garway. To these may be added St Dubricius' chapel in Woolhope and Hardwick Chapel, Kenderchurch, mentioned about 1300 in a Cartulary of Ewyas Harold Priory. The incidence of lost chapels is far greater in Shropshire; Duke recorded 105 in 1844.

Villages and homesteads

The Marches today exhibits a mixture of villages, hamlets, isolated farms and outlying cottages. The emphasis on dispersal was long interpreted as a legacy from a Celtic pattern consisting mainly of enclosed fields and scattered farms, but while the Celtic influence may have been important, it is now appreciated that many of the dispersed elements in the present pattern are not original. The historical evidence from part of Shropshire for this view has been set out in Volume VIII of the *Victoria County History* for that county, but the most useful archaeological model to guide further investigation is that put forward for East Anglia by Wade-Martins, who has demonstrated continued migration within parishes since Anglo-Saxon times. The gradual shift of houses from old to new focuses is in marked contrast to the more familiar processes in the English Midlands and Yorkshire, where villages often disappeared suddenly following seventeenth-century sheep enclosure or were dispersed equally rapidly when the farmhouses moved out to their fields as a result of later parliamentary enclosure. In either case, by the time the village was abandoned or stripped of its main farms, its population was large, and so too was its mark on the landscape. The deserted villages of the Midlands, since maintained under grass, show extensive plans of deeply hollowed streets and well-defined house platforms, often accompanied by a lonely church; desertion usually meant depopulation and was late enough to be verified in national tax returns.

The search for similar evidence in the Welsh Marches is difficult. Hamlets are widespread and do not attract the ancillary settlement that may sustain a nucleated village through hard times. Secondly, although it is now recognized that open-field agriculture was widespread in both English and Welsh areas, most land on the border was enclosed early, while settlements were still small enough to be covered by the barns of a modern farm; over 80% of Shropshire, for example, was enclosed by 1675. Thirdly, such enclosure was probably accompanied by migration within the parish rather than by depopulation; so, in the absence of maps, it will be difficult to identify the changes, for their early date means there are few historical records to illuminate them. It is therefore futile to approach border settlement studies in the same frame of mind as used for the Midlands. Even the terminology leads to confusion, for there are few border sites to compare with those of Warwickshire, for example. As a result interest becomes attached to shrunken sites and often the same term 'deserted village' is used of shrunken villages or hamlets with gaps in their street frontage.

Hamlets are especially common in parts of Cheshire, west Shropshire, south Herefordshire and the Welsh counties, where they are often a Celtic legacy. Many were recorded as Welshries in Domesday Book, and their use of open-field agriculture is indicated by the narrow strips which survive as a pattern of ridge and furrow at Braggington and Old Marton, the latter presumed to be the site of the vill of Merton from which the Welsh inhabitants were evicted for joining the rebellion of 1280. Some manors included more than one settlement even in the time of Edward the Confessor, also perhaps reflecting the Celtic background, although other reasons would not be far to seek since border warfare may have disrupted or stunted the growth of many villages both before and after the Conquest. Many manors, especially in the west, were waste in 1086, and others are lost from subsequent record.

One area that has been intensively studied by Rowley, is Corve Dale and the Clee Hills in south-east Shropshire (*fig 61*). Documentary evidence indicates that there were large numbers of hamlets in the Middle Ages, many of which are now represented only by a farm, a church, or a few cottages. In the absence of maps or detailed terriers it is not possible to be certain that medieval population figures refer to the location now bearing the name. Many of these hamlets do have earthworks indicative of more extensive building, though three-quarters are without earthworks or are occupied by extensive modern farm-buildings which are presumed to cover the medieval houses.

Some of the possible oscillations of settlement history are indicated at Abdon on the north side of Brown Clee Hill. About 1.3 hectare of irregular earthworks lies between the isolated church and the surviving farms and cottages. Late medieval decline is indicated from the records and a long-house site excavated near the church yielded no

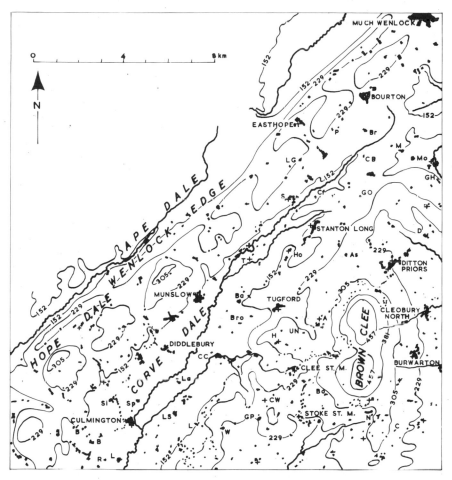

Fig 61   Rural settlement in Corve Dale (Source: Rowley 1972). All buildings are shaded. Shrunken or deserted settlements are indicated by initial letters. Contours in metres above OD.

A Abdon	CB Corve Barn	M Monk Hall
As Ashfield	D Derrington	Mo Monkhopton
B Bache	GH Gt Hudwick	N Newton
Ba Baucott	GO Gt Oxenbold	P Patton
Bo Bockleton Ct	GP Greater Poston	R Ruckley
Br Bradley	H Heath	S Shipton
Bro Broncroft	Ho Holdgate	Si Siefton
Bu Burley	L Langley	Sp Sparchford
C Coldgreen	LG Larden Grange	T Thonglands
CW Cold Weston	La Lawton	UN Upper Norncott
CC Corfham Castle	LS Little Sutton	W Witchcot
Cf Corfield	Ly Lydehole	

finds later than about 1300. Another house site about 135 metres away was occupied in the sixteenth century when mining and quarrying became important locally; but the village was in decline again by the end of the eighteenth century.

Abdon is at 274 metres high up on marginal land, and it is possible that climatic deterioration or soil exhaustion encouraged its fourteenth-century desertion. Such might also have been the case with other Brown Clee Hill sites like Heath and Cold Weston, both at about 244 metres and possessing extensive village earthworks. Like Abdon, Heath has an isolated chapel and Cold Weston a lonely church. Heath's earthworks seem to require more than the seven families assessed for tax in 1327 and point to the difficulty sometimes encountered of relating earthworks to records when the components of the earthworks are not individually dated by document or excavation. Cold Weston was virtually deserted by 1341.

At Detton Hall, just east of the Clee Hills, a large field known as Chapel Field once contained hollow ways and platforms (fig 62).

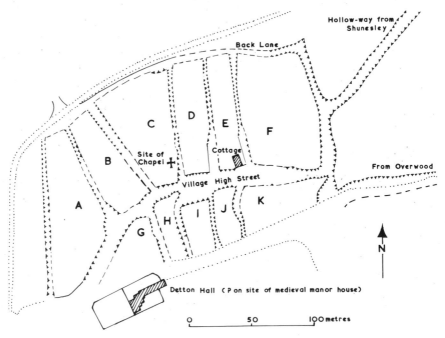

Fig 62 Detton Hall, Shropshire, the crofts (A–K) of the medieval settlement as indicated by earthworks before being levelled in 1960. Modern features unrelated to medieval alignments are shown by dotted lines (After Stanford 1965, fig 16)

Excavation failed to produce structural evidence for any medieval buildings, which were presumably constructed in timber and laid without stone sills on the old ground surface. Pottery showed the site to have been abandoned around 1300. At its maximum extent there were probably, in addition to the existing manor house, at least two other large farms occupying the large crofts at the east end of the village street. The chapel, of which traces remained in the nineteenth century, held a central position on the street and there were half a dozen narrower crofts, presumably the property of cottagers. The whole settlement may have held forty or fifty people. This may be compared with a total Domesday Book population of seven serfs, one villein, four bordars and one 'radman' (probably a free man). Multiplying by 3.5 to obtain total Domesday population from the recorded inhabitants, we arrive at a figure of forty-five people for Detton, within the estimate based on earthworks.

Detton Hall is at only 152 metres, as too is Sidbury, a severely shrunken site, also east of the Clee Hills. Other deserted or shrunken sites occur at lower levels still, down to Corfham Castle on the bank of the Corve around 125 metres. Climatic deterioration will not account for the whole range of such sites; other factors must be involved. These will include the early enclosure of common fields and the establishment of new farms on consolidated holdings away from the old nucleus, the growth of certain land holdings at the expense of others, and the success or otherwise of waste-land squatter settlement in acquiring a share of the old arable land.

At Hampton Wafer in north-east Herefordshire there is today only a single farm, but in the early nineteenth century the ruins of what was probably the chapel survived nearby. Deeply eroded hollow ways and house platforms, together with a pond that proved to be the flooded stockyard of a farm, suggest that the settlement here was about the same size as Detton, although less clearly defined. The pottery from several house sites showed that occupation went back at least to the eleventh century and ended perhaps around 1300. The archaeological date for desertion is thus close enough to 1330 when the manor passed to the FitzAllens who held Hampton Court by the Lugg. Most of their resources went into the latter manor, and the consequent neglect of upland Hampton Wafer may have encouraged enclosure and the consequent transfer of population to new outlying farms. There is however no evidence of an early fourteenth century date for these farms, so it remains to be seen whether there was a hiatus between the decline of the settlement and the re-establishment of a dispersed farm pattern in the seventeenth century or thereabouts. The problem is not confined to Hampton Wafer and in considering it we cannot overlook the susceptibility of hamlets to epidemics and their possible reduction by plague. Between Hampton Wafer and Detton Hall, though still on the Herefordshire side of the Teme, we have already noted that the churches of Great and Little Collington were united in 1352, and those of Whyle and Pudleston in 1364, on the petition that the plague had depopulated the area.

Of similar size to Detton Hall and Hampton Wafer are Runston and St Brides Netherwent in Gwent, both with isolated chapels beside village earthworks. After a long period of decline from the Middle Ages, Runston was eventually abandoned some time between about 1772 and 1800; eight house sites have been identified within it. At St Brides ten possible house sites have been located. The lateness of the final abandonment of Runston draws attention to the evidence elsewhere for the long-continued decline of small nucleated settlements. Near Hereford the village of Stretton Sugwas contained eleven cottages as late as 1757. There are none there now and when the church was pulled down in 1877 and the new one built a kilometre to the south-west, only the Court Farm was left on the old village site. East of the Lugg at Preston Wynne the church stands alone beside a large field corrugated by the typical hollow ways and platforms of a deserted settlement.

The voluntary or enforced removal of the labourers from the neighbourhood of the manor farm led frequently to straggling unplanned settlements on waste hillside land, or at the edge of the forest, or near the parish boundary in the waste beyond the common fields. Such peripheral settlements are widespread; but just because they were occupied by the least well organized members of the community they were particularly vulnerable in times of rural depression and many were abandoned or severely depleted earlier this century. The earthworks of such an abandoned forest-edge hamlet may be seen on Garnons Hill, Bishopstone, where there were ten houses in 1886 but now none. It looks as though there has been a double desertion, first from Bishopstone to Garnons Hill and then from the hill to extra-parochial destinations.

The re-organization of labourers' accommodation for the benefit of the owners of the great hall is thought to have been behind the abandonment of Braggington on the Shropshire-Powys border. The hamlet had probably been established in waste land after the Norman Conquest and excavation of a house site, within an extensive moated area, showed that it had been abandoned in the seventeenth century, possibly about the time that Braggington Hall was built nearby in

1675. At Pitchford, eight kilometres south of Shrewsbury, an extensive medieval village was formerly to be seen on the ground below the hall where still stands the parish church. The hall was built about 1560–1570, and possibly at that time the rest of the village community was removed to the main road where most of the houses are today. At Morville in east Shropshire the village centre was cleared for landscaping in the late sixteenth century, but the inhabitants need not have moved far away, simply to the edge of the village.

Gaps in other villages may have been occasioned when houses were abandoned by people moving to industrial sites at the edge of the parish or on marginal land elsewhere. Such would have been the potteries, charcoal burning places, brick and lime kilns, quarries and mines. With the decline of such industries in the last century hundreds of house sites and paddocks have been neglected, many completely deserted. At Hangstree Gate, Willey, a sixteenth-century map showed a sizeable hamlet, presumably occupied by iron-workers, but there are no houses there now.

Apart from the widespread examples of house or hamlet desertion it must be remembered that there is probably not a village or hamlet that does not today exhibit house platforms that are unoccupied and hollow ways that lead nowhere. To this extent almost every Welsh border village is a shrunken settlement. The seeds of dispersal may have been there before the Conquest but the construction of castles and moated establishments within and without the village accelerated the process of community fragmentation. It continued for a variety of reasons until very recently, when planning authorities started to encourage the infilling of the gutted skeletons of our remaining villages.

While the search must continue for the earthworks and documentary records of abandoned sites the processes of settlement evolution will only be properly understood by attention to the whole parish, involving historical and cartographical research, earthworks survey, place-name study and hedgerow dating. The last technique involves counting the shrub species in thirty-metre sections: the older the hedge the more species there will be. The success of such search is not to be judged by the number of sites accepted by Midland standards as 'Deserted Medieval Villages' but by the extent to which it can locate on the ground the homes of all the people in the records and identify and date all the house and barn sites in the parish. Only then can the physical background to changing political and social attitudes be adequately assessed.

CHAPTER ELEVEN

The Archaeology of Rural Industries

The post-medieval development of an increasingly literate and cen-tralized state has given the historian masses of documents from which to reconstruct society in the recent past; but there remain small unlit areas where archaeological techniques are still called for, especially in the industrial field. This is not the place to dispute the label 'industrial archaeology' for a subject that is primarily the province of the economic historian, historical geographer and engineer, but it will be useful to set aside those areas in which the archaeological content must always be a minor component. These are normally areas where indus-try has persisted into the era of detailed Ordnance Survey maps and where the relics of such activities are abundant and often conspicuous, regions like the Forest of Dean, the Shelve district, Coalbrookdale and the Clwyd coalfield. Nor are specifically archaeological techniques likely to provide the major contribution to the study of post-medieval transport, to the tramways, canals, railways and roads, though these and their associated stations, wharves, toll-houses and even mile-stones are usually brought under the wide umbrella of industrial archaeology.

Welsh Marches industry (*fig 63*) has always taken place in a rural setting, even since the Industrial Revolution, but the activities which are our main concern here are further distinguished by their dispersal and small-scale organization; so that in decline their remains have slipped easily into grass-grown mounds and have merged with the agricultural scene. Because of its less intensive development in mod-ern times the border offers especially rewarding conditions for the study of such industries, though little systematic archaeological effort has yet been devoted to them.

In the pre-steam age the need to derive power from water and fuel from wood, as charcoal, was a common locating factor for industry. The ungraded character of most border streams ensured an adequacy of breaks in profiles to encourage the proliferation of water mills and, particularly south of the middle Severn, the steep-sided narrow tributary valleys were readily dammed for mill-ponds.

In Herefordshire there were ninety-two mills recorded in 1086, while Taylor's map of 1786 showed 209 mills and two former mills widely distributed on all the county's streams. In 1835 Bryant showed only 186 working mills and sixteen former mills. Today a recognizable mill is a rarity, and an intact one, like the paper mill at Mortimer's Cross, is scheduled as an ancient monument. An indication of the long period of use to be expected of most mills is given by the finds from excavated water-mill sites. At Troy mill on the Trothy, Gwent, they ranged from about the fourteenth to the eighteenth century. At Welsh Newton in Herefordshire twelfth-century pottery was found in the earliest part of the mill, which was finally destroyed about 1700. Lower down the Mally Brook the mill at Dixton spanned the period from about 1200 to 1650. Histories of this order are pointers to some of the problems that await the correct identification and dating of the attendant weirs, pools and leats.

In connection with the upstream works of water-mills it will be remembered that leats and weirs were also constructed to irrigate pastures, and a particularly famous set of such works was constructed by Rowland Vaughan in the early seventeenth century at Turnastone in the Golden Valley of south-west Herefordshire. A Trench Royal was dug along the far side of the valley from the river, three metres wide and 1.2 metres deep; it was to be five kilometres long and could be used for transport on the farm. A sixty-millimetre 'topping' trench was dug beside the river, about 1.2 metres from it. With the aid of sluices these arrangements permitted some 121 hectares of meadow to receive the muddy flood waters of winter, to be watered again in April if need be, and to be drowned once more two or three days before mowing. Flooding could also be used to clear snow from the meadows.

The liberal occurrence of marginal land has guaranteed plenty of woodland. Much of this was coppiced to provide the small wood favoured by charcoal burners, and the stools of oak and ash often survive to betray such woodland management. On the steep slopes available for coppicing it was necessary to excavate terraces, roughly circular and about ten metres in diameter, on which the wood stack could be built for firing. Their inhospitable locations, indifferent of aspect and slope, usually make confusion with hut terraces unlikely,

245

and confirmation of their function is often given by the black soil of their mole-hills. Charcoal burning must go back to prehistoric times, and some of the terraces may be ancient; but it has continued into recent years, as late as 1963, for example, on the steep southern slopes of Credenhill.

Most intensive charcoal-burning sites were probably related to a specialized local fuel requirement for iron-working, lime-burning or pottery manufacture. Consequently the charcoal-burners' terraces are often accompanied at no great distance by the earthworks and scars of such industry. Most frequent among these are deep hollow ways scored on the hillside by iron-rimmed cart-wheels and eroded more with every storm, leading to the terraces and connecting them with quarries and forges. A complex of such tracks, small limestone quarries and charcoal-burning terraces may be seen below Croft Ambrey, strung along the lower part of the Aymestrey Limestone escarpment of Leinthall Earls common. The chances are that they are all related to the provison of burnt lime for local agricultural use. On a larger scale in the Fishpool Valley south-east of Croft Ambrey a large quarry and the remains of a lime kiln show a more organized preparation of lime to meet the needs of the Croft Castle estate. On the same limestone near Leintwardine a triple series of kilns with interconnecting stone chambers stands in a large quarry (*pl 42*), and north-eastwards, on the dip-slope of Wenlock Edge, bulldozers broke into lost lime kilns on the hillside above Siefton Forest Farm. The preparation of lime for agricultural and building use was widespread and similar relics occur not only on the major limestone outcrops like the Dean and Trelleck Plateau, and the Woolhope Dome, but along thinner bands like the

Fig 63   Navigations, tramways and some early and rural industrial sites in the Marches. Iron forge or furnace f Glass furnace g Lime kiln k Pottery p

C Coalbrookdale	W Wombridge
E Elmbridge	Wi Withington
G Gunns Mills	WV Whitchurch Vagas
MC Mortimer's Cross	WW Wrockwardine Wood

Canals

bac Brecon and Abergavenny	lc Leominster
bc Birmingham	mgc Montgomeryshire
bljc Birmingham and Liverpool Junction	moc Monmouthshire
cc Chester	sc Shropshire
ec Ellesmere	swc Staffordshire and Worcestershire
hgc Herefordshire and Gloucestershire	syc Shrewsbury
kc Ketley	tmc Trent and Mersey

Plate 42   Lime kilns at Mocktree, Leintwardine

Psammosteus Limestone which appears around the upper slopes of many of the Old Red Sandstone hills of Herefordshire. Like the large disused sewers of major houses and abbeys, the kilns are commonly reported as caves, tombs and escape tunnels.

Potters too have made heavy demands on the forest, although we have little knowledge of the organization of their industry until after the Middle Ages. The discovery of fourteenth/fifteenth century was-ters of jugs, storage vessels and ridge tiles at Ewloe, Clwyd, in an area associated with post-medieval potteries may point towards continuity and encourage the search for medieval potteries in the vicinity of known post-medieval kilns. In that part of Clwyd the earliest post-medieval pottery known at present, indicated by three waster pits exposed in a cable trench, is at Buckley and dates to the mid or late seventeenth century.

An important group of kiln sites of roughly this date is known in north-west Herefordshire with no fewer than six within an area of twenty square kilometres, mostly in the ancient royal forest of Deerfold. Their depredations caused the warden to be charged in 1616 with permitting their activity for his own personal gain from the sale of wood to the tune of forty pounds over the previous five years. Similar pottery has been found on other Herefordshire kiln sites at St Margarets, Whitney-on-Wye and Upton Bishop. The latter lead us towards Gwent potteries of the same period at Abergavenny, Gwehelog near Usk, and Cwmcarvan, south-west of Monmouth. Such rural potteries died away in the face of competition from mass-produced slipware from Staffordshire which was coming into the border from about 1700.

Mention must be made here of the discovery of the bed of the glass furnace built at Glasshouse Farm, St Weonards, probably by Lorrainers around 1600, which produced drinking glasses, window glass and linen smoothers. Since such furnaces were only the size of a large bread oven their discovery depends on the re-appearance of glass wasters as happened during bulldozing at Ruyton Park on fields named Glasshouse Bank on a survey of 1771. Both sites were probably in use only for two or three decades since Lorraine glassmakers did not begin to settle in England until 1567, and in 1615 the use of timber as fuel for this purpose was banned. Some time after 1616 a coal-fired glasshouse was built by Mansell at Newnham-on-Severn, and early seventeenth-century glass may be seen built into the walls of houses there; but most of the glass-makers came to concentrate on the coal-field around Stourbridge – where too were suitable refractory clays for crucibles.

The association of charcoal burning with iron working presents a somewhat different pattern since iron-working requires water for washing the ore and water power to operate the furnace bellows and forge hammers. The charcoal terraces will thus be on the hillside at some distance from the stream-side forge or furnace. In the Forest of Dean the combination of haematite from the Crease Limestone and wide areas of infertile or uncultivable terrain fit only for woodland made this an important iron-working area. To produce one tonne of iron could require as much as a tonne and a half of charcoal; so, not surprisingly, the industry spread beyond the outcrop of the ore-bearing limestone and the limits of the Forest. Such dispersal was not peculiar to the seventeenth and eighteenth centuries, for at Whitchurch Vagas, and at Monmouth, Roman and medieval iron slags have been found near sites known to have had ironworks in modern times. As well as Whitchurch there were eighteenth-century blast furnaces on tributaries of the Wye at Tintern, Redbrook, Lydbrook, Bishopswood and St Weonards, while the Forest was flanked on east and south by furnaces at Elmbridge, Gunns Mills, Flaxley, Blakeney, and Lydney. The first commercially successful blast furnace in the area, at Lydbrook, was operated by William Herbert, Earl of Pembroke, in 1608; and in the eighteenth century the Foleys held the major part of the furnaces and forges. What may have been one of their furnaces was excavated at Coed Ithel just north of Tintern. Probably built about 1650, it was stone-lined with a pyramidal top half and a conical bottom half; it measured 7.3 metres square and would have been about six metres high, with a capacity of about twelve cubic metres. Forging of the iron took place elsewhere, often far from the Forest and the furnaces, at places like Llancillo, Peterchurch and Upleadon, where water power and charcoal were assured. The charcoal furnaces and forges mostly failed before the end of the eighteenth century against the competition of coke-fired plant. They carried their names, if only as 'Old Forge' or 'Old Furnace', to nineteenth-century maps and so are easy to locate, though in most cases it would require excavation to determine their form and layout.

In the Angidy valley at Tintern, where Britain's first water-powered wire-drawing works were built in 1566, there were twenty water-wheels in use by 1821. Today the ponds are the main evidence for the works that were only closed in 1901.

Just as the Dean iron industry extended into the quiet valleys and dingles of south Herefordshire and Gwent, so did the ramifications of the Coalbrookdale industry reach into the valleys of the central Marches when the introduction of the blast furnace – earlier here than in the Forest of Dean – required extra fuel from the forests before the general adoption of coke allowed concentration around Coalbrookdale. A furnace was built at Cleobury Mortimer about the same time as that at Shifnal, 1562. It was one of a small group of ironworks that were to be established in the valleys of the Clee and Rea Brooks using ore from Clee Hill, whose heyday was in the eighteenth century but whose origins may, like Cleobury Mortimer's, go back to the seventeenth; it may require archaeological investigation to determine the matter. There were two forges on the Rea Brook at Cleobury Mortimer, and two more about five kilometres upstream at Prescott and Hardwick. On the Clee Brook at Charlcotte, another six kilometres to the north, the Cinder Hill Farm furnace is well preserved, built of stone, six metres square and 7.3 metres high, with the foundations of a store-house and large mounds of charcoal blast furnace slag nearby. Most of the pig iron from Charlcotte went to Bringewood, Bewdley and Stourport forges, and the difficulties of transport from such upland valley furnaces, coupled with the competition of coke-iron, led to decline in the late eighteenth century. There is no evidence that Charlcotte was working after 1792.

Charlcotte's furnace was first mentioned in 1712 when the manor was acquired by Richard Knight, ironmaster, of Bringewood, where an interesting early industrial complex was built in the wooded gorge where the Teme spills out of the Vale of Wigmore. Relics of this pioneering period include an eighteenth-century bridge over the Teme, a fine horse-shoe weir, and remains of the wharf and tin-plating works. A famous collection of cast-iron tomb covers from Bringewood is at nearby Burrington Church (pl 43).

Plate 43   Iron tomb covers at Burrington church

North of Coalbrookdale the iron industry was also established in the Severn's tributary valleys. Wrockwardine and Wombridge were among the earlier furnaces, and the valley of the Tern accounted for seven of Shropshire's fifteen forges in 1717. There were at least five large works in the fourteen kilometres between Moreton Corbet and the Severn, manufacturing 800–900 tons of wrought iron per annum. Moreton Corbet forge was probably working by 1666 and continued till the late eighteenth century; Wytheford Forge, with its dam, pool and watercourse system, is documented over the same period and there was a forge at Withington, probably near the confluence of the Tern and Roden. The waterworks associated with Upton Forge originate at Duncote and extend for three kilometres; the forge was established by about 1675 and continued until at least about 1820. At Atcham, by Attingham Hall, the Tern has been harnessed to drive a mill since at least the thirteenth century, and in 1710 the Tern Forge was established there with waterworks extending upstream for three kilometres and including a pool, weirs, locks and wharfs. It closed in 1757.

With Abraham Darby's successful smelting of iron with coke instead of charcoal at Coalbrookdale in 1709 it was inevitable that coal would become the major locating factor for the iron industry, and this was confirmed when the development of steam engines removed the need for water power. The countryside furnaces and forges, hampered by transport costs, fell into second place behind the ironmasters of Coalbrookdale. There may be seen the foundations of the furnace, built in 1638, in which the important coke smelt of 1709 took place. This success led Darby to build a second furnace here in 1715 and to construct new furnaces nearby at Horsehay and Ketley between 1753 and 1756. There was no going back to dispersed industry now. As work concentrated in the gorge and on the hills of either bank Coalbrookdale hauled the world into new approaches to construction and transport. The first cast-iron waggon wheels were made there in 1767.

Ten years later a huge iron beam inscribed ABRAHAM DARBY 1777 was cast as part of a major rebuilding of the Old Furnace towards satisfying the extra demand for iron occasioned by the decision to build the world's first iron bridge (pl 44), started in the same year and opened on 1 January 1781. Magnificently arched over the Severn, its single span integrated the resources in minerals and personnel on both banks while permitting the increased river traffic to proceed unhindered. With its main ribs weighing 5.8 tonnes each and a total of 384.6 tonnes of iron in all, the bridge was more than a technological triumph; it symbolized a new era as Industrial Man stepped along the

252

Plate 44   The Ironbridge from the east bank of the Severn
        (David Hibbert)

road to new conceptions in communication. The world's first iron boat, The Trial, was built in 1787 for use on the Severn. In 1788 the Ketley canal was completed, incorporating the first inclined plane to be successfully used in Britain to take the boats down twenty-two metres to the ironworks. By 1793 the Hay incline, dropping sixty-three metres to the Severn within the Blists Hill Museum area, and the Windmill incline just to the north, were in use taking the Shropshire Canal to Coalport. In 1796 a trough of cast iron made at Ketley was employed for the first time in an aqueduct carrying the Shrewsbury Canal over the Tern at Longdon.

Meanwhile the completion of the Staffordshire and Worcestershire Canal and its junction with the Birmingham Canal in 1772 had linked the Trent and Severn; and by 1777 the Midlands network had an outlet to the Mersey. At the Severn terminus of this canal system

Plate 45   The Stourport canal basin in 1926 looking north (*Aerofilms Ltd*)

settlement and industry were attracted to the canal basin that was opened in 1771 (*pl 45*), and the new town of Stourport came into being. Despite the failure of the project to link it with the Wye (*see p 256*) and the difficulties of navigation on the fluctuating waters of the Severn, the town maintained its interest in canal traffic and its basin survives in the modern town centre as a tranquil reminder of a past era.

The success of the early canals close to the ironworks and coal-mines encouraged their large-scale development through the country. On the south-west border of the Marches the industrial archaeologist may not only view but navigate the restored Brecon and Abergavenny Canal with its 343-metre tunnel at Ashford, its fine stone aqueduct over the Usk, its locks and winding holes and variety of bridges, formerly more than a hundred in the fifty-three kilometres of restored canal. Work had started on this, as the Monmouthshire Canal, in 1792 and by the beginning of the nineteenth century it had a number of tramway feeders bringing iron, coal and limestone to its wharfs. Such tramways, their waggons pulled by horses, sometimes came to be built along routes where canal projects had failed to materialize, as between Brecon and Hereford, and also between Hay and Kington. Their courses may still be traced intermittently across country; occasionally the sleepers are still in place, as south of Pandy on the Abergavenny-Hereford route.

In the south-east of our region a canal was started in 1793 from Gloucester to Hereford. It was opened as far as Oxenhall in 1796 and with the completion of the Oxenhall tunnel reached Ledbury two years later. The price of coal there fell forthwith from 24/- to 13/6 a ton, but shortage of water only allowed the canal to be used for a few months in the year and it remained difficult to attract capital. Nothing more was done until 1839 when the extension to Hereford was started, but before this was completed in 1845 the company was already considering the possibility of selling out to the railways. The canal was eventually acquired by the Great Western Railway and after 1877 the stretches not used for the railway itself were sold off in small lots. This was the last main line British canal to be completed save for the Manchester Ship Canal of 1894. Many relics survive along its course. South of the Oxenhall tunnel 'Lock Cottage' stands beside a series of four locks and the entrances to the Ashperton and Aylestone Hill tunnels, 366 and 402 metres long respectively, may still be seen. The embankments that carried the canal across the plains of the Frome and Lugg remain as prominent features in the landscape.

In 1777, when work was beginning on the Ironbridge, Robert Whitworth was appointed to survey three canal schemes for the central Marches – one connecting Leominister and Stourport, another Leominster and Hereford, and a third Bridgnorth and Leintwardine via Corve Dale. He also considered possible links from Leintwardine to Hereford via Leominster and, alternatively, via Dilwyn and Canon Pyon. The extent of these enquiries indicates the conviction that this mode of transport could benefit the rural communities as well as the mine-owners and iron-smiths. Time made a mockery of this enthusiasm for, like the shareholders of the Hereford-Gloucester Canal, those who subscribed to the Stourport-Leominster-Kington Canal project that emerged from Whitworth's deliberations received neither interest nor repayment of capital during the lifetime of the canal. When it was eventually handed over to the Shrewsbury and Herefordshire Railway Company in 1858 the shareholders received only £16 for each £100 share.

The route had been authorized by Act in 1791 and in 1793 there were celebrations at Tenbury when the *Royal George* was launched at the new wharf. Difficulties with the Putnal tunnel, 320 metres long, delayed the opening of the section from Marlbrook near Southnet Farm to Leominster until 1796. Meanwhile there had been a collapse in the 1143-metre Southnet tunnel, and although this tunnel was completed no work seems to have been undertaken on the proposed 3.5 kilometre Pensax tunnel or the ambitious flight of locks planned to lower the canal sixty-three metres to Stourport. West of Leominster there was only some preparatory digging and aqueduct pier construction at Kingsland. Elsewhere, although sometimes no more than a curving cropmark in the fields north of Leominster, there is still much to see, notably the entrances to the Southnet, Newnham and Putnel tunnels, the Rea aqueduct and the embanked approach to the site of the Teme aqueduct, demolished as an exercise in World War II.

In country better suited to canals, those of the northern Marches are still apparent on the modern map and many miles are still in use. An early one, the Shrewsbury Canal, was authorized in 1793 and opened in 1797. With the Shropshire Canal it linked Shrewsbury with the industrial area north of Coalbrookdale. The 887-metre Berwick tunnel on the Shrewsbury Canal is an early example of a tunnel provided with a towpath; usually the boatmen had to leg it along the tunnel roof. On the same canal the cast-iron trough of the Longdon aqueduct has already been mentioned; in order to reach the level of the earlier Wombridge Canal eleven locks were required and the final ascent at Trench was achieved with a twenty-three-metre climb on an inclined plane.

The imagination and skill of the canal engineers culminated in two outstanding monuments, the Chirk and Pont Cysyllte aqueducts. These were started to carry a projected Chester – Wrexham – Shrewsbury canal over the Ceiriog and the Dee. Before they were finished the main line route was changed so that the canal from Lower Frankton to Llangollen became simply a branch of the Ellesmere Canal, authorized in 1793. The Pont Cysyllte aqueduct, built by Telford, is 307 metres long, carrying the canal in a cast-iron trough supported by nineteen stone arches thirty-seven metres above the Dee. It is a fitting memorial to the canal era, daring in conception and thrilling in prospect. It was opened in 1805, three years after the world's first railway locomotives were built at Coalbrookdale.

By 1833, when the Shropshire Union Canal, formed by the amalgamation of the Ellesmere and Chester Canals in 1813, was joined to the country's main network near Middlewich, the railways were poised to take over the markets sought by the canal operators. Just as the latter had underestimated the physical problems involved in their schemes for the Marches and had overestimated the potential traffic, so too were the railway men to push their projects beyond the limits of profitability. They tunnelled the Malverns and threw their splendid brick viaduct across the Leadon valley in order to link Hereford with Worcester and the industrial Midlands. As they struggled to thread their branch lines through the hills of Gwent, north Herefordshire and south Shropshire, to market towns with populations of only 1500 or so, the illusion that there were yet riches to be won in the west evaporated and the railways joined the list of contributors to monuments of the industrial age that started in Coalbrookdale in 1709.

Today the furnaces of the Coalbrookdale Company's successor still burn to produce iron for domestic boilers in a district where archaeology, history and modern industry combine to create a real sense of continuity with the past. Here the Coalbrookdale Gorge Museum Trust has made it possible for us to experience something of the atmosphere of experiment and industry that led the world into the Industrial Age. In this, the birthplace of industrial archaeology, we may inspect early blast-furnaces and machinery, follow the line of early plateways and look upon chimney pots, lamp-posts and window frames produced by the world's pioneers in modern cast-ironwork. About us are the architectural adjuncts of the industrial village that just about became a town, the church of 1854 and the Literary and Scientific Institute of 1859 built by the ironmasters, some of whose large houses still stand close to the Works beside the terraced cottages of the labour force.

✯

At Coalbrookdale the mainstream of industrial development was diverted from the greater part of the Marches where the impress of industrialization and urbanization has been slight. As a result the region holds a great store of information about our past and it must be hoped that the conservation and exploration of this will form major aspects of future planning policies.

Among the issues that await exploration are the medieval village and the relationship of farms, manors and castles. We have no idea what villages or hamlets had existed to be destroyed or taken over by the English in the seventh century and little to enable us to assess the legacy left by Rome, let alone the success or failure of the Imperial occupation as far as the former hillfort communities were concerned. The origin of these people is unknown. Were they invaders, responsible for the last major pioneering phase in the Marches, or descendants of a local Bronze Age population that awaits documentation? In much earlier times were the Beaker people, perhaps, the last great prehistoric invaders in the west or was their invasion simply a cultural one of copper tools, new pots and new religious rites? In a rural area we need no special excuse to be curious about the Neolithic and the very beginnings of farming hereabouts.

The field is so large, and our ignorance so great, that it would be presumptuous to suggest where the next advances should be made. With archaeologists increasingly absorbed in rescuing information from sites that are to be destroyed by changes in land use the choice of site is often dictated by non-archaeological considerations. Yet this need not cramp the expansion of knowledge. Rescue work revealed the Bromfield cemetery and the crowded buildings in the hillforts of Moel y Gaer, the Breidden, the Wrekin and Credenhill. In the same way the legionary base at Usk and much information about Chester and Caerleon has been revealed. The Saxon defences of Hereford were uncovered by rescue work and most of the investigation of moated sites has been on the same basis. These examples are not put forward to justify the destruction of sites at short notice, causing excavations to be skimped and hurried; but where long-term planning is possible, notably in quarries, a rescue operation can approximate to research conditions; and from it new understandings are bound to emerge, raising new questions and causing old ones to be re-phrased.

APPENDICES

Maps and museums

The appreciation of the Welsh Marches will be much enhanced by pondering over the Ordnance Survey 1:50,000 sheets 117, 126, 127, 137, 138, 149, 150, 162 and 171. For local detail the relevant 1:25,000 sheets should be consulted. The Ordnance Survey's period maps, and particularly those of *Southern Britain during the Iron Age* and *Roman Britain*, will help to place the Marches in a wider context. For the geological background the Geological Survey's regional handbooks *The Welsh Borderland, Central England, South Wales* and *Bristol and Gloucester* are recommended.

Many major finds from Welsh border sites will be found in the British Museum and the National Museum of Wales, Cardiff; some of the material from Bromfield and Midsummer Hill Camp is at present on loan to Birmingham City Museum from Ludlow and Hereford City Museums respectively. Other museums in the border itself are the Grosvenor Museum, Chester, Rowley's House Museum, Shrewsbury, Wroxeter Site Museum, Acton Scott Farm Museum, Ironbridge and Blist Hills Museums, Hartlebury Museum, Clun Museum, Leominster Museum, Abergavenny Museum, Monmouth Museum, Caerleon Museum and Chepstow Museum. The archaeological collections at Chester, Shrewsbury and Caerleon are especially important.

Societies and publications

Information about local journals, societies, archaeological groups and university extramural courses in local archaeology can usually be obtained from the main public libraries.

A short list of important sites normally open to the public
Further information may be traced from the Index.

ACTON BURNELL Medieval fortified house in the guardianship of the Department of the Environment. SJ 533 019. 11 km SE of Shrewsbury midway between the A458 and A49.

ARTHUR'S STONE   Neolithic chamber tomb in the guardianship of the Department of the Environment. SO 318 432. Beside the ridgeway lane 1 km N of Dorstone (B4348) and 2 km SE of Bredwardine (B4352). The nearest town is Hay-on-Wye, 9 km to the west.

BEESTON CASTLE   Medieval castle in the guardianship of the Department of the Environment. SJ 537 592. 17 km N of Whitchurch and 2 km W of the A49.

BROCKHAMPTON MANOR   Moated hall and gatehouse owned by the National Trust. SO 688 560. 3 km NE of Bromyard, approached by drive from the A44.

BURY DITCHES   Multivallate hillfort in Forestry Commission woods. SO 327 835. 4 km S of Bishop's Castle via B4385 and the lane through Brockton and Lower Down.

CAER CARADOC   Hillfort, 3 km NE of Church Stretton, whence it may be reached by path. SO 478 953.

CAERLEON   Roman legionary fortress and Museum, with barracks and amphitheatre in the guardianship of the Department of the Environment within the environs of the town itself. ST 340 905.

CAERWENT   Roman town of Venta Silurum; town walls, temple and houses within the modern village in the guardianship of the Department of the Environment. ST 470 905. 6 km SW of Chepstow, just off the A48.

CHEPSTOW CASTLE   with Norman and later work, in the guardianship of the Department of the Environment. ST 533 941. Within the town which is on the A48.

CHESTER   Roman legionary fortress of Deva with the amphitheatre in the guardianship of the Department of the Environment. The medieval town walls, in part on the Roman line, may still be seen, notably along the north side of the old town. SJ 404 663.

COALBROOKDALE   Early iron furnace and museum, SJ 669 045, with an open-air display of industrial monuments and machinery at Blists Hill SJ 696 035. The former is on the B4373, 6 km S of Wellington, Salop; Blists Hill is 3 km E of Coalbrookdale and reached by minor road from B4373 at Ironbridge.

COED Y BWNYDD CAMP   Multivallate hillfort owned by the National Trust. SO 365 068. 6 km N of Usk and reached by a narrow lane from Bettws Newydd.

CROFT AMBREY   Multivallate hillfort occupied throughout the Iron Age. SO 445 668. Part of the National Trust's Croft Castle estate and reached by path from Croft Castle (see below).

CROFT CASTLE   Late medieval fortified house owned by the National Trust.

SO 450 654. 9 km NW of Leominster, off the B4362 at Cock Gate.

DINEDOR CAMP Hillfort occupied in the Iron Age and Roman periods; owned by the Hereford City Corporation. SO 523 364. 4 km S of Hereford via A49, B4399 and a minor road right from this.

GOODRICH CASTLE with Norman keep and later work, in the guardianship of the Department of the Environment. SO 577 199. 4 km SW of Ross-on-Wye approached by path from Goodrich village on B4229.

HAROLD'S STONES Three Neolithic or Bronze Age standing stones in the guardianship of the Department of the Environment. SO 499 050. Just east of the B4293, 250 metres SW of Trelleck.

HEREFORDSHIRE BEACON CAMP (or BRITISH CAMP) Multi-phase hillfort with a Norman ringwork on the summit, owned and maintained on behalf of the public by the Malvern Hills Conservators. SO 760 400. Just S of the A449, 6 km NE of Ledbury and the same distance S of Great Malvern.

LONGTOWN CASTLE and borough enclosure partly in the guardianship of the Department of the Environment. SO 321 291. 15 km N of Abergavenny and reached by minor road from Pandy on the A465.

LUDLOW CASTLE with Norman and later work, in private ownership but open to the public most days. In the centre of the town, SO 509 746.

LYDNEY PARK Hillfort and Roman temple in private ownership, open Wednesdays and Sundays in the summer. SO 615 026. Off A48 2 km SW of Lydney.

MIDSUMMER HILL CAMP Hillfort, occupied from about 400 BC until the Roman conquest. Owned by the National Trust. SO 760 374. 5 km E of Ledbury, off the A438 at Hollybush.

MITCHELL'S FOLD Neolithic or Bronze Age stone circle, SO 304 984; 2 km W of the A488 10 km N of Bishop's Castle.

MORETON CORBET Medieval fortified house in the guardianship of the Department of the Environment. SJ 561 231. Just east of the B5063 at Moreton Corbet, 2 km N of the A53 at Shawbury.

NORDYBANK CAMP Hillfort on a spur of the Brown Clee Hill common. SO 576 847. 15 km NE of Ludlow and 4 km N of the B4364 via Stoke St. Milborough and Clee St Margaret.

OLD OSWESTRY Multivallate hillfort, the defences in the guardianship of the Department of the Environment. SJ 295 310. 1 km N of Oswestry railway station along a minor road from the A483.

SKENFRITH CASTLE Medieval castle in the guardianship of the Department of the Environment. SO 457 202. 9 km NW of Monmouth via B4347 and B4521.

STOKESAY CASTLE   Medieval fortified manor in private ownership but open to the public. SO 436 817. Just off the A49, 10 km NW of Ludlow.

SUDBROOK CAMP   Multivallate coastal hillfort, occupied in the Iron Age and Roman periods. ST 504 873. 6 km SW of Chepstow via A48 and B4245 through Portskewett to Sudbrook.

WAPLEY CAMP   Multivallate hillfort in Forestry Commission woods. SO 346 623. 4 km SE of Presteigne. Reached by footpath from the lane to Stansbatch from Byton Hand on the B4362.

WHITE CASTLE   Llantilio Crossenny, with Norman and later work, in the guardianship of the Department of the Environment. SO 380 168. 1 km S of the B4521, 8 km NE of Abergavenny.

WREKIN CAMP   Multi-phase hillfort. SJ 628 081. 4 km SW of Wellington, Salop, approached by minor roads from the A5.

WROXETER   Roman town of Viroconium Cornoviorum in the guardianship of the Department of the Environment, with the public baths and forum colonnade displayed. Site museum. SJ 560 088. 8 km SE of Shrewsbury via A5 and B4380.

BIBLIOGRAPHY

ABERG, F. A. (Ed). 1978. *Medieval Moated sites*. Council for British Archaeology Research Report 17.

ADAMS, D. R. 1970. *Survey of Llanymynech Ogof, Roman copper mine*. Newport, Salop.

ALCOCK, L. 1963. *Dinas Powys*. Cardiff.

ALCOCK, L. 1964. The Defences and Gates of Castell Collen Auxiliary Fort. *Archaeol Cambrensis*. 113, 64–96.

ALCOCK, L., KING, D. J. C., PUTNAM, W. G. and SPURGEON, C. J. 1968. Excavations at Castell Bryn Amlwg. *Montgomeryshire Collect*. 60, 8–27.

ANTHONY, I. E. 1958. *The Iron Age Camp at Poston, Herefordshire*. Hereford.

ASHMORE, P. J. and F. M. 1973. Excavations at Abergavenny Orchard site 1972. *Monmouthshire Antiq*. 3, 104–110.

ATKINSON, D. 1942. *Report on Excavations at Wroxeter 1923–1927*. Oxford.

AW: *See* COUNCIL FOR BRITISH ARCHAEOLOGY. *Archaeology in Wales*.

BABBIDGE, A. V. 1971. Excavations at Coed-y-Bwnydd, Bettws Newydd, 1970 season. *Monmouthshire Antiq*. 3, 59–60.

BAGNALL-OAKELEY, M. E. 1889. *Rude Stone Monuments in Monmouthshire*.

BAKER, A. 1968. Viroconium: a study of the defences from aerial reconnaissance. *Trans Shropshire Archaeol Soc*. 58, 197–219.

BAKER, A. 1970a. Results in Herefordshire from aerial reconnaissance in 1969. *Trans Woolhope Natur Fld Club*. 40, 45–48.

BAKER, A. 1970b. Aerial reconnaissance over Viroconium and military sites in the area in 1969. *Trans Shropshire Archaeol Soc*. 59, 24–31.

BARKER, P. A. 1959. The Excavation of an enclosure at Uppington, Salop. *Trans Shropshire Archaeol Soc*. 56, 158–63.

BARKER, P. A. 1961a. Excavations on the Town Wall, Roushill, Shrewsbury. *Medieval Archaeol*. 5, 181–210.

BARKER, P. A. 1961b. A pottery sequence from Brockhurst Castle, Church Stretton 1959. *Trans Shropshire Archaeol Soc*. 57, 63–80.

BARKER, P. A. 1964. Pontesbury Castle Mound Emergency Excavations 1961 and 1964. *Trans Shropshire Archaeol Soc*. 57, 206–23.

BARKER, P. A. 1966. The deserted medieval hamlet of Braggington. *Trans Shropshire Archaeol Soc*. 58, 122–39.

BARKER, P. A. 1970. *The medieval pottery of Shropshire from the Conquest to 1400*. Shrewsbury.

BARKER, P. A. 1975. Excavations on the site of the baths basilica at Wroxeter, 1966–74: an interim report. *Britannia*. 6, 106–17.

BARKER, P. A. 1977. Hen Domen, Montgomery, 1960–77. *Archaeol. J.* 134, 101–4.

BARLEY, M. W. (Ed). 1975. *The plans and topography of medieval towns in England and Wales*. Council for British Archaeology Research Report 14.

BARNETT, C. 1961. A find of Roman pottery at Uskmouth. *Monmouthshire Antiq*. 1, 12–13.

BERESFORD, M. W. 1967. *New Towns of the Middle Ages*. London.

BIRLEY, E., DOBSON, B. and JARRETT, M. (Eds). *Roman Frontier Studies 1969*. Cardiff.

BLAKE, J. E. H. 1913. Some remains of the Bronze Age at Mathon. *Trans Proc Birmingham Archaeol Soc*. 39, 90–3.

BOON, G. C. 1972. *Isca*. Cardiff.

BOON, G. C. and LEWIS, J. M. (Eds). 1976. *Welsh Antiquity*. Cardiff.

BOWEN, E. G. 1956. *The settlements of the Celtic Saints in Wales*. Cardiff.

BRIDGEWATER, N. P. 1959a. The Whitchurch Vagas. *Trans Woolhope Natur Fld Club*. 36, 228–33.

BRIDGEWATER, N. P. 1959b. Ancient buried roads in south Herefordshire. *Trans Woolhope Natur Fld Club*. 36, 218–27.

BRIDGEWATER, N. P. 1962. The Huntsham Romano-British Villa – First Report. *Trans. Woolhope Natur Fld Club*. 37, 179–91.

BRIDGEWATER, N. P. 1963. Glasshouse Farm, St Weonards: a small glass-working site. *Trans Woolhope Natur Fld Club*. 37, 300–15.

BRIDGEWATER, N. P. 1965. Romano-British Iron Working near Ariconium. *Trans Woolhope Natur Fld Club*, 38, 124–35.

BRIDGEWATER, N. P. 1970. The Medieval Homestead of Wallingstones. *Trans Woolhope Natur Fld Club*. 40, 75–116.

BRIGGS, S. 1977. Stone axe trade or glacial erratics? *Current Archaeol*. 57, 303.

BROWN, A. E. 1961. Records of surface finds in Herefordshire. *Trans Woolhope Natur Fld Club*. 37, 77–91.

BROWN, R. ALLEN. 1976 *English Castles*. (3rd ed). London.

BRYANT, A. 1835. *Map of Herefordshire*. London.

BU'LOCK, J. D. 1956. The hill-fort at Helsby, Cheshire. *Trans Lancashire Cheshire Antiq Soc*. 66, 107–12.

BU'LOCK, J. D. 1960. The Celtic, Saxon and Scandinavian settlement at Meols in Wirral. *Trans Hist Soc Lancashire Cheshire*. 112, 1–28.

BURGESS, C. B. 1962. A socketed axe from central Monmouthshire and its significance for the Bronze Age in Wales and the Marches. *Monmouthshire Antiq*. 1, 17–27.

BURGESS, C. 1974. The Bronze Age. In RENFREW (Ed)., 165–232.

BURGESS, C., COOMBS, D., and DAVIES, D. G. 1972. The Broadward Hoard and Barbed Spearheads. In LYNCH and BURGESS (Eds)., 211–84.

BURGESS, C. B. and COWEN, J. D. 1972. The Ebnal Hoard and Early Bronze Age Metal-working traditions. In LYNCH and BURGESS (Eds)., 167–81.

BURNHAM, C. P. 1964. The soils of Herefordshire. *Trans Woolhope Natur Fld Club*. 38, 27–35.

BURTON, J. R. 1890. *History of Kidderminster*.

BUTLER, L. A. S. 1960. Excavations at Black Friars, Hereford, 1958. *Trans Woolhope Natur Fld Club*. 36, 334–62.

BUTLER, L. A. S. 1965. St Kynemark's Priory, Chepstow. *Monmouthshire Antiq*. 2, 33–41.

CAMERON, K. 1976. *The significance of English place-names*. London.

CARVER, M. O. H. 1974. Early Shrewsbury: an archaeological definition in

1975. *Trans Shropshire Archaeol Soc.* 59, 225–63.

CBA: *See* COUNCIL FOR BRITISH ARCHAEOLOGY.

CHAPLIN, R. E. 1969. A forgotten Industrial valley. *Shropshire News Letter.* 36, 1–6.

CHITTY, L. F. 1925. Three bronze implements from the Edgebold brickyard, Meole Brace. *Antiq. J.* 5, 109–14.

CHITTY, L. F. 1926a. Notes on prehistoric implements *Trans Shropshire Archaeol Soc.* 43, 233–46.

CHITTY, L. F. 1926b. The Hoar Stone or Marsh Pool Circle. *Trans Shropshire Archaeol Soc.* 43, 247–53.

CHITTY, L. F. 1927a. Bronze implements found near Castle Bryn Amlwg, Bettws-y-Crwyn. *Trans Shropshire Archaeol Soc.* 44, v–vii.

CHITTY, L. F. 1927b. Dug-out canoes from Shropshire. *Trans Shropshire Archaeol Soc.* 44, 113–33.

CHITTY, L. F. 1928. The Willow Moor Bronze Hoard, Little Wenlock, Shropshire. *Antiq J.* 8, 30–47.

CHITTY, L. F. 1929. Notes on recent acquisitions to the prehistoric section, Shrewsbury Museum. *Trans Shropshire Archaeol Soc.* 45, 61–74.

CHITTY, L. F. 1947. Report on bronze implements stated to have been found at Netherwood, Thornbury, N.E. Herefordshire. *Trans Woolhope Natur Fld Club.* 32, xlv–xlix.

CHITTY, L. F. 1949. Subsidiary Castle Sites West of Shrewsbury. *Trans Shropshire Archaeol Soc.* 53, 86–90.

CHITTY, L. F. 1952. A Late Bronze Age Spearhead from the Great Doward. *Trans Woolhope Natur Fld Club.* 34, 21–3.

CHITTY, L. F. 1963. The Clun-Clee Ridgeway: a prehistoric trackway across South Shropshire. In FOSTER and ALCOCK (Eds)., 171–92.

CLARK, G. T. 1884. *Medieval Military Architecture.* London.

CLARK, R. M. 1975. A calibration curve for radiocarbon dates. *Antiquity.* 49, 251–66.

CLIFFORD, E. M. 1961. *Bagendon: A Belgic Oppidum.* Cambridge.

COHEN, I. 1954. Archaeological Report for 1954. *Trans Woolhope Natur Fld Club.* 34, 296–301.

COHEN, I. 1957. The Leominster – Stourport Canal. *Trans Woolhope Natur Fld Club.* 35, 267–86.

COHEN, I. 1959. The Herefordshire and Gloucestershire Canal. *Trans Woolhope Natur Fld Club.* 36, 167–79.

COLEMAN, V. H. 1964. The Kington Railway. *Trans Woolhope Natur Fld Club.* 38, 16–26.

COLVIN, H. M. (Ed)., BROWN, R. A. and TAYLOR, A. J. 1963. *The History of the King's Works, Vols 1, 2: The Middle Ages.* London.

CORCORAN, J. X. W. P. 1972. Multi-period construction and the origins of the chambered long cairn in Western Britain and Ireland. In LYNCH and BURGESS (Eds)., 31–64.

COUNCIL FOR BRITISH ARCHAEOLOGY. 1971. *Archaeological site index to radiocarbon dates for Great Britain and Ireland* (Compiler C. Lavell). London.

COUNCIL FOR BRITISH ARCHAEOLOGY. Group 2 Annual newsletter. *Archaeology in Wales* (Abbr. AW).

COUNCIL FOR BRITISH ARCHAEOLOGY. Group 8. *West Midlands Archaeol News Sheet* (Abbr. WMANS).

CRASTER, O. E. 1956. *Tintern Abbey Gwent.* (Official Guide). London.

CRASTER, O. E. 1967. Skenfrith Castle: When was it built? *Archaeol Cambrensis.* 116, 133–58.

CRASTER, O. E. and LEWIS, J. M. 1963. Hen Gwrt moated site, Llantilio Crossenny, Monmouthshire. *Archaeol Cambrensis.* 112, 159–83.

CRAWFORD, O. G. S. 1925. *Long Barrows of the Cotswolds.* Gloucester.

CROSSLEY, D. W. 1968. Excavations at Pen y Gaer Roman fort, Brecknock, 1966. *Archaeol Cambrensis.* 106, 92–102.

CUNLIFFE, B. 1966. The Somerset Levels in the Roman Period. In THOMAS (Ed)., 68–73.

CURNOW, P. E. and THOMPSON, M. W. 1969. Excavations at Richard's Castle, Herefordshire 1962–64. *J Brit Archaeol Ass.* 32, 105–27.

DANIEL, G. 1950. *Prehistoric Chamber Tombs of England and Wales.* Cambridge.

DANIELS, C. M., JONES, G. D. B. and PUTNAM, W. G. 1970. Excavations at Caersws 1968. *Montgomeryshire Collect.* 61, 37–42.

DAVEY, P. J. and FORSTER, E. 1975. *Bronze Age Metalwork from Lancashire and Cheshire.* Liverpool.

DAVISON, B. K. 1969. Early earthwork castles: a new model. In TAYLOR (Ed)., 45–6.

DIXON, P. 1976. Crickley Hill, 1969–72. In HARDING (Ed)., 162–75.

DUKE, T. F. 1844. *Antiquities of Shropshire from an old manuscript of Edward Lloyd Esquire of Drenewydd.* Shrewsbury.

EKWALL, E. 1960. *The concise Oxford dictionary of English place-names.* (4th ed). Oxford.

EMERY, A. 1975. The development of Raglan castle and keeps in late medieval England. *Archaeol J.* 132, 151–86.

EVANS, Sir J. 1881. *Ancient Bronze Implements of Great Britain.* London.

FORDE-JOHNSTON, J. 1962. The Hillforts of Lancashire and Cheshire. *Trans Lancashire Cheshire Antiq Soc.* 72, 9–46.

FORDE-JOHNSTON, J. 1965. Hill-forts of the Clwyds. *Archaeol Cambrensis.* 114, 146–78.

FORDE-JOHNSTON, J. 1976. *Hillforts of the Iron Age in England and Wales.* Liverpool.

FORTEY, C. 1885. Explorations upon the Old Field near Ludlow, December 1884. *Trans Shropshire Archaeol Soc.* 8, 445–9.

FOSTER, I. L. and ALCOCK, L. (Eds). 1963. *Culture and Environment.* London.

FOWLER, P. J. (Ed). 1975. *Recent work in rural archaeology.* Bradford-on-Avon.

FOX, SIR CYRIL. 1952. *The Personality of Britain.* (4th ed). Cardiff.

FOX, SIR CYRIL. 1955. *Offa's Dyke.* London.

FOX, SIR CYRIL. 1959. *Life and death in the Bronze Age.* London.

FRERE, S. S. 1967. *Britannia.* London.

GAVIN-ROBINSON, R. S. 1954. Prehistoric Man in Herefordshire. In

Woolhope Club, 1954, 107–19.

GAYDON, A. T. (Ed). 1968. *Victoria History of Shropshire – Vol. viii*. Oxford.

GELLING, M. 1978. *Signposts to the Past*. London.

GELLING, P. S. 1963. Excavations at Caynham Camp, near Ludlow – Final Report. *Trans Shropshire Archaeol Soc*. 57, 91–100.

GELLING, P. S. and PEACOCK, D. P. S. 1966. The pottery from Caynham Camp. *Trans Shropshire Archaeol Soc*. 58, 96–100.

GELLING, P. S. and STANFORD, S. C. 1965. Dark Age Pottery or Iron Age Ovens? *Trans Proc Birmingham Archaeol Soc*. 82, 77–91.

GEMMELL, A. M. D. and GEORGE, P. K. 1972. The Glaciation of the West Midlands: A Review of Recent Research. *N. Staffordshire J Fld Stud*. 12, 1–20.

GRIMES, W. F. 1930. Holt, Denbighshire, the works depot of the Twentieth legion at Castle Lyons. *Y Cymmrodor*. 41.

GRIMES, W. F. 1939. The Excavation of Ty-isaf Long Cairn, Brecknockshire. *Proc Prehist Soc*. 5, 119–42.

GRIMES, W. F. 1951. *The prehistory of Wales*. Cardiff.

GRIMES, W. F. 1963. The Stone Circles and Related Monuments of Wales. In FOSTER and ALCOCK (Eds)., 93–153.

GUILBERT, G. C. 1975a. Planned hillfort interiors. *Proc Prehist Soc*. 41, 203–21.

GUILBERT, G. C. 1975b. Ratlinghope/Stitt Hill, Shropshire: Earthwork enclosures and cross-dykes. *Bull Board Celtic Stud*. 26, 363–73.

GUILBERT, G. C. 1976a. Moel y Gaer (Rhosesmor) 1972–1973: An area excavation of the interior. In HARDING (Ed)., 303–17.

GUILBERT, G. C. 1976b. Caer-din ring, Salop. *Archaeol Cambrensis*. 125, 165–9.

HADFIELD, C. 1966. *The canals of the West Midlands*. Newton Abbott.

HADFIELD, C. 1967. *The canals of South Wales and the Border*. (2nd ed). Newton Abbott.

HAMILTON, W. G. 1938. Bronze Age burial site, Mathon. *Trans Woolhope Natur Fld Club*. 24, 120–7.

HARDEN, D. B. (Ed). 1956. *Dark Age Britain*. London.

HARDING, D. W. (Ed). 1976. *Hillforts: Later Prehistoric Earthworks in Britain and Ireland*. London.

HENCKEN, T. C. 1939. The Excavation of the Iron Age Camp on Bredon Hill, Gloucestershire. *Archaeol J*. 95, 1–111.

HEYS, F. G. 1963. Excavations on a medieval site at Breinton, Herefordshire. *Trans Woolhope Natur Fld Club*. 37, 272–94.

HEYS, F. G. and THOMAS, M. 1962. Excavations on the defences of Kenchester. *Trans Woolhope Natur Fld Club*. 37, 149–78.

HILL, D. 1974. The inter-relation of Offa's and Wat's dykes. *Antiquity*. 48, 309–12.

HILLABY, J. G. 1970. The Boroughs of the Bishops of Hereford in the late 13th century, with particular reference to Ledbury. *Trans Woolhope Natur Fld Club*, 40, 10–35.

HILLABY, J. G. 1976. The origins of the diocese of Hereford. *Trans Woolhope Natur Fld Club* 42, 16–52.

HILLABY, J. G. and PEARSON, E. D. (Eds). 1970. *Bromyard – A local history.* Bromyard.

HODGSON, J. M. 1972. *The Soils of the Ludlow District.* Harpenden.

HOGG, A. H. A. 1975. *Hill-forts of Britain.* London.

HOGG, A. H. A. and KING, D. J. C. 1963. Early castles in Wales and the Marches. *Archaeol Cambrensis.* 112, 77–124.

HOGG, A. H. A. and KING, D. J. C. 1967. Masonry castles in Wales and the Marches. *Archaeol Cambrensis.* 116, 71–132.

HOGG, A. H. A. and KING, D. J. C. 1970. Castles in Wales and the Marches: Additions and Corrections. *Archaeol Cambrensis.* 119, 119–24.

HOPE, W. H. ST. JOHN. 1908. The Castle of Ludlow. *Archaeologia.* 61, 257–328.

HOPE, W. H. ST. JOHN. 1909. The ancient topography of the town of Ludlow. *Archaeologia.* 61, 383–88.

HOPE, W. H. ST. JOHN and BRAKSPEAR, H. 1909. Haughmond Abbey, Shropshire. *Archaeol J.* 66, 281–310.

HOUGHTON, A. W. J. 1958. A note on excavations at the Roman villa at Lea Cross during 1956–57. *Trans Shropshire Archaeol Soc.* 56, 26–7.

HOUGHTON, A. W. J. 1960. The Roman Road from Greensforge through the Central Welsh March. *Trans Shropshire Archaeol Soc.* 56, 233–43.

HOULDER, C. 1961. Rescue excavations at Moel Hiraddug. *Flintshire Hist Soc Publ.* 19, 1–20.

HUME, C. R. and JONES, G. W. 1959. Excavations on Nescliff Hill. *Trans Shropshire Archaeol Soc.* 56, 129–32.

IRON, D. 1953. Excavations at Clifford Castle during 1953. *Trans Woolhope Natur Fld Club.* 34, 82–4.

JACK, G. H. 1924. *Excavations on the site of Ariconium.* Hereford.

JACK, G. H. and HAYTER, A. G. K. 1924. Excavations on the site of Caplar Camp. *Trans Woolhope Natur Fld Club.* 83–8.

JACK, G. H. and HAYTER, A. G. K. 1926. *Excavations on the site of the Romano-British Town of Magna, Kenchester, Herefordshire, II.* Hereford.

JARRETT, M. G. (Ed). 1969. *The Roman Frontier in Wales.* Cardiff.

JONES, G. B. D. and WEBSTER, P. V. 1968. Mediolanum: excavations at Whitchurch, 1965–6. *Archaeol J.* 125, 193–254.

JONES, H. C. 1936. A prehistoric burial in Clun Valley. *Caradoc Trans.* 10, 74–80.

JONES, H. C. 1940. Archaeological notes from the Clun Valley. *Caradoc Trans.* 11, 126–31.

JOPE, E. M. (Ed). 1961. *Studies in building history.* London.

KENYON, K. M. 1942. Excavations at the Wrekin, Shropshire. *Archaeol. J.* 99, 99–109.

KENYON, K. M. 1954. Excavations at Sutton Walls. *Archaeol J.* 110, 1–87.

KING, D. J. C. and PERKS, J. C. 1956. Llangibby Castle. *Archaeol Cambrensis.* 105, 96–132.

KING, D. J. C. and SPURGEON, C. J. 1965. The Mottes in the Vale of Montgomery. *Archaeol Cambrensis.* 114, 69–85.

LEACH, G. B. 1960. Excavations at Hen Blas, Coleshill Fawr, Near Flint – Second Report. *Trans Flints Hist Soc.* 18, 13–60.

LEACH, P. J. 1967. Archaeological Report from Hereford City Muscum 1967. *Trans Woolhope Natur Fld Club.* 39, 175–6.

LEACH, P. J. 1969. Hereford City Museum Archaeological Report 1969. *Trans Woolhope Natur Fld Club.* 39, 479–80.

LEACH, P. J. 1971. Hereford Castle excavations 1968–69. *Trans Woolhope Natur Fld Club.* 40, 211–24.

LEE-ROBERTS, R. 1927. Farlow, an ancient Herefordshire parish. *Trans Woolhope Natur Fld Club.* 193.

LEWIS, M. J. T. 1966. *Temples in Roman Britain.* Cambridge.

LOBEL, M. D. (Ed). 1969. *Historic Towns. Vol. 1.* London and Oxford.

LOCKE, S. 1973. The post glacial deposits of the Caldicot Level and some associated archaeological discoveries. *Monmouthshire Antiq.* 3.1, 1–16.

LYNCH, F. and BURGESS, C. (Eds). 1972. *Prehistoric Man in Wales and the West.* Bath

LYNCH, F. 1976. Towards a chronology of Megalithic tombs in Wales. In BOON and LEWIS (Eds)., 63–76.

MANNING, W. H. 1978. Usk – Roman legionary fortress. *Current Archaeol.* 62, 71–7.

MARGARY, I. D. 1967. *Roman roads in Britain.* London.

MARSHALL, G. 1930–2. Report on the discovery of two Bronze Age cists in the Olchon Valley, Herefordshire. *Trans Woolhope Natur Fld Club.* 147–53.

MARSHALL, G. 1946. Potteries in North Herefordshire. *Trans Woolhope Natur Fld Club.*, 1–12.

MARTIN, S. H. 1954. The chapel of St. Dubric in Woolhope. *Trans Woolhope Natur Fld Club.* 34, 229–32.

MELLARS, P. A. 1974. The Palaeolithic and Mesolithic. In RENFREW (Ed)., 41–93.

MORGAN, F. C. 1956. Herefordshire Potteries. *Trans Woolhope Natur Fld Club.* 35, 133–8.

MORRIS, J. 1973. *The age of Arthur: a history of the British Isles from 350–650.* London.

MORRIS, J. A. 1926. Excavations at Stowe, Shropshire. *Trans Shropshire Archaeol Soc.* 10, iv.

MUSSON, C. 1976. Excavations at the Breiddin 1969–73. In HARDING (Ed)., 293–99.

MUTTON, N. 1965. Charlcotte Furnace. *Trans Shropshire Archaeol Soc.* 58, 84–8.

NASH-WILLIAMS, V. E. 1933. An Early Iron Age hill-fort at Llanmelin near Caerwent, Monmouthshire. *Archaeol Cambrensis.* 88, 237–346.

NASH-WILLIAMS, V. E. 1939. An Early Iron Age coastal camp at Sudbrook. *Archaeol Cambrensis.* 94, 42–79.

NEAL, S. COOPER. 1927. An ancient cottage pottery in Upton Bishop parish. *Trans Woolhope Natur Fld Club.*, 144–6 and 207–8.

NEWTON, R. G. and RENFREW, C. 1970. British faience beads reconsidered. *Antiquity.* 44, 199–206.

NOBLE, F. 1964. Medieval Boroughs of West Herefordshire. *Trans Woolhope Natur Fld Club.* 38, 62–70.

NOBLE, F. 1969. *The Shell Book of Offa's Dyke Path.* London.

NORWOOD, J. N. L. 1957. Prehistoric accessions to Hereford Museum. *Trans Woolhope Natur Fld Club.* 35, 316–320.

NORWOOD, J. N. L. 1963. Prehistoric accessions to Hereford Museum. *Trans Woolhope Natur Fld Club.* 37, 345–50.

O'NEIL, B. St. J. *Usk castle.* (Official Guide). Usk.

O'NEIL, B. St. J. 1934. Excavations at Titterstone Clee Hill Camp, 1932. *Archaeol Cambrensis.* 89, 83–111.

O'NEIL, B. St. J. 1937. Excavations at Breiddin Hill Camp, Montgomery-shire 1933–35. *Archaeol Cambrensis.* 92, 86–150.

O'NEIL, B. St. J. 1942. Excavations at Ffridd Faldwyn Camp, Montgomeryshire 1937–39. *Archaeol Cambrensis.* 97, 1–57.

ORDNANCE SURVEY. 1956. *Map of Roman Britain.* (3rd ed). Chessington.

ORDNANCE SURVEY. 1962. *Map of Southern Britain in the Iron Age.* Chessington.

ORDNANCE SURVEY. 1973. *Britain before the Norman conquest.* Southampton.

PAAR, H. W. and TUCKER, D. G. 1975. The old wireworks and ironworks of the Angidy Valley at Tintern, Gwent. *Hist Metall.* 9(1), 1–14.

PALMER, A. N. 1907. History of Holt, 1. *Archaeol Cambrensis.* 62, 311–4, 389–402.

PALMER, A. N. 1908. History of Holt, 2. *Archaeol Cambrensis.* 63, 155–63.

PEACOCK, D. P. S. 1967. Romano-British pottery production in the Malvern district of Worcestershire. *Trans Worcestershire Archaeol Soc.* 1, 15–29.

PEACOCK, D. P. S. 1968. A petrological study of certain Iron Age pottery from Western England. *Proc Prehist Soc.* 34, 414–27.

PEACOCK, D. P. S. 1969. A contribution to the study of Glastonbury ware from south-western Britain. *Antiq J.* 49, 41–61.

PERKS, J. C. 1955. *Chepstow Castle.* (Official Guide). London.

PEVSNER, N. 1958. *The Buildings of England: Shropshire.* Harmondsworth.

PHILLIPS, C. W. 1931. Final report on excavations at Merlin's Cave. *Proc Univ Bristol Spelaeol Soc.* 4, 11–32.

POCOCK, R. W. and WHITEHEAD, T. H. 1948. *British Regional Geology – The Welsh Borderland.* (2nd ed). London.

POLLARD, E., HOOPER, M. D. and MOORE, N. W. 1974. *Hedges.* London.

POWELL, T. G. E. 1966. *Prehistoric Art.* London.

PRICE, F. G. H. 1880. Camps on the Malvern Hills. *Trans Woolhope Natur Fld Club.* 217–27.

PROBERT, L. A. 1976. Twyn-y-Gaer hill-fort, Gwent: an interim assessment. In BOON and LEWIS (Eds)., 105–14.

PSAL: *See* SOCIETY OF ANTIQUARIES OF LONDON – PROCEEDINGS.

PRYCE, F. N. and PRYCE, T. D. 1930. The Forden Gaer. Third interim report (excavations of 1929). *Archaeol Cambrensis.* 85, 115–30.

RADCLIFFE, F. and KNIGHT, J. 1973. Excavations at Abergavenny, 1962–69; II Medieval and later. *Monmouthshire Antiq.* 3, 65–103.

RADFORD, C. A. R. 1946. *Grosmont Castle, Monmouthshire.* (Official Guide). London.

RADFORD, C. A. R. 1956. Imported pottery found at Tintagel, Cornwall. In HARDEN (Ed)., 59–70.

RADFORD, C. A. R. 1958. The Medieval Defences of Shrewsbury. *Trans Shropshire Archaeol Soc.* 56, 15–20.

RADFORD, C. A. R. 1961. Acton Burnell Castle. In JOPE (Ed)., 94–103.

RADFORD, C. A. R. 1962. *White Castle.* (Official Guide). London.

RAHTZ, P. 1968. Hereford. *Current Archaeology.* 9, 242–6.

RCHM: *See* ROYAL COMMISSION ON HISTORICAL MONUMENTS.

RENFREW, C. (Ed). 1974. *British Prehistory – A new outline.* London.

RENN, D. F. 1958. The Water Tower at Chester. *J. Chester and N. Wales Architect Archaeol and Hist Soc.* 45, 56–60.

RENN, D. F. 1961. The Round Keeps of the Brecon Region. *Archaeol Cambrensis.* 110, 129–43.

RENNELL, LORD. 1963. The Land of Lene. In FOSTER and ALCOCK (Eds)., 303–26.

RENNELL, LORD. 1970. A Roman road from Mortimer's Cross to Clyro/Hay. *Trans Woolhope Natur Fld Club.* 40, 36–44.

RICHARDS, M. 1973. The 'Lichfield' gospels (Book of St Chad). *Nat Libr of Wales J.* 18.

RICHMOND, I. A. 1963. The Cornovii. In FOSTER and ALCOCK (Eds)., 251–62.

RICHMOND, SIR IAN. 1968. *Hod Hill II.* London.

RIDGWAY, M. H., and KING, D. J. C. 1959. Beeston Castle, Cheshire. *J. Cheshire and N. Wales Archaeol Soc.* 46, 1–23.

RIVET, A. L. F. 1970. The British Section of the Antonine Itinerary. *Britannia.* 1, 34–82.

ROBERTS, B. K. 1964. Moats and Mottes. *Medieval Archaeol.* 8, 219–22.

RODWELL, W. and ROWLEY, T. (Eds). 1975. *The small towns of Roman Britain.* Oxford.

ROE, D. A. 1968. *A gazetteer of British Lower and Middle Palaeolithic sites.* London.

ROWLANDS, M. J. 1976. *Middle Bronze Age metalworking.* Oxford.

ROWLEY, T. 1972. *The Shropshire Landscape.* London.

ROYAL COMMISSION ON HISTORICAL MONUMENTS. 1931. *Herefordshire I – South-west.* London.

ROYAL COMMISSION on HISTORICAL MONUMENTS. 1932. *Herefordshire II, East.* London.

ROYAL COMMISSION ON HISTORICAL MONUMENTS. 1934. *Herefordshire III North-West.* London.

RUSSELL, J. C. 1948. *British Medieval Population.*

St Joseph, J. K. S. 1951. Roman forts on Watling Street near Penkridge and Wroxeter. *Trans Birmingham Archaeol Soc.* 69, 53–6.

St Joseph, J. K. S. 1961. Aerial reconnaissance in Wales. *Antiquity.* 35, 263–75.

St Joseph, J. K. S. 1965. Air reconnaissance in Britain, 1961–4. *J. Roman Stud.* 55, 74–89.

St Joseph, J. K. S. 1973. Air reconnaissance in Roman Britain 1970–72. *J. Roman Stud.* 63, 214–46.

St Joseph, J. K. S. 1977. Air reconnaissance: recent results, 42. *Antiquity.* 51, 55–60.

Saunders, A. D. 1977. Five castle excavations – introduction. *Archaeol J.* 134,1–10.

Saville, A. 1974. A collection of flint artifacts from the south-east Shropshire region. *Trans Shropshire Archaeol Soc.* 59, 198–208.

Savory, H. N. 1940. A Middle Bronze Age barrow at Crick, Monmouthshire. *Archaeol Cambrensis.* 95, 169–91.

Savory, H. N. 1948. A bronze socketed axe of South Wales type from Llanfair Cilgedyn, Mon. *Bull. Board Celtic Stud.* 13, 55–6.

Savory, H. N. 1960. Excavations at Dinas Emrys, Beddgelert, Caernarvonshire, 1954–56. *Archaeol Cambrensis.* 109, 13–77.

Savory, H. N. 1963. The Southern Marches of Wales in the Neolithic and Early Bronze Age. In foster and alcock .(Eds)., 25–52.

Savory, H. N. 1971. *Excavations at Dinorben, 1965–9.* Cardiff.

Shoesmith, R. 1971. Hereford City excavations 1970. *Trans Woolhope Natur Fld Club.* 40, 225–40.

Shoesmith, R. 1972. Hereford (Saxon defences). *Current Archaeol.* 3, 256–8.

Shotton, F. W., Chitty, L. F. and Seaby, W. A. 1951. A new centre of stone axe dispersal on the Welsh Border. *Proc. Prehist Soc.* 17, 159–67.

Shropshire Archaeological Society – *Shropshire News Letter.* (Abbr. SN).

Simpson, G. 1964. *Britons and the Roman army.* London.

Smith, R. A. 1907. The timekeepers of the Ancient Britons. *Proc Soc Antiq. London.* 21, 319–34.

SN: *See* shropshire archaeological society.

Society of Antiquaries of London – Proceedings. (Abbr. PSAL).

Stanford, S. C. 1959. Excavations at the Roman Outpost at Clifton-on-Teme, Worcestershire. *Trans Worcestershire Archaeol Soc.,* 19–32.

Stanford, S. C. 1965. A medieval settlement at Detton Hall. *Trans Shropshire Archaeol Soc.* 58, 27–47.

Stanford, S. C. 1966. Excavations in Bath Street, Hereford 1966. *Trans Woolhope Natur Fld Club.* 38, 204–10.

Stanford, S. C. 1967. The Deserted Medieval Village of Hampton Wafer, Herefordshire. *Trans Woolhope Natur Fld Club.* 39, 71–92.

Stanford, S. C. 1968a. The Roman marching camp at Bromfield (Salop). *Trans Shropshire Archaeol Soc.* 58, 195–6.

Stanford, S. C. 1968b. The Roman forts at Leintwardine and Buckton. *Trans Woolhope Natur Fld Club.* 39, 222–326.

STANFORD, S. C. 1970. Credenhill Camp, Herefordshire. *Archaeol J.* 127, 82–129.

STANFORD, S. C. 1972a. Welsh Border Hill-forts. In THOMAS (Ed)., 25–36.

STANFORD, S. C. 1972b. The Function and Population of hill-forts in the central Marches. In LYNCH and BURGESS (Eds)., 307–20.

STANFORD, S. C. 1973. *The Malvern Hill-forts.* Ledbury.

STANFORD, S. C. 1974a. *Croft Ambrey.* Leominster.

STANFORD, S. C. 1974b. Native and Roman in the central Welsh borderland. In BIRLEY, DOBSON and JARRETT (Eds)., 44–60.

STANFORD, S. C. (Ed). 1976. *Guide to prehistoric and Roman sites in Herefordshire.* Woolhope Club Hereford.

STENTON, SIR FRANK (Ed). 1957. *The Bayeux Tapestry.* New York.

STONE, J. F. S. and THOMAS, I. C. 1956. The use and distribution of faience in the ancient East and prehistoric Europe. *Proc. Prehist Soc.* 22, 37–84.

SYLVESTER, D. and NULTY, G. (Eds). 1958. *The historical atlas of Cheshire.* Chester.

SYMONDS, W. S. 1871. On the contents of a hyaena's den on the Great Doward, Whitchurch, Ross. *Geological Magazine.* 8, 433.

TACITUS (trans. M. Grant 1956). *Tacitus on Imperial Rome.* London.

TAYLOR, A. J. 1951. Monmouth Castle. (Official Guide). London.

TAYLOR, A. J. 1961. White Castle in the thirteenth century: a reconsideration. *Medieval Archaeol.* 5, 169–75.

TAYLOR, A. J. 1965. Chepstow Castle. *Archaeol J.* 122, 226–8.

TAYLOR, A. J. (Ed). 1969. *Chateau Gaillard European Castle Studies III.* Chichester.

TAYLOR, H. 1928. Second Report on King Arthur's Cave. *Proc Univ Bristol Spelaeol Soc.* 3, 59–83.

TAYLOR, J. 1754 *Map of Herefordshire.*

THOMAS, C. (Ed). 1966. *Rural settlement in Roman Britain.* Council for British Archaeology Research Report 7.

THOMAS, N. 1960. *A guide to Prehistoric England.* London.

THOMAS, N. 1972. An Early Bronze Age Stone Axe-Mould from the Walleybourne below Longden Common, Shropshire. In LYNCH and BURGESS (Eds)., 161–66.

THOMPSON, F. H. 1959. *Deva – Roman Chester.* Chester.

THOMPSON, F. H. 1965. *Roman Cheshire.* Chester.

THOMPSON, F. H. 1975. The excavation of the Roman amphitheatre at Chester. *Archaeologia.* 105, 127–240.

TOMS, G. S. G. 1970 2a St. Alkmund's Place – A late Saxon and Medieval site in Shrewsbury. *Trans Shropshire Archaeol Soc.* 59, 32–42.

TRANSACTIONS SHROPSHIRE ARCHAEOLOGICAL SOCIETY (Abbr. TSAS).

TRINDER, B. 1973. *The Industrial Revolution in Shropshire.* London and Chichester.

TSAS: *See* TRANSACTIONS SHROPSHIRE ARCHAEOLOGICAL SOCIETY.

VARLEY, W. J. 1935. Maiden Castle, Bickerton: Preliminary excavations 1934. *Liverpool Univ Annals of Archaeol and Anthropol.* 22, 97–110.

VARLEY, W. J. 1936. Further excavations at Maiden Castle, Bickerton, 1935. *Liverpool Univ Annals of Archaeol and Anthropol.* 23, 101–12.

VARLEY, W. J. 1948. The hill-forts of the Welsh Marches. *Archaeol J.* 105, 41–60.

VARLEY, W. J. 1950. Excavations of the Castle Ditch, Eddisbury 1935–38. *Trans Hist Soc Lancashire and Cheshire.* 102, 1–68.

VARLEY, W. J., JACKSON, J. W., and CHITTY, L. F. 1940. *Prehistoric Cheshire.* Chester.

VCH: *See* VICTORIA COUNTY HISTORY.

VICTORIA COUNTY HISTORY (Abbr. VCH). 1908a. *Shropshire – I.* London.

VICTORIA COUNTY HISTORY (Abbr. VCH). 1908b. *Herefordshire – I.* London.

WACHER, J. 1975a. *The Towns of Roman Britain.* London.

WACHER, J. 1975b. Village fortifications. In RODWELL and ROWLEY (Eds)., 51–2.

WADE-MARTINS, P. 1975. The origins of rural settlement in East Anglia. In FOWLER (Ed)., 137–57.

WAINWRIGHT, G. J. 1967. *Coygan Camp.* Cardiff.

WALKER, C. I. 1965. Excavation at the Roman fort at Walltown Farm, Shropshire 1960–1961. *Trans. Shropshire Archaeol Soc.* 58, 8–18.

WALLER, D. 1970. Lost Beginnings. In HILLABY and PEARSON (Eds)., 5–6.

WARG: *See* WOOLHOPE ARCHAEOLOGICAL RESEARCH GROUP NEWS-SHEET.

WATKINS, A. 1926. Excavations at the Queen Stone. *Trans Woolhope Natur Fld Club.,* 189–93.

WATKINS, A. 1948. *The old straight track.* (4th ed). London.

WEBSTER, G. 1953. The Lead-mining industry in N. Wales in Roman Britain. *Trans Flintshire Hist. Soc.* 13, 3–31.

WEBSTER, G. W. 1954. The Roman Fort at Tedstone Wafer. *Trans Woolhope Natur Fld Club.* 34, 284–7.

WEBSTER, G. 1956. An investigation of an earthwork at Linley Hill, More. *Trans Shropshire Archaeol Soc.* 55, 119–21.

WEBSTER, G. 1975. *The Cornovii.* London.

WEBSTER, G. and DUDLEY, D. R. 1965. *The Roman Conquest of Britain.* London.

WHEELER, R. E. M. 1926. The Roman fort at Brecon. *Y Cymmrodor.* 37.

WHEELER, R. E. M. and T. V. 1928. The Roman amphitheatre at Caerleon, Monmouthshire. *Archaeologia.* 78, 111–218.

WHEELER, R. E. M. 1932. *The Excavation of the Prehistoric, Roman and post-Roman Site in Lydney Park.* Rep Res Comm Soc Antiq. London No. 11.

WHEELER, R. E. M. 1943. *Maiden Castle, Dorset.* Rep Res Comm Soc Antiq. Oxford. No. 12.

WILSON, D. R. 1968. Roman Britain in 1967. I – Sites explored. *J. Roman Stud.* 58, 176–206.

WILSON, D. R. 1974. Roman Britain in 1973. I – Sites explored. *Britannia* 5, 396–460.

WMANS: *See* COUNCIL FOR BRITISH ARCHAEOLOGY. Group 8. *West Midlands Archaeological News Sheet.*

Wood, M. E. 1950. Thirteenth-century domestic architecture in England. *Archaeol J.* 105, Suppl., 64–9.

Woolhope Club. 1954. *Herefordshire*. Gloucester.

Woolhope Archaeological Research Group News-Sheet (Abbr. WARG).

Wray, A. (1805–74). Metalwork of the Bronze Age, Vol. 2. *Soc of Antiq of London Library*.

Wright, C. F. 1964. Craswall Priory – report of a field study made in 1962. *Trans Woolhope Natur Fld Club.* 38, 76–81.

Wright, T. 1872. *Uriconium*. London.

Wright, R. P. and Jackson, K. H. 1968. A late inscription from Wroxeter. *Antiq J.* 48, 296–300.

Wymer, J. J. and Bonsall, C. J. (Eds). 1977. *Gazetteer of Mesolithic and Upper Palaeolithic sites in England and Wales*. Council for British Archaeology Research Report No. 20.

INDEX

With the exception of places quoted simply as examples of place-name types or church dedications, sites mentioned are in the index, most of them with their National Grid Reference. All of them, save for most ecclesiastical and medieval settlement sites on pages 232–8, will also appear on a map, and the reference to this, as to any other figure or plate illustrating a place or object in the text, will be found in the index. The main bibliographical references appear in the site entries with author's name and year of publication; full details can then be obtained from the bibliography on pages 263–75.

Where technical terms have been used they are explained in the text when first introduced and this reference can be found by looking up the first page reference following the term in the index.

Numbers in italics denote pages on which drawings or photographs appear.

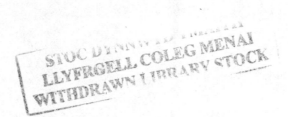